The Romanovs, Rasputin, & Revolution
Fall of the Russian Royal Family

Rasputin and the Russian Revolution

Princess Catherine Radziwill
(Count Paul Vassili)

With a Short Account Rasputin: His Influence
and His Work from 'One Year at the
Russian Court: 1904-1905'
by Renee Elton Maud

LEONAUR

The Romanovs, Rasputin, & Revolution
Fall of the Russian Royal Family
Rasputin and the Russian Revolution
by Princess Catherine Radziwill
(Count Paul Vassili)
With a Short Account Rasputin: His Influence and His Work from 'One Year at the
Russian Court: 1904-1905'
by Renee Elton Maud

FIRST EDITION

Leonaur is an imprint of Oakpast Ltd

Copyright in this form © 2017 Oakpast Ltd

ISBN: 978-1-78282-648-4 (hardcover)
ISBN: 978-1-78282-649-1 (softcover)

http://www.leonaur.com

Publisher's Notes

The Romanovs, Rasputin, & Revolution

GREGORY RASPUTIN
"THE BLACK MONK OF RUSSIA"

Contents

Initial Publisher's Foreword   9

Part 1 Rasputin   11

Part 2 The Great Revolution   119

Part 3 The Riddle of the Future   195

Rasputin: His Influence and His Work   209

My dear Mr. Finot:—

Allow me to offer you this little book, which may remind you of the many conversations we have had together, and of the many letters which we have exchanged. In doing so, I am fulfilling one of the pleasantest of duties and trying to express to you all the gratitude which I feel towards you. Without your kind help, and without your advice, I could never have had the courage to take a pen in my hand, and all the small success I may have had in my literary career is entirely due to you, and to the constant encouragement which you have always given to me, and which I shall never forget, just as I shall always remember that it was in the *Revue* that the first article I ever published appeared. Permit me today to thank you from the bottom of my heart, and believe me to be,

Always yours most affectionately,

Catherine Radziwill

(Catherine Kolb-Danvin)

Initial Publisher's Foreword

When the book called *Behind the Veil at the Russian Court* was published the Romanoffs were reigning and, considering the fact that she was living in Russia at the time, the author of it, had her identity become known, would have risked being subjected to grave annoyances, and even being sent to that distant Siberia where Nicholas II is at present exiled. It was therefore deemed advisable to produce that work as a posthumous one, and "Count Paul Vassili" was represented as having died before the publication of "his" Memoirs. This however was not the case, because on the contrary "he" went on collecting information as to all that was taking place at the Russian Court as well as in the whole of Russia, and, consigning this information to a diary, "he" went on writing.

If one remembers, "Count Vassili" distinctly foresaw and prophesied in "his" book most of the things that have occurred since it was published. This fact will perhaps give added interest to the present account of the Russian Revolution which now sees the light of day for the first time. Though devoid of everything sensational or scandalous it will prove interesting to those who have cared for the other books of "Count Vassili," for it contains nothing but the truth, and has been compiled chiefly out of the narrations of the principal personages connected in some way or other with the Russian Revolution. The facts concerning Rasputin, and the details of this man's extraordinary career, are, we believe, given out now for the first time to the American public, which, up to the present moment, has been fed on more or less untrue and improbable stories or, rather, "fairy tales," in regard to this famous adventurer. The truth is far simpler, but far more human, though humanity does not shine in the best colours in its description.

GREGORY RASPUTIN

Part 1 Rasputin

INTRODUCTION

This *exposé*, based on facts which have come to my knowledge, though probably far from being complete, aims at depicting the recent state of things in Russia, and thus to explain how the great changes which have taken place in my country have been rendered possible. A lot of exaggerated tales have been put into circulation concerning the Empress Alexandra, the part she has played in the perturbations that have shaken Russia from one end to another and the extraordinary influence which, thanks to her and to her efforts in his behalf, the sinister personage called Rasputin came to acquire over public affairs in the vast empire reigned over by Nicholas II. for twenty-two years. A good many of these tales repose on nothing but imagination, but nevertheless it is unfortunately too true that it is to the conduct of the Empress, and to the part she attempted to play in the politics of the world, that the Romanoffs owe the loss of their throne.

Alexandra Feodorovna has been the evil genius of the dynasty whose head she married. Without her it is probable that most of the disasters that have overtaken the Russian armies would not have happened, and it is certain that the crown which had been worn by Peter the Great and by Catherine II. would not have been disgraced. She was totally unfit for the position to which chance had raised her, and she never was able to understand the character or the needs of the people over which she ruled.

Monstrously selfish, she never looked beyond matters purely personal to her or to her son, whom she idolised in an absurd manner. She, who had been reared in principles of true liberalism, who had had in her grandmother, the late Queen Victoria, a perfect example of a constitutional sovereign, became from the very first day of her arrival in Russia the enemy of every progress, of every attempt to civilise the

11

nation which owned her for its empress. She gave her confidence to the most ferocious reactionaries the country possessed. She tried, and in a certain degree succeeded, in inspiring in her husband the disdain of his people and the determination to uphold an autocratic system of government that ought to have been overturned and replaced by an enlightened one.

Haughty by nature and by temperament, she had an unlimited confidence in her own abilities, and especially after she had become the mother of the son she had longed for during so many years, she came to believe that everything she wished or wanted to do had to be done and that her subjects were but her slaves. She had a strong will and much imperiousness in her character, and understood admirably the weak points in her husband, who became but a puppet in her hands.

She herself was but a plaything in the game of a few unscrupulous adventurers who used her for the furtherance of their own ambitious, money-grubbing schemes, and who, but for the unexpected events that led to the overthrow of the house of Romanoff, would in time have betrayed Russia into sullying her fair fame as well as her reputation in history.

Rasputin, about whom so much has been said, was but an incident in the course of a whole series of facts, all of them more or less disgraceful, and none of which had a single extenuating circumstance to put forward as an excuse for their perpetration.

He himself was far from being the remarkable individual he has been represented by some people, and had he been left alone it is likely that even if one had heard about him it would not have been for any length of time.

Those who hated him did so chiefly because they had not been able to obtain from him what they had wanted, and they applied themselves to paint him as much more dangerous than he really was. They did not know that he was but the mouthpiece of other people far cleverer and far more unscrupulous even than himself, who hid themselves behind him and who moved him as they would have done pawns in a game of chess according to their personal aims and wants. These people it was who nearly brought Russia to the verge of absolute ruin, and they would never have been able to rise to the power which they wielded had not the Empress lent herself to their schemes. Her absolute belief in the merits of the wandering preacher, thanks to his undoubted magnetic influence, contrived to get hold of her mind and to persuade her that so long as he was at her side nothing evil could befall her or her family.

It is not generally known outside of Russia that Alexandra Feodorovna despised her husband, and that she made no secret of the fact. She considered him as a weak individual, unable to give himself an account of what was going on around him, who had to be guided and never left to himself. Her flatterers, of whom she had many at a time, had persuaded her that she possessed all the genius and most of the qualities of Catherine II., and that she ought to follow the example of the latter by rallying around her a sufficient number of friends to effect a palace revolution which would transform her into the reigning sovereign of that Russia which she did not know and whose character she was unable to understand.

Love for Nicholas II. she had never had, nor esteem for him, and from the very first moment of her marriage she had affected to treat him as a negligible quantity. But influence over him she had taken good care to acquire. She had jealously kept away from him all the people from whom he could have heard the truth or who could have signalled to him the dangers which his dynasty was running by the furtherance of a policy which had become loathsome to the country and on account of which the war with Germany had taken such an unexpected and dangerous course.

The empress, like all stupid people, and her stupidity has not been denied, even by her best friends, believed that one could rule a nation by terror. She, therefore, always interposed herself whenever Nicholas II. was induced to adopt a more liberal system of government and urged him to subdue by force aspirations it would have been far better for him to have encouraged. She had listened to all the representatives of that detestable old bureaucratic system which gave to the police the sole right to dispose of people's lives and which relied on Siberia and the knout to keep in order an aggrieved country eager to be admitted to the circle of civilised European nations.

Without her and without her absurd fears, it is likely that the first *Duma* would not have been dissolved. Without her entreaties, it is probable that the troops composing the garrison at St. Petersburg would not have been commanded to fire at the peaceful population of the capital on that January day when, headed by the priest Gapone, it had repaired to the Winter Palace to lay its wrongs before the *czar*, whom it still worshipped at that time. She was at the bottom of every tyrannical action which took place during the reign of Nicholas II.

And lately she was the moving spirit in the campaign, engineered by the friends of Rasputin, to conclude a separate peace with Germany.

In the long intrigue which came to an end by the publication of the Manifesto of Pskow, Rasputin undoubtedly played a considerable part, but all unconsciously. Those who used him, together with his influence, were very careful not to initiate him into their different schemes. But they paid him, they fed him, they gave him champagne to drink and pretty women to make love to in order to induce him to represent them to the empress as being the only men capable of saving Russia, about which she did not care, and her crown, to which she was so attached.

With Rasputin she never discussed politics, nor did the emperor. But with his friends she talked over every political subject of importance to the welfare of the nation, and being convinced that they were the men best capable of upholding her interests, she forced them upon her husband and compelled him to follow the advice which they gave. She could not bear contradiction, and she loved flattery. She was convinced that no one was more clever than herself, and she wished to impose her views everywhere and upon every occasion.

Few sovereigns have been hated as she has been. In every class of society her name was mentioned with execration, and following the introduction of Rasputin into her household this aversion which she inspired grew to a phenomenal extent. She was openly accused of degrading the position which she held and the crown which she wore. In every town and village of the empire her conduct came to be discussed and her person to be cursed. She was held responsible for all the mistakes that were made, for all the blunders which were committed, for all the omissions which had been deplored. And when the plot against Rasputin came to be engineered it was as much directed against the person of Alexandra Feodorovna as against that of her favourite, and it was she whom the people aimed to strike through him.

Had she shown some common sense after the murder of a man whom she well knew was considered the most dangerous enemy of the Romanoff dynasty things might have taken a different course. Though everyone was agreed as to the necessity of a change in the system of government of Russia, though a revolution was considered inevitable, yet no one wished it to happen at the moment when it did, and all political parties were agreed as to the necessity of postponing it until after the war. But the exasperation of the empress against those who had removed her favourite led her to trust even more in those whom he had introduced and recommended to her attention. She threw herself with a renewed vigour into their schemes, urging her husband to dishonour himself, together with his signature, by turning traitor to his allies and to his promises.

She wanted him to conclude a peace with Germany that would have allowed her a free hand in her desires to punish all the people who had conspired against her and against the man upon whom she had looked as a saviour and a saint. Once this fact was recognised the revolution became inevitable. It is to the credit of Russia that it took place with the dignity that has marked its development and success.

This, in broad lines, is the summary of the causes that have brought about the fall of the Romanoff dynasty, and they must never be lost sight of when one is trying to describe it. It is, however, far too early to judge the Russian revolution in its effects because, for one thing, it is far from being at an end, and may yet take quite an unexpected turn. For another, the events connected with it are still too fresh to be considered from an objective point of view. I have, therefore, refrained from expressing an opinion in this narrative. My aim has been to present to my readers a description of the personality of Rasputin, together with the part, such as I know it, that he has played in the development of Russian history during the last five years or so, and afterward to describe the course of the revolution and the reasons that have led to its explosion in such an unexpected manner.

Chapter 1

We live in strange times, when strange things happen which at first sight seem unintelligible and the reason for which we fail to grasp. Even in Russia, where Rasputin had become the most talked-of person in the whole empire, few people fully realised what he was and what had been the part which he had played in Russia's modern history. Yet during the last ten years his name had become a familiar one in the palaces of the great nobles whose names were written down in the Golden Book of the aristocracy of the country, as well as in the huts of the poorest peasants in the land. At a time when incredulity was attacking the heart and the intelligence of the Russian nation the appearance of this vagrant preacher and adept of one of the most persecuted sects in the empire was almost as great an event as was that of Cagliostro during the years which preceded the fall of the old French monarchy.

There was, however, a great difference between the two personages. One was a courtier and a refined man of the world, while the other was only an uncouth peasant, with a crude cunning which made him discover soon in what direction his bread could be buttered and what advantages he might reap out of the extraordinary positions to which events, together with the ambitions of a few, had carried him. He was a perfect impersonation of the kind of individual known in the annals of Russian history as "*Wremienschtchik,*" literally "the Man of the Day." an appellation which since the times of Peter the Great had clung to all the different favourites of Russian sovereigns. There was one difference, however, and this a most essential one. He had never been the favourite of the present *czar,* who perhaps did not feel as sorry as might have been expected by his sudden disappearance from the scene of the world.

I shall say a thing which perhaps will surprise my readers. Personally, Rasputin was never the omnipotent man he was believed to be, and more than once most of the things which were attributed to him were not at all his own work. But he liked the public to think that he had a finger in every pie that was being baked. And he contrived to imbue Russian society at large with such a profound conviction that he could do absolutely everything he chose in regard to the placing or displacing of people in high places, obtaining money grants and government contracts for his various "*protégés,*" that very often the persons upon whom certain things depended hastened to grant them to those who asked in the name of Rasputin, out of sheer fright of finding this terrible being in their way. They feared to refuse compliance with any request preferred to them either by himself or by one who could recommend himself on the strength of his good offices on their behalf.

But Rasputin was the tool of a man far more clever than himself, Count Witte. It was partly due to the latter's influence and directions that he tried to mix himself up in affairs of state and to give advice to people whom he thought to be in need of it. He was an illiterate brute, but he had all the instincts of a domineering mind which circumstances and the station of life in which he had been born had prevented from developing. He had also something else—an undoubted magnetic force, which allowed him to add auto-suggestion to all his words and which made even unbelieving people succumb sometimes to the hypnotic practices which he most undoubtedly exercised to a considerable extent during the last years of his adventurous existence.

Amidst the discontent which, it would be idle to deny, had existed in the Russian empire during the period which immediately preceded the great war the personality of Rasputin had played a great part in giving to certain people the opportunity to exploit his almost constant presence at the side of the sovereign as a means to foment public opinion against the emperor and to throw discredit upon him by representing him as being entirely under the influence of the cunning peasant who, by a strange freak of destiny, had suddenly become far more powerful than the strongest ministers themselves. The press belonging to the opposition parties had got into the habit of attacking him and calling his attendance on the imperial court an open scandal, which ought in the interest of the dynasty to be put an end to by every means available.

In the *Duma,* his name had been mentioned more than once, and always with contempt. Every kind of reproach had been hurled at him, and others had not been spared. He had become at last a fantastic kind of creature, more exploited than exploiting, more destroyable than destructive, one whose real "role" will never be known to its full extent, who might in other countries than Russia and at another time have become the founder of some religious order or secret association. His actions when examined in detail do not differ very much from those of the fanatics which in Paris under the reign of Louis XV. were called the "*Convulsionnaires,*" and who gave way to all kind of excesses under the pretext that these were acceptable to God by reason of the personality of the people who inspired them.

In civilised, intelligent, well-educated Europe such an apparition would have been impossible, but in Russia, that land of mysteries and of deep faiths, where there still exist religious sects given to all kinds of excesses and to attacks of pious madness (for it can hardly be called by any other name), he acquired within a relatively short time the affections of a whole lot of people. They were inclined to see in him a prophet whose prayers were capable of winning for them the Divine Paradise for which their hungry souls were longing. There was nothing at all phenomenal about it. It was even in, a certain sense quite a natural manifestation of this large Russian nature, which is capable of so many good or bad excesses and which has deeply incrusted at the bottom of its heart a tendency to seek the supernatural in default of the religious convictions which, thanks to circumstances, it has come to lose.

The American public is perhaps not generally aware of the character of certain religious sects in Russia, which is considered to be a country of orthodoxy, with the *czar* at its head, and where people think there is no room left for any other religion than the official one to develop itself. In reality, things are very different, and to this day, outside of the recognised nonconformists, who have their own bishops and priests, and whose faith is recognised and acknowledged by the State, there are any number of sects, each more superstitious and each more powerful than the other in regard to the influence which they exercise over their adherents. These, though not numerous by any means, yet are actuated by such fanaticism that they are apt at certain moments to become subjects of considerable embarrassment to the authorities. Some are inspired by the conviction that the only means to escape from the clutches of the devil consists in suicide or in the murder of other people.

For instance, the Baby Killers, or *Dietooubitsy*, as they are called, think it a duty to send to Heaven the souls of new-born infants, which they destroy as soon as they see the light of day, thinking thus to render themselves agreeable to the Almighty by snatching children away from the power of the evil one. Another sect, which goes by the name of Stranglers, fully believes that the doors of Heaven are only opened before those who have died a violent death, and whenever a relative or friend is dangerously ill they proceed to smother him under the weight of many pillows so as to hasten the end. The *Philipovtsy* preach salvation through suicide, and the voluntary death of several people in common is considered by them as a most meritorious action. Sometimes whole villages decide to unite themselves in one immense holocaust and barricade themselves in a house, which is afterward set on fire.

An incident that occurred during the reign of Alexander II. is remembered to this day in Russia. A peasant called Khodkine persuaded twenty people to retire together with him into a grotto hidden in the vast forests of the government of Perm, where he compelled them to die of hunger. Two women having contrived to escape, the fanatics, fearing that they might be denounced, killed themselves with the first weapons which fell under their hand. It was their terror that they might find themselves compelled to renounce their sinister design, and thus fall again into the clutches of that Satan for fear of whom they had made up their minds to encounter an awful death.

Even as late as the end of the last century, (19th), such acts of fanaticism could be met with here and there in the east and centre of Russia. In 1883, under the reign of the father of the last *czar*, a peasant in the government of Riazan, called Joukoff, burnt himself to death by setting fire to his clothes, which he had previously soaked in paraffin, and expired under the most awful torments, singing hymns of praise to the Lord.

Among all these heresies there are two which have attracted more than the others the attention of the authorities, thanks to their secret rites and to their immoral tendencies. They are the Skoptsy, or Voluntary Eunuchs, about which it is useless to say anything here, and the *Khlysty*, or Flagellants, which to this day has a considerable number of adepts and to which Rasputin undoubtedly belonged, to which, in fact, he openly owed allegiance. This sect, which calls itself "Men of God," has the strangest rites which human imagination can invent. According to its precepts, a human creature should try to raise its soul toward the Divinity with the help of sexual excesses of all kinds. During their assemblies, they indulge in a kind of waltz around and around the room, which reminds one of nothing so much as the rounds of the Dancing *Dervishes* in the East. They dance and dance until their strength fails them, when they drop to the floor in a kind of trance or ecstasy, during which, being hardly accountable for their actions, they imagine that they see Christ and the Virgin Mary among them. They then threw themselves into the embrace of the supposed divinities.

As a rule, the general public knows very little concerning these sects, but I shall quote here a passage out of a book on Russia by Sir Donald Mackenzie Wallace, which is considered to this day as a standard work in regard to its subject:

> Among the '*Khlysty*,' there are men and women who take upon themselves the calling of teachers and prophets, and in this character they lead a strict, ascetic life, refrain from the most ordinary and innocent pleasures, exhaust themselves by long fasting and wild ecstatic religious exercises and abhor marriage. Under the excitement caused by their supposed holiness and inspiration, they call themselves not only teachers and prophets, but also Saviours, Redeemers, Christs, Mothers of God. Generally speaking, they call themselves simply gods and pray to each other as to real gods and living Christs and Madonnas.
>
> When several of these teachers come together at a meeting they dispute with each other in a vain, boasting way as to which of them possesses most grace and power. In this rivalry, they sometimes give each other lusty blows on the ear, and he who

bears the blows the most patiently, turning the other cheek to the smiter, acquires the reputation of having the most holiness. Another sect belonging to the same category and which indeed claims close kindred with it is the Jumpers, among whom the erotic element is disagreeably prominent. Here is a description of their religious meetings, which are held during summer in a forest and during winter in some outhouse or barn. After due preparation prayers are read by the chief teacher, dressed in a white robe and standing in the midst of the congregation.

At first, he reads in an ordinary tone of voice and then passes gradually into a merry chant. When he remarks that the chanting has sufficiently acted on the hearers he begins to jump. The hearers, singing likewise, follow his example. Their ever-increasing excitement finds expression in the highest possible jumps. This they continue as long as they can—men and women alike yelling like enraged savages. When all are thoroughly exhausted, the leader declares that he hears the angels singing, and then begins a scene which cannot be here described.

I have quoted this passage in full because it may give to the reader who is not versed in the details of Russian existence and Russian psychology the key to the circumstances that helped Rasputin to absorb for such a considerable number of years the attention of the public in Russia, and which, in fact, made him possible as a great ruling, though not governing, force in the country. In some ways, he had appealed to the two great features of the human character in general and of the Russian character in particular—mysticism and influence of the senses. It is not so surprising as it might seem at first sight that he contrived to ascend to a position which no one who knew him at first ever supposed he would or could attain.

At the same time I must, in giving a brief sketch of the career of this extraordinary individual, protest against the many calumnies which have associated him with names which I will not mention here out of respect and feelings of patriotism. It is sufficiently painful to have to say so, but German calumny, which spares no one, has used its poisoned arrows also where Rasputin came to be discussed. It has tried to travesty maternal love and anxiety into something quite different, and it has attempted to sully what it could not touch.

There have been many sad episodes in this whole story of Rasputin, but some of the people who have been mentioned in connection with them were completely innocent of the things for which they have been reproached. Finally, the indignation which these vile and unfounded accusations roused in the hearts of the true friends and servants of the people led to the drama which removed forever from the surface of Russian society the sectarian who unfortunately had contrived to glide into its midst.

The one extraordinary thing about Rasputin is that he was not murdered sooner. He was so entirely despised and so universally detested all over Russia that it was really a miracle that he could remain alive so long a time after it had been found impossible to remove him from the scene of the world by other than violent means. It was a recognised fact that he had had a hand in all kinds of dirty money matters and that no business of a financial character connected with military expenditure could be brought to a close without his being mixed in it. About this, however, I shall speak later on in trying to explain how the Rasputin legend spread and how it was exploited by all kinds of individuals of a shady character, who used his name for purposes of their own. The scandal connected with the shameless manner in which he became associated with innumerable transactions more or less disreputable was so enormous that unfortunately it extended to people and to names that should never have been mentioned together with him.

It must never be forgotten, and I cannot repeat this sufficiently, that Rasputin was a common peasant of the worst class of the Russian *moujiks*, devoid of every kind of education, without any manners and in his outward appearance more disgusting than anything else. It would be impossible to explain the influence which he undoubtedly contrived to acquire upon some persons belonging to the highest social circles if one did not take into account this mysticism and superstition which lie at the bottom of the Slav nature and the tendency which the Russian character has to accept as a manifestation of the power of the divinity all things that touch upon the marvellous or the unexplainable. Rasputin in a certain sense appeared on the scene of Russian social life at the very moment when his teachings could become acceptable, at the time when Russian society had been shaken to its deepest depths by the revolution which had followed upon the Japanese war and when it was looking everywhere for a safe harbour in which to find a refuge.

At the beginning of his career and when he was introduced into the most select circles of the Russian capital, thanks to the caprices and the fancies of two or three fanatic orthodox ladies who had imagined that they had found in him a second Savonarola and that his sermons and teachings could provoke a renewal of religious fervour, people laughed at him and at his feminine disciples, and made all kinds of jokes, good and bad, about him and them. But this kind of thing did not last long and Rasputin, who, though utterly devoid of culture, had a good deal of the cunning which is one of the distinctive features of the Russian peasant, was the first to guess all the possibilities which this sudden *"engouement"* of influential people for his person opened out before him and to what use it could be put for his ambition as well as his inordinate love of money.

He began by exacting a considerable salary for all the prayers which he was supposed to say at the request of his worshippers, and of all the ladies, fair or unfair, who had canonised him in their enthusiasm for all the wonderful things which he was continually telling them. He was eloquent in a way and at the beginning of his extraordinary thaumaturgic existence had not yet adopted the attitude which he was to assume later on—of an idol, whom everyone had to adore.

He was preaching the necessity of repenting of one's sins, making due penance for them after a particular manner, which he described as being the most agreeable to God, and praying constantly and with unusual fervour for the salvation of orthodox Russia. He contrived most cleverly to play upon the chord of patriotism which is always so developed in Russians, and to speak to them of the welfare of their beloved fatherland whenever he thought it advantageous to his personal interests to do so. He succeeded in inspiring in his adepts a faith in his own person and in his power to save their souls akin to that which is to be met with in England and in America among the sect of the Christian Scientists, and he very rapidly became a kind of Russian Mrs. Eddy.

A few hysterical ladies, who were addicted to neuralgia or head-aches, suddenly found themselves better after having conversed or prayed with him, and they spread his fame outside the small circle which had adopted him at the beginning of his career. One fine day a personal friend of the reigning empress, Madame Wyroubourg, in-troduced him at Tsarskoie Selo, under the pretext of praying for the health of the small heir to the Russian throne, who was occasioning some anxiety to his parents. It was from that day that he became a personage.

His success at court was due to the superstitious dread with which he contrived to inspire the empress in regard to her son. She was constantly trembling for him, and being very religiously inclined, with strong leanings toward mysticism, she allowed herself to be persuaded more by the people who surrounded her than by Rasputin himself. She believed that the man of whose holiness she was absolutely persuaded, could by his prayers alone obtain the protection of the Almighty for her beloved child. An accidental occurrence contributed to strengthen her in this conviction.

There were persons who were of the opinion that the presence of Rasputin at Tsarskoie Selo was not advantageous for many reasons. Among them was Mr. Stolypine, then Minister of the Interior, and he it was who made such strong representations that at last Rasputin himself deemed it advisable to return to his native village of Pokrovskoie, in Siberia. A few days after his departure the little grand duke fell seriously ill and his mother became persuaded that this was a punishment for her having allowed the vagrant preacher to be sent away. Rasputin was recalled, and after this no one ever spoke again of his being removed anywhere. From that time, all kinds of adventurers began to lay siege to him and to do their utmost to gain an introduction.

Russia was still the land where a court favourite was all-powerful, and Rasputin was held as such, especially by those who had some personal interest in representing him as the successor to Menschikoff under Peter the Great, Biren under the Empress Anne and Orloff under Catherine II. He acquired a far greater influence outside Tsarskoie Selo than he ever enjoyed in the imperial residence itself, and he made the best of it, boasting of a position which in reality he did not possess. The innumerable state functionaries, who in Russia unfortunately always have the last word to say everywhere and in everything and whose rapacity is proverbial, hastened to put themselves at the service of Rasputin and to grant him everything which he asked, in the hope that in return he would make himself useful to them.

A kind of bargaining established itself between people desirous of making a career and Rasputin, eager to enrich himself no matter by what means. He began by playing the intermediary in different financial transactions for a substantial consideration, and at last he thought himself entitled to give his attention to matters of state. This was the saddest side of his remarkable career as a pseudo-Cagliostro. He had a good deal of natural intelligence, and while being the first to laugh at fair ladies who clustered around him, he understood at once that he could make use of them. This he did not fail to do. He adopted toward them the manners of a stern master, and treated them like his

THE EX-CZAR AND FAMILY

humble slaves.

At last he ended by leading the existence of a man of pleasure, denying himself nothing, especially his fondness for liquor of every kind. At that time, there was no prohibition in Russia and, like all Russian peasants, Rasputin was very fond of vodka, to which he never missed adding a substantial quantity of champagne whenever he found the opportunity.

I shall abstain from touching upon the delicate point of the orgies to which it is related that Rasputin was in the habit of addicting himself, the more so because I do not really believe these ever took place in those higher circles of society where it was said they regularly occurred. That strange things may have happened among the common people, who in far greater numbers than it has ever been known, used to attend the religious meetings which he held, I shall not deny.

It must always be remembered that Rasputin belonged to the religious sect of the *Khlysty*, of whose assemblies we have read the description, and it is quite likely, and even probable, that the assemblies of these sectarians at which he presided were not different from the others to which these heretics crowded. But I feel absolutely convinced that as regards the relations of the adventurer with the numerous ladies of society silly enough to believe in him and in his gifts of prophecy, these consisted only of superstitious reverence on one side and exploitation of human stupidity on the other.

I must once more insist on the point that the apparition of Rasputin in Russian society had nothing wonderful about it, and that the only strange thing is that such a fuss was made. Before his time people belonging to the highest social circles had become afflicted with religious manias of one kind or another out of that natural longing for something to believe in and to worship which lies hidden at the bottom of the character of every Russian who has the leisure, or the craving, to examine seriously the difficult and complicated problems of a future life and of the faith one ought to follow and to believe in.

In 1817, there was discovered in the very heart of St. Petersburg, holding its meetings in an imperial residence (the Michael Palace), a religious sect of most pronounced mystical tendencies, presided over by a lady belonging to the best circles of the capital—the widow of a colonel, Madame Tatarinoff. In her apartments used to gather officers, State functionaries, women and girls of good family and excellent education who, with slight variations, practised all the religious rites of the *Khlystys*.

One of the ministers of Alexander I., Prince Galitzyne, was suspected of having honoured these assemblies with his presence. Thanks to a letter which accidentally fell into the hands of the police, the government became aware of what was going on, and Madame Tatarinoff, this Russian Madame Guyon, expiated in exile in a distant province of Siberia the ecstasies which she had practised and which she had allowed others to practise under her roof. Some of her disciples were prosecuted, but the greater number escaped scot free. The authorities did not care to increase the scandal which this affair had aroused in the capital.

Much later, in 1878, after the Russo-Turkish war, which, like the Japanese affair, had been followed by a strong revolutionary movement in the country that culminated in the assassination of the *czar*, Alexander II., another prophet, this time of foreign origin, appeared on the social horizon of St. Petersburg society, where he made a considerable number of converts. This was the famous Lord Radstock, whose doctrines were taken up by a gentleman who up to that time had been known as one of the gayest among the gay, a colonel in the Guards—Mr. Basil Paschkoff.

He was enormously rich, and put all his vast fortune at the service of the religious craze which had seized him. He used his best efforts to convert to the doctrine of salvation through faith only not alone his friends and relatives, but also the poorer classes of the population of the capital, devoting in particular his attention to the cab drivers. All these people used to meet at his house, where they mingled with persons of the highest rank and standing, such as Count Korff, and a former Minister, Count Alexis Bobrinsky. Later on, the whole Tchertkoff family, to which belonged the famous friend of Count Leo Tolstoy, associated itself with them, and, indeed, displayed the greatest fanaticism in regard to its participation in the doctrines of the new sect.

The Paschkovites, as they came to be called, had nothing at all in common with the *Khlystys*. Their morals were absolutely unimpeachable, and what they preached was simply the necessity to conform one's morals were absolutely unimpeachable, and what they explained and commented upon, each person according to his own light. They were Protestants in a certain sense, inasmuch as their views were distinctly Protestant ones.

But they had much more in common with the nonconformists than the real followers of Luther or of Calvin. They were a kind of refined Salvation Army, if this expression can be forgiven me; though they never acquired the importance, nor did the good which the latter has done, perhaps because they could never make any practical application of the principles and of the ideas which animated them. But at one time the Paschkovist craze was just as strong as the Rasputin one became later on, and Lord Radstock and Mr. Paschkoff were considered just as much prophets among their own particular circle as was Rasputin among the fanatical ladies who had taken him up.

These crises of religious mania are regular occurrences in Russian higher social circles when unusually grave circumstances arrive to shake their equanimity. Seen from this particular point of view, the apparition of Rasputin and the importance which his personality acquired in the life of the Russian upper classes present nothing very wonderful. Before him other so-called prophets had kept the attention of the public riveted upon their doings and their actions.

What distinguished his short passage was the fact that it was made the occasion by the natural enemies of the empire, consisting of the discontented at home, and of the Germans outside the frontier, to discredit the dynasty as well as those whose life was spent in its immediate vicinity and to present this figure of the vagrant half-monk and half-layman, who preached a new relation to those foolish enough to listen to him, as being one of almost gigantic importance, who could at his will and fancy direct the course of public affairs and lead them wherever he wanted.

My object in this study will be to show Rasputin for what he really was, and in retracing the different vicissitudes of his strange career, not to give way to the many exaggerations, which, in familiarising people abroad with his person and with his name, have made out of him something quite wonderful, and almost equal in power with the *czar* himself. It is time to do away with such legends and to bring Rasputin back to his proper level—a very able and cunning, half-cultured peasant, who owed his successes only to the fanaticism of the few, and to the interest which many had in dissimulating themselves behind him, in order to bring their personal wishes to a successful end. It is not Rasputin who performed most of the actions put to his credit. It was those who influenced him, who pushed him forward and who, thanks to him, became both rich and powerful. He has disappeared. I wish we could be as sure that they have disappeared along with him.

CHAPTER 2

The beginning of the career of Gregory Rasputin is shrouded with a veil of deep mystery. He was a native of Siberia, of a small village in the government of Tobolsk, called Pokrovskoie. Some people relate that when quite a youth he was compromised in a crime which attracted some attention at the time—the murder of a rich merchant who was travelling from Omsk to Tobolsk to acquire from an inhabitant of the latter town some gold diggings, of which he wished to dispose. This merchant was known to carry a large sum of money, and as he never reached his destination inquiries were started. At last his body was found, with the head battered by blows, hidden in a ditch by the high road, together with that of the coachman who had driven him. The murderers were never discovered, but dark rumours concerning the participation of the youth Rasputin in the deed spread all over the village.

Whether it was the desire to put an end to them, or remorse for an action of which he knew himself to be guilty, it is difficult to say, but the fact remains that suddenly Gricha, as he was called, developed mystical tendencies and took to attending some religious meetings at which a certain wandering pilgrim used to preach. The latter used to go from place to place in Siberia predicting the end of the world and the advent of the dreaded day of Judgment when Christ would once again appear to demand from humanity an account of its various good or bad actions. For something like two years Rasputin followed him, until at last he began himself to assume the character of a lay preacher, to apply himself to the study of the Scriptures and to try to establish a sect of his own, the principles of which he exposed to his followers in these terms:

> I am possessed of the Holy Spirit, and it is only through me that one can be saved. In order to do so, one must unite oneself with me in body and soul. Everything which proceeds from me is holy, and cleanses one from sin.

On the strength of this theory, Rasputin declared that he could do whatever he liked or wished. He surrounded himself with worshippers of both sexes, who believed that by a close union with him they could obtain their eternal salvation, together with divine forgiveness for any sins they might have committed during their previous existence.

Strange tales began to be related concerning the religious assemblies at which the new prophet presided. But, nevertheless, the whole village of Pokrovskoie, whither he had returned after his few years' wanderings, accepted his teachings and submitted to his decrees with scarcely any exceptions. These unbelievers were looked upon askance by the majority of the inhabitants, who had succumbed to the "monk's" power of fascination and hypnotism. It was with nothing else that Rasputin kept his "flock" subjugated. He introduced among them the cult of his own person, together with certain rites which he called "sacrifice with prayer."

According to the narratives of some people, who out of curiosity had attended these ceremonies, this is how they proceeded: In the night, as soon as the first stars had become visible in the sky, Rasputin, with the help of his disciples, dragged some wood into a deep ditch dug for the purpose and lighted a huge bonfire. On a tripod placed in the midst of this fire was put a cup full of incense and different herbs, around which people began to dance, holding themselves by the hand all the while, and singing in a voice which became louder and louder as the wild exercise became more and more accelerated different hymns which always ended with the phrase: "Forgive us our sins, O Lord, forgive us our sins."

The dance went on until people fell exhausted to the ground and groans and tears replaced the former singing. The fire died out slowly and, when darkness had become complete, the voice of Rasputin was heard calling upon his disciples to proceed to the sacrifice which God required them to perform. Then followed a scene of general orgy.

As one can see by this tale, the strange practices introduced by the seer, about whom people were already beginning to talk, differed in no way from those generally in use among the *Khlysty*, and, indeed, Rasputin made no secret of his allegiance to this particular form of heresy, in which, however, he had introduced a few alterations. For instance, he did not admit that the souls of his followers could be saved by a general prayer, but only thanks to one uttered in common with him, and by a complete submission to his will.

Some persons have alleged that during the early wanderings of Rasputin he had gone; as far as China and Thibet, and there learned some Buddhist practices, but this is hardly probable, as; in that case, his instruction would have been more developed than it was. It is far more likely that during his travels he had met with exiled sectarians belonging to the different persecuted religious Russian communities, of which there exist so many in the whole Oural region, and that they initiated him into some of their rites and customs. They also made him attentive to the hypnotic powers, which he most undoubtedly possessed, teaching him how to use them for his own benefit and advantage.

Very soon Rasputin found that Pokrovskoie was not a field wide enough for his energies, and he took to travelling, together with a crowd of disciples that followed him everywhere over the eastern and central Russian provinces. There he contrived to win every day new adherents to the doctrines in which free love figured so prominently. Among the towns where he obtained the most success can be mentioned those of Kazan, Saratoff, Kieff and Samara.

Concerning his doings in Kazan, people became informed through a letter which one of his victims addressed to the bishop of that diocese, Monsignor Feofane, who had shown at the beginning of Rasputin's career a considerable interest in him and who had protected him with great success. In this letter, which later on found its way into the press, the following was said among other things:

> Your Reverence, I absolutely fail to understand how it is possible that you continue to this day to know and see Gregory Rasputin. He is Satan in person and the things which he does are worthy of those that the Antichrist alone is supposed to perform, and prove that the latter's advent is at hand.

The writer then proceeded to explain that Rasputin had completely subjugated the mind of her two daughters, one of whom was aged twenty, whilst the second had not yet attained her sixteenth year. This unfortunate mother writes:

> One afternoon, I met in the street, coming out of a bathhouse, Rasputin, together with my two girls. One must be a mother to understand the feelings which overpowered me at this sight. I could find no words to say, but remained standing motionless and silent before them. The prophet turned to me and slowly said: 'Now you may feel at peace, the day of salvation has dawned for your daughters!'

Another woman, who had also fallen under the spell of Rasputin, wrote as follows about him:

> I left my parents, to whom I was tenderly attached, to follow the prophet. One day when we were travelling together in a reserved first-class carriage, talking about the salvation of souls and the means to become a true child of God, he suddenly got up, approached me, and .. .. proceeded to cleanse me of all my sins. Towards evening I became anxious and asked him: 'Perhaps

what we have been doing today was a sin, Gregory Efimitsch?' 'No, my daughter,' he replied, 'it was not a sin. Our affections are a gift from God, which we may use as freely as we like.'

Bishop Feofane finally was obliged to recognise the evil which Rasputin was constantly doing, and he bitterly repented having been taken in by him and by his hypocrisy. He reproached himself especially for having given him a letter of recommendation to the famous Father John of Cronstadt, through whom Rasputin was to become acquainted with some of the people who were later on to pilot him in the society of St. Petersburg. The bishop was not a clever man by any means, but he had been sincere in his admiration for Rasputin, a fact which added to the consternation that overpowered him when the truth about the famous sectarian became known to him.

He assembled a kind of judicial court, composed of one bishop, one monk and three well-known and highly respected civil functionaries, and called upon the prophet to come and explain himself before this court as to the actions which were imputed to him. Among these figured his general conduct in regard to the women who had enrolled themselves in the ranks of his disciples. But somehow the adventurer succeeded in dispelling the suspicions that had become attached to his name and conduct, and he explained in a more or less plausible manner the things which had been told about him. His leanings towards feminine society, and his invariable custom of bathing with women, he declared to be quite innocent things, and only a proof of his desire to show that it was quite possible for human beings to rise above every kind of carnal temptation.

In spite of this episode, which would have interfered with the career of anyone but Rasputin, the fame of the latter grew with every day that passed. He established himself at last in the town of Tiumen in Siberia, where he hired the whole of a large house for himself and some of his most favoured disciples, and he began to turn his activity into another and more profitable channel. He established reception hours every day, when all his followers, admirers and friends could come to speak with him about any business they liked. Hundreds of people used to attend those receptions, among them some very influential persons curious to see and speak with the modern Peter the Hermit, who declared that he had been called by God to save Holy Russia.

In some mysterious manner, he acquired the reputation of having great influence in high quarters, where (this must be noticed) he was at the time still quite unknown. Governors fearing dismissal, rapacious functionaries whose exactions had become too flagrant, as well as business men in quest of some good "*geschaft*," to use the German expression employed before the war among financial circles in Russia, crowded round him, waiting sometimes hours for an opportunity to speak with him, and fully believing in his capacities for obtaining what they required.

Rasputin soon became a kind of business agent and surrounded himself with a number of secretaries of both sexes, whose occupation consisted in attending to his correspondence—he could himself hardly read or write—and in receiving the numerous offerings which were being brought to him daily. These secretaries, among whom figured a sister of the Bishop of Saratoff, Warnava, made an immense amount of money themselves because no one was ever admitted into the presence of Rasputin without having previously paid dearly for this favour. Very soon they established a tax in regard to the audiences granted by their master.

Besides this sister of Bishop Warnava, Rasputin had another female secretary, and they both accompanied him in all his travels, calling themselves his spiritual sisters. They constituted, so to say, his bodyguard, and wherever he went, even in St. Petersburg, they never left off attending him and seeing to all his wants. They were the channel through which everything had to go, and without their consent no one was ever admitted into the presence of the "Saint," as they already had begun to call him.

Gregory Rasputin very often used to visit Tobolsk, where he was always received with great ceremony and pomp, as if he had been really the important personage he believed himself. The policeman in the streets saluted him as he passed; the carriage in which he drove was escorted or preceded by a high police functionary, and the governor asked him to dinner. The same kind of thing used to take place in other Siberian cities. In one of them the staterooms reserved at the railway station for any high authority on a visit to the place were thrown open to him. In another, triumphal arches were erected in his honour, while in a third he was met by deputations in the midst of which could be seen civil functionaries and religious dignitaries.

How all this happened no one knew or could explain. In what consisted the fame of Rasputin and what he had done to deserve all these honours nobody could tell. But fame he had acquired, honours he had obtained, and where another person gifted with a smaller amount of impudence than he was possessed of, would have been put into prison or sent to a madhouse, Gricha had it all his own way, and defied governors and judges with an equal indifference, sure that none among them would be daring enough to try to put a stop to his progress or to his avidity.

Most friendly, not to say intimate, relations were established between Rasputin and Bishop Warnava, especially after the latter's elevation to the Episcopal See of Tobolsk. The first sermon which Warnava preached in that town he dedicated to the wife of Rasputin. One need not say that the whole clergy of the town and of the diocese trembled before Rasputin, who did not fail to exact from it large sums of money, which he extorted, thanks to the promises which he made but never meant in the least to keep.

During the course of the year 1909 complaints about Rasputin's behaviour increased to a considerable extent. He was once more called before an ecclesiastical court to give explanations in regard to his general conduct. Among his judges figured again Bishop Feofane. This time Rasputin could not clear himself of the charges preferred against him, and he was invited to retire for one year into a monastery by way of penance. But Rasputin refused to submit to this sentence and categorically declined to do as he had been told. He gave as a reason for his disobedience to the commands of his ecclesiastical superiors that his conscience obliged him to resist because it would be impossible for his "spiritual sisters and daughters" to accompany him in his retreat and live together with him in the monastery they wished him to enter.

At the time this incident took place Rasputin was already living in St. Petersburg, whither he had repaired on the invitation of some of his admirers and protectors, who had the opportunity to listen to his preachings in Kieff and other Russian towns. Among them figured the Countess Sophy Ignatieff, a woman of high standing, irreproachable reputation and great influence in some circles of the capital, where her salon was considered the centre of the conservative orthodox party. Bishops and priests figured among her daily visitors, and it was among her *habitués* that the most important ecclesiastical appointments in the Empire were discussed. Often it was the candidates whom she honoured with her protection who were chosen for a bishop's place or for that of a superior to one of those rich monasteries the heads of which are quite personages in the state.

The countess was already an old woman, widow of a man who

had been murdered during the revolution of 1905, and, incapable of being even suspected of any frailties of conduct. She was the mother of a large family, and though by no means brilliant, was yet clever in her way, with a slight propensity to intrigue. She was extremely devout, with a strong tendency to exaltation where religious matters came into question, and was continually lamenting what she called the relaxation of modern society in those practices of strict church discipline which Russians belonging to the higher classes have lately taken to forgetting. She would not have missed attending any of the long church services, sometimes so tiring in the Orthodox faith, which are celebrated on Sundays and many feast days, and she strictly fasted at prescribed times. Indeed, her whole existence was, as regards its daily routine, more that of a nun than of a woman of the world. But for all that, she liked to keep herself well informed as to all that was going on around her, and politics was her especial hobby.

Among those who frequented her house were Mr. Sabler, then Procurator of the Holy Synod, together with his future successor, Mr. Loukianoff; a good sprinkling of ministers—she was distantly related to Mr. Stolypine, a fact that had considerably added to her importance during the latter's lifetime—and a few influential dames belonging to the immediate circle of friends of the imperial family. All this constituted a *coterie* that had gradually assumed perhaps more importance than it really deserved, but that brought into St. Petersburg society an element with which it would not have been wise to trifle and which it was impossible to overlook, for anyone caring to concern himself or herself with the course that public affairs were taking and assuming.

A few years before the time I am referring to, that is about 1908 or 1909, a good deal of interest was excited not only in St. Petersburg, but in the whole of Russia, by a monk called Illiodore, who also preached a new gospel to those willing to listen. There was, however, about him none of the peculiarities which distinguished Rasputin, and no one had ever found one word to say against his morals. But he tried also to found a religion of his own in the sense that he attempted to develop on a higher scale, and with certain Protestant leanings, the feelings of fervour of the people.

At Saratoff, where he lived, he did a great deal of good, and he had built there a large church, Orthodox, of course, which soon became a centre of pilgrimage to which flocked thousands and thousands of people desirous of hearing him and of listening to his inflamed speeches. They reminded one of those crusades that in the Middle

Ages had stirred whole nations to rise and rush to deliver the Holy Sepulchre from the yoke of the infidels. He was far more a Peter the Hermit than Rasputin, and had, moreover, education, which the other lacked.

But ecclesiastical authorities in St. Petersburg did not approve of his teachings, and he soon came into conflict with them, together with the Bishop of Saratoff, who had all along supported him and who considered him as being really a good and pious man. This conflict led to a quarrel, the result of which was that Illiodore was confined in a monastery, whence, however, with the help of his disciples and adherents, he contrived to make his escape. There was also a whole series of lawsuits, into the details of which it is useless to enter here.

At last the monk was unfrocked for rebellion to his superiors, by a decree issued from the Holy Synod, and compelled to take back his secular name of Trufanoff. He became fearful of further annoyance and managed to get hold of a false passport, with the help of which he made his way into Norway, where we shall find him presently mixed up in a most extraordinary adventure with which Rasputin was concerned. But before all this had occurred there was a brief period when Illiodore was quite an important personage in Russia, and the salons of the Countess Ignatieff and of other ultra-devout ladies used to see a lot of him whenever he happened to be in St. Petersburg. These feminine listeners were very fond of him, and did their best to spread his reputation all over the capital.

During Rasputin's wanderings, he had come across Illiodore at Saratoff, and the latter, like so many others before and after him, had succumbed to the hypnotic spell which "Gricha" was casting around him. He had believed him to be a real servant of God, and he had engaged him to come to St. Petersburg and to preach there before some of the people who had already listened to his (Illiodore's) sermons. He had introduced him to the celebrated Father John of Cronstadt, this saintly priest who was so famous for his virtues and his good deeds. And, strange though this may appear, Father John also had been struck by Rasputin's eloquence and had believed him to be really inspired by the Lord.

In order to explain the state of mind prevalent at the time among the orthodox clergy one must say that the clergy, or at least some of their important members, were trying to bring about a revival of religious fervour in the Orthodox Church, especially among persons belonging to the upper classes, who had, during the last twenty-five years or so, become more than indifferent in regard to spiritual matters, and who had considered religion more a question of "convenience" than anything else. Since the religious censorship had been suppressed and books to any amount treating of every conceivable subject had been allowed to circulate freely in the country, the former attachment to the Mother Church had waxed fainter and fainter, until this Church appeared in the eyes of many as simply a question of good breeding, to which it was necessary to conform when one belonged to good society, but which, beyond this, was treated entirely as a matter devoid of importance.

In view of this fact, those Prelates and Dignitaries who lamented over this state of things were not sorry to find that there were still in the world people capable of arousing in the minds of others an interest in religion and religious matters. This explains partly why the craze which seized some persons in regard to Illiodore at first, and to Rasputin later on, was not viewed with the dissatisfaction one might have expected by the Russian ecclesiastical authorities. They argued that surely it was better for people to pray in the way these two so-called "saints" told them to do than not to pray at all. It was only much later, after Illiodore's rebellion to the orders of his superiors, and Rasputin's ever-growing personal influence had begun to alarm them, that there were found some bishops in Russia who made a stand against both, until at last a catastrophe removed these two men from the scene of their previous labours and successes.

Rasputin and Illiodore were in time to become mortal enemies, but at first a great friendship united them, and when Rasputin was sentenced to enter a convent in the manner already related, Illiodore took up his cause most warmly and telegraphed to one of the former's admirers, an ecclesiastic of high rank in St. Petersburg, in the following terms:

> Neither Bishop Feofane nor Archimandrite Serge has behaved fairly in regard to the 'Blessed Grigory.'

Illiodore's efforts, however, did not avail and Rasputin was ordered to leave the capital immediately. But instead of being compelled to enter the convent whither they had wished to confine him at first, he was allowed to return to his native village of Pokrovskoie. Before doing so he bethought himself of calling on his former patron, Bishop Feofane, but the latter met him with the exclamation:

> Don't approach me, Satan! Thou art not a blessed thing, but

only a vulgar deceiver!

At Pokrovskoie Rasputin surrounded himself with twelve sisters, of whom the oldest was barely twenty-nine years of age. They all lived in his house, which was extremely well arranged and richly furnished. Rasputin's wife, together with her children, was also there and occupied a suite of five rooms, whilst each of the sisters had a separate room to herself.

People wondered that the woman who ought to have been the sole mistress in the place had consented to share her authority with all these girls, and some even thought that she was just as bad as her husband. In reality, the "Prophet's" consort had done all that she could to persuade her husband to give up the "mission" which he declared had been imposed upon him by the Almighty and to return to his former life of a simple peasant. Her efforts had remained fruitless, and Rasputin had replied to all her entreaties that his past existence had come forever to an end, and that he knew his star was about to shine in a wonderful way within a short time.

He commanded his wife not to attempt to interfere in the matter of his own personal relations with the "Sisters" living under their roof. Though she tried to submit to his will, yet there were occasions when terrible scenes occurred between husband and wife. Then the latter would attack violently the girls, whom she accused of all kinds of dreadful things, and would then fall on the ground in attacks of strong hysterics, screaming so dreadfully that people heard her from the street. But tears and submission were equally of no avail and Rasputin did not trouble about his wife's rage or grief any more than he had troubled in general with any other impediment he had found in his way. As concerns the kind of life which the "Sisters" were leading at Pokrovskoie this is how one of them describes it:

> It is now already six months since I am here, living in a kind of nightmare. I do not know to this day whether the "Blessed" Gricha is a saint or the greatest sinner the earth has ever known. I cannot find a quiet place in this miserable village. I would like to run away, to return to St. Petersburg, but I dare not do so. I am so afraid, so terribly afraid of the "Blessed" one. His large, grey, piercing eyes crush me, enter into my very soul and absolutely terrify me. At a distance of 5,000 *versts* I feel his presence near me. I feel that he has got extraordinary powers, that he can do everything that he wishes with me.

For two whole years Rasputin was not allowed to show himself in the Russian capital, but the influential friends he had there never left off trying to get the decree of banishment rescinded. Among others, the Archbishop of Saratoff, Hermogene, and Illiodore worked most actively in his favour, and the latter in one of his sermons did not hesitate to call Rasputin the "greatest saint which the modern Russian Church had ever known." At last the efforts of his friends proved successful and Rasputin, toward the end of the year 1912, reappeared in St. Petersburg, where this time his progress was far more rapid than it had been formerly, and here his reputation of a latter-day saint grew with every hour, until at last he came to be looked upon as a real manifestation of the Divinity upon earth.

It was about that time that he was seen more frequently at Tsarskoie Selo, where the poor empress was eating her heart away in anxiety over the health of her only son, the little heir to the throne, whose days seemed to be numbered. Rasputin, who had been introduced to her as a pious, good man, whose prayers had already worked miracles, was very quickly able to influence her in the sense that he persuaded her that the small grand duke could only be cured if constant prayers were said for him by people who were agreeable to the Lord. It is not to be denied that the pseudo-saint had cultivated to a considerable; extent the science of hypnotism and that he used it in regard to the consort of the sovereign in the sense; that she grew really to believe that the presence of the "Prophet" by the side of her sick child might cure the latter. There was nothing else in their relations to each other, which remained always, in spite of all that has been said, purely official ones.

Rasputin was far too clever ever to say one word capable of offending the empress, whose proud temperament would never have forgiven him any familiarity had he dared to venture upon it. Whenever he was in her presence he kept a most humble attitude, and certainly never discussed with her any matters of state and never dared entertain her with aught else than religious questions. He was far less guarded with regard to what he told the emperor, with whom it is unfortunately true that he sometimes allowed himself remarks he would have done better to keep to himself.

But the *czar* never looked upon him in any other light than in that of a jester whose sayings were absolutely devoid of any importance whatever, but who could amuse him at times by the daring manner in which he would touch upon things and criticise people whose names no one else would ever have dared to mention in a disparaging tone before Nicholas II. But between that and the possession of any real power and influence, there was an abyss which, unfortunately, in view of the turn that events were to take, no one noticed among all those who lamented over the almost constant presence of Rasputin at Tsarskoie Selo.

All that I have said, however, refers only to the emperor and empress. In regard to some people who surrounded them it was not quite the same. It is certain that from the first day that the "Prophet" was introduced at Tsarskoie Selo some intriguing persons applied themselves to make use of him for their own special benefit and advantage, and tried to create around him a legend that had hardly anything in common with the real truth. It is useless to mention the names of these people, whose influence it must be hoped is now at an end. But it is impossible not to speak of their activity in regard to the spreading of these rumours which attributed to Rasputin an importance he was never really in possession of.

This caused no small damage to the prestige of the dynasty. Rasputin ought to have been considered for what he was—that is, a kind of jester, "*un fou du roi*," who, like Chicot in Dumas' famous novels, allowed himself to say all that he thought to his sovereign and whose words or actions no one could take seriously into account. Instead of this some ambitious men and women, mostly belonging to that special class of Tchinovnikis or civil functionaries that has always been the curse of Russia and that, happily, is losing every day something of its former power, profited by the circumstance that the solitary existence led by the Imperial Court in its various residences did not allow any outside rumours to penetrate to the ears of the rulers of the country. They intentionally transformed Rasputin into a kind of *deus ex machina*, whose hand could be traced in every event of importance which occurred and who could at will remove and appoint ministers, generals, ladies in waiting, court officials and at last induce the *czar* himself to deprive his uncle, the Grand Duke Nicholas, of the supreme command of the army and to assume it himself.

These different tales were repeated and carried about all over Russia with alacrity, and all the enemies of the reigning house rejoiced in hearing them. They were untrue nine times out of ten, and generally invented for a purpose. Rasputin did not influence the *czar*, who is far too intelligent to have ever allowed this uneducated peasant to guide or to advise him, but unfortunately, he influenced other people, who really believed him to be all powerful. A kind of camarilla formed itself around Rasputin that clung to him and used him for its own purposes, and that went about saying that he was the only man in the whole of Russia capable of obtaining what one wanted, provided it pleased him to do so. One declared that he could persuade the empress, always trembling for the health of her only son, to discuss with her imperial spouse any subject that he might suggest. In reality no such thing ever took place.

Alexandra Feodorovna always kept Rasputin at arms' length, and for one thing had far too much faith in his absolute disinterestedness even to imagine offering him any reward or gratification. But it is a fact that he was often called by her to pray at the bedside of the little boy, who represented the best hope of Russia. This circumstance was cleverly exploited. No one was ever present at his interviews with the *czar* or with the empress; it was therefore easy for him to say what he liked about them, certain that no one could ever contradict him, with the exception of the interested persons themselves, and these could never get to hear or to learn anything about the; wild tales which it pleased him, together with his friends, to put into circulation regarding the position which he occupied at the court. Thanks to his persuasive powers and to the undoubted magnetic force he was possessed of, he contrived to imbue even earnest and serious people with the conviction that he was at times the echo of the voices of those placed far above him, and that they had called upon him to say to others what it embarrassed them to mention themselves.

In Russia, as a general rule, the people in power were all cringing before the *czar*, whom they never dared to contradict. There were at the time I am writing about some ministers who believed, or affected to believe, in all the extraordinary tales which it pleased Rasputin to repeat, and who thought it useful to follow the indications which it pleased him to give to them. He was only too delighted to be considered the most powerful personage in the whole of the Russian Empire. He helped as much as he could to accredit all the legends going about among the public in regard to his own person, and he imagined that the best way to add to his reputation as a man who did not care for the opinions of the world was to treat this world with disdain and with contempt, and to transform into his humble slaves, ladies belonging to the highest social ranks, just as he had transformed into his handmaidens the peasant girls who had fallen under his spell.

That he magnetised most of the people with whom he prayed

seems but too true. Perhaps they did not notice it, and perhaps this was done with the consent of those on whom he exercised his hypnotic strength—it is difficult to know exactly—but that his prayer meetings were the scene of spiritist and magnetic experiences all who have ever been present agree in saying. He made no secret about the fact, and openly acknowledged the use which he made of the state of trance in which he liked to throw his disciples, especially those belonging to the weaker sex. He practiced to the full all the customs of the "*Khlystys*," but he added to them a cunning such as is but rarely found in a human being, and a rough knowledge of human nature which gave him the facility to exploit the passions of the many vile people who thought that he was their instrument while in reality it was they who were playing fiddle to his tune.

After his return to St. Petersburg he applied himself to the task of setting aside all his former patrons, such as Illiodore, against whom he contrived to irritate several important members of the Holy Synod with false reports about remarks which the now disgraced monk was supposed to have made. He contrived also to bring about the exile of the Archbishop of Saratoff, Hermogene, from whom he feared disagreeable revelations concerning his own past life and certain episodes connected with the days when he had preached his so-called doctrine in the town and government of Saratoff.

On the other hand, he toadied to other ecclesiastical dignitaries eager for promotion, and in that way obtained their support in the Synod. Very soon he turned his thoughts to more practical subjects than religious fervour or religious reforms, and sought the society of business and financial people. Among these he soon obtained the opportunities he longed for and established a kind of large shop of concern where everything in the world could be bought or sold, from a pound of butter to a minister's portfolio.

It is no exaggeration to say that there was a time when nothing of importance ever occurred in the political, social and administrative life of the Russian capital that was not attributed to Rasputin, and the result of this was that there crowded about him all kinds of dark personalities, who hoped, thanks to his support and influence, to obtain this or that favour. Everything interested him, everything attracted his attention; railway concessions, bank emissions, stock exchange speculations, purchase of properties, acquisition of shares in industrial concerns, arranging of loans for persons in need of them—nothing seemed too small or too important for his activity. He liked to think himself necessary to all these high-born people, whom he compelled to wait for hours in his antechambers, just as if he had been a sovereign.

And for even favour he granted, for every word which he promised to say, he exacted payment in the shape of a pound of flesh, which consisted, according to circumstances, in a more or less important commission. Ministers and functionaries feared him. They knew that he could do them an infinitude of harm by causing to be circulated against them rumours of a damaging character, the result of which would have undoubtedly been their disgrace or removal to another sphere of action very probably not at all desirable. He was credited for an infinitude of things he had never thought of performing, and he was supposed to have been privy to all kinds of governmental changes that either pleased or displeased those who criticised them.

As time went on one accused him among other things of the dismissal of the procurator of the Holy Synod, Mr. Loukianoff, with whom he had for a long period been at daggers drawn and who had openly expressed his disapproval of the "Prophet" and his disbelief in his miraculous powers. The elevation of the Archimandrite Warnava, one of his warmest patrons in the past, to the Episcopal See of Tobolsk was also said to have been Rasputin's work, and the public persisted so entirely in seeing his hand everywhere and in everything that it was even rumoured that it was he who was answerable for the decision of the censor forbidding the representation of a drama by the celebrated author Leonide Andreieff called, *Anathema*, on the eve of the day when it was to be produced—a decision which caused an immense sensation in the society of the Russian capital.

It was natural that among the many people who crowded around Rasputin some secret police agents found their way. One of these who was later to become the hero of more than one scandal, a certain Mr. Manassevitsch Maniuloff, bethought himself of becoming the mentor of the "Prophet." He was in close relation with Count Witte, always eager for his own return to power, and desirous of overturning every individual in possession of the posts which he had formerly occupied himself.

The two men tried to imbue Rasputin with the idea that he had great political talents, and that it was a pity he had not yet turned these into account for the good and the welfare of Holy Russia. Rasputin did not believe in the sincerity of his newly acquired advisers, but he was shrewd enough to see that their help would be of wonderful value to him. He willingly entered into the plans which they unfolded to him between two glasses of brandy or two cups of champagne as the occasion presented itself. Count Witte was very well aware of all the secret influences which were paramount at Tsarskoie Selo, and he contrived to turn them in favour of Rasputin, suggesting at the same time to the latter the things which he ought to say, when in presence of certain personages.

It was easy to throw in a word now and then, either in the shape of a jest, or of a remark uttered inadvertently and unintentionally, but yet sure to bear fruit in the future. The great thing was to give to Rasputin the idea that he was a personage of importance. This was not a very difficult matter considering the very high opinion which he already had of his own capacities, coupled with his set resolution to make the most hay whilst the sun was shining, and never to miss an opportunity of asserting his personality no matter on what occasion or with what purpose.

The Balkan war gave Rasputin a golden opportunity for exercising his various talents, and it is pretty certain that he made at the time strenuous efforts in favour of peace, repeating to whomsoever wished to hear him that he had had visions which predicted that the greatest calamities were awaiting Russia, if she mixed herself up in it. This feeling was shared by 1 numerous party, and the sovereign himself was the most resolute adversary of any military intervention: in this unfortunate affair. It is likely that even without Rasputin Russia would not have drawn her sword either for Bulgaria or for Serbia, but nevertheless it pleased his friends to say that without him this would have most undoubtedly occurred. And it also pleased him to assert that on this occasion he had proved to be the saviour of his native land. We shall see him repeat this legend with great relish during a conversation which I had with him personally just before the creaking out of the present war.

There was also another incident in which Rasputin most certainly was implicated. This was the dismissal of Mr. Kokovtsoff, then Prime Minister and President of the Council, followed by the appointment in his place of old and tottering Mr. Goremykine, to whom no one in the whole of Russia had ever given a thought as a possible candidate for this difficult post. Count Witte was the personal enemy of Mr. Kokovtsoff, whom he had never forgiven for his so-called treason in regard to himself, and he never missed any opportunity to attack him in the Council of State, of which they were both members, criticising his financial administration and making fun of the splendid budgets which were regularly presented to the *Duma*.

These Witte declared to be entirely artificial, reposing on a clever manipulation of figures. In some ways, it was easy to find fault with Mr. Kokovtsoff, whose name had been mixed up far too much for the good of his personal reputation in all kind of financial transactions and Stock Exchange operations. But, then, the same thing had been said about Count Witte with perhaps even more reason than about Mr. Kokovtsoff, whose wife, at least, had never been suspected of any manipulations with her banking account. Indeed, no finance minister in Russia had escaped accusations of the kind from his detractors or his adversaries, and it had never interfered with their administrative careers nor prevented them from sleeping soundly.

So far, so well; but then this was more the work of events as they had unfolded themselves naturally than the merit of Rasputin; yet he was openly congratulated by his friends, or so-called ones, on the success which he had obtained in driving Mr. Kokovtsoff away. The ultra-orthodox party which hailed the advent to power of one of its members—Mr. Goremykine having always been considered as one of the pillars of the conservative faction—not only cheered the "Prophet" with enthusiasm but also started to proclaim anew his genius and clear understanding of the needs of the Russian people. Thus, a ministerial crisis culminated in the apotheosis of a man whose only appreciation of the qualities and of the duties of a minster consisted in the knowledge of that minister's existence as a public functionary.

CHAPTER 3

Among Rasputin's adversaries was Mr. Stolypine, who, with strong common sense and great intelligence, had objected to the importance which certain social circles in St. Petersburg had tried to give to the soothsayer. At first, he had regarded the whole matter as a kind of wild craze which was bound to subside in time, as other crazes of the same sort had dwindled into insignificance in the past. Later on, however, some reports that had reached him concerning the persons who frequented Rasputin's society had given him reason to think that there might be something more than stupid enthusiasm in the various tales which had come to his ears in regard to the Prophet of Pokrovskoie. He, therefore, expressed the wish to see him, so as to be able to form a personal judgment of the man, and a meeting was arranged in due course at the house of one of the ladies who patronised Rasputin.

It is related that after he had cast his eyes upon him Mr. Stolypine, when asked to give his opinion on the personality of the individual about whom he had heard so many conflicting reports, had simply replied:

"The best thing to do with him is to send him to light the furnace; he is fit for nothing else."

The words were repeated and circulated freely in St. Petersburg; they reached Rasputin, and enraged him the more, because, shortly afterwards, it was Mr. Stolypine who had insisted on having him expelled from the capital, and who for two whole years had refused to allow him to enter it again. When, therefore, in the early autumn of 1912 the "prophet" at last was allowed to return to St. Petersburg, it was with the feelings of the deepest enmity against the Minister who had exiled him. He had the satisfaction of finding that during his enforced absence the popularity of Mr. Stolypine had decreased, and that a considerable number were openly talking about overthrowing him.

Rasputin very soon discovered the use which could be made of this state of things, which surpassed by far any hopes he might have nursed of being able to be revenged upon the President of the Cabinet for the injury which he imagined that the latter had done to him. He proceeded in all his sermons to compare him with the Antichrist, and to say that Russia would never be quiet so long as he remained one of its rulers.

The police agent, whose name I have already mentioned, Mr. Manassevitsch Maniuloff, who always had his eye on Rasputin, and who had hastened to call upon him as soon as he had seen him return to the capital, was not slow to notice the now outspoken animosity of the latter in regard to the prime minister, who was offensive to him as well as to the whole secret police. The latter, finding that it could no longer do what it pleased, and that it had to respect the private liberty and life of the peaceful Russian citizens, or else be called to account by Mr. Stolypine, who ever since his appointment had been working against the occult powers of the "*Okhrana*," had but one idea; and this was to get rid by fair means or by foul of a master determined to control the police.

It is known in Russia that Mr. Stolypine's assassination was the work of the secret police itself, who had found the murderer in the person of one of its own agents, to whom it had furnished even the revolver with which to kill the unfortunate Stolypine. But few people dared relate all that they suspected in regard to this heinous crime, and fewer still were aware of all its details, and of the manner in which it had been planned.

The truth of the story is that Mr. Maniuloff secretly took to Rasputin's house two or three police agents, to whom the latter said that God himself had revealed to him that Russia could never be saved from the perils of revolution until the removal of Mr. Stolypine. He even blessed the officers, together with a pistol with which he presented them. It turned out afterwards that this pistol was the very weapon which the Jew Bagroff fired at the prime minister in the theatre of Kieff during the gala performance given there in honour of the emperor's visit to the town.

When Stolypine had succumbed to his wounds, Rasputin made no secret of the satisfaction which his death had occasioned to him, and exerted himself in favour of several people who were supposed to have been privy to the plot that had been hatched against the life of the prime minister. He told his disciples that the fate which had overtaken the unhappy Stolypine did not surprise him at all, and that every one of those who would venture to oppose him would meet with a similar one in the future.

In a certain sense, this threat had an effect on those before whom it was uttered. People began to dread Rasputin, not on account of any supernatural powers he might have been endowed with, but because they saw that he had managed to get into association with individuals utterly unscrupulous and ready to resort to every means, even to assassination, in order to come to their own ends. They thought it better and wiser, therefore, to get out of his way and not to attempt to thwart him. He became associated in the mind of Russian society with conspirators similar to the Italian *carbonari* or Camorrists.

The conviction that under the veil of religious fervour he was able to persuade his satellites to do whatever he pleased, and to hesitate at nothing in the way of infamy and crime, gradually established itself everywhere until it was thought advisable to have nothing to do with him, or else to submit to him absolutely and in everything. It was very well known that he had had a hand in the murder of Mr. Stolypine, but not one single person could be found daring enough to say so, and an atmosphere of impunity enveloped him together with those who worshipped at his shrine or who had put themselves under his protection.

It was during this same winter of 1912-13 that the name of Rasputin became more and more familiar to the ears of the general public, which until that time had only heard about him vaguely and had not troubled about him at all. It was also then that rumours without number concerning the prayer meetings at which he presided began to circulate. Innumerable legends arose in regard to those meetings, which were compared to the worst assemblies ever held by *Khlysty* sectarians. In reality nothing unmentionable took place during their course.

Rasputin was far too clever to apply to the fine ladies, whose help he considered essential to the progress of his future career, the same means by which he had subjugated the simple peasant women and provincial girls whom he had depraved. He remained strictly on the religious ground with his aristocratic followers, and he tried only to develop in them feelings of divine fervour verging upon an exaltation which was close to hysteria in its worst shape or form. In a word, it was with him and them a case like that of the nuns of Loudun in the sixteenth century. Had he lived in the middle ages it is certain that Rasputin would have been burnt at the first stake to be found for the purpose, which, perhaps, would not have been such great misfortune.

I have seen a photograph representing the "Prophet" drinking tea with the ladies who composed the nucleus of the new church or sect, which he prides himself upon having founded. It is a curious production. Rasputin is seen sitting at a table before *samovar* or tea urn slowly sipping out of a saucer the fragrant beverage so dear to Russian hearts. Around him are grouped the Countess I., Madame W., Madame T. and other of his feminine admirers, who, with fervent eyes, are watching him. The expression of these ladies is most curious, and makes one regret that one could not observe it otherwise than in a picture. Their faces are filled with an enthusiasm that bears the distinct stamp of magnetic influence, and it is easy to notice that they are plunged into that kind of trance when one is no longer accountable for one's actions.

The method used by Rasputin was to humiliate all the women of the higher circles whom he had subjugated, and who had been silly enough to allow themselves to fall under his spell. Thus, he liked to compel them to kiss his hands and feet, to lick the plates out of which he had been eating, or to drink out of the glass which he had just drained. He made them say long prayers in a most fatiguing posture, compelled them sometimes to remain for hours prostrate on the ground before some sacred image, or to stand for a whole day in one place without moving, as a penance for their sins; or again to go for hours without food. Once he commanded one of them to walk

RASPUTIN AND HIS COURT

in one night to the village of Strelna, a distance of about twenty-five miles from St. Petersburg, and to return immediately, without giving herself any rest at all, with a twig from a certain tree he had designated to her.

In a word, Doctor Charcot would have found in him an invaluable assistant in the experiments he was so fond of making. But he did not go further than these eccentricities. Orgies did not take place during the prayer meetings in which Rasputin exerted to the utmost the magnetic powers which he undoubtedly possessed. While he had been preaching to the humble followers he had at the beginning of his career of thaumaturgy the theory of free love, to his St. Petersburg disciples he declared that sensuality was the one great crime which the Almighty never forgave to those who had rendered themselves guilty of it. It was in order to subdue the flesh and the devil that he commanded his victims to mortify themselves together with their senses, and that he submitted them to the most revolting practices of self-penitence before which they would have recoiled with horror had they been of sound mind.

There is a curious account of an interview with him which was published in the *Retsch*, the organ of the Russian Liberal party, immediately after the death of Rasputin by Prince Lvoff, who had had the curiosity to speak with the "Prophet." The prince was one of the leaders of the progressive faction of the *Duma*. This is what he wrote, which I feel certain will interest my readers sufficiently for them to forgive me for quoting it *in extenso*:

I have had personally twice in my life occasion to speak with Rasputin. The first time was toward the end of the year 1915, when I was invited by Prince I. W. Gouranoff to meet him.

When I arrived, Rasputin was already there, sitting beside a large table, with a numerous company gathered around him, among which figured, in the same quality as myself, as a curious stranger, the present chief of the military censorship in Petrograd, General M. A. Adabasch, who was the whole time attentively watching the "Prophet" from the distant corner whither he had retired.

Rasputin was dressed in his usual costume of a Russian peasant and was very silent, throwing only now and then a word or two into the general conversation or uttering a short sentence, after which he relapsed into his former silence. In his dress and in

49

his manners, he was absolutely uncouth, and when, for instance, he was offered an apple he cut a hole at its top with his own very dirty pocket knife, after which he put the knife aside and tore the fruit in two with his hands, eating it, peel and all, in the most primitive manner. After some time, he got up and went to the next room, where he sat down on a large divan with a few ladies who had joined him, toward whom his manner left very much to be desired.

I had kept examining him the whole time with great attention, seeking for that extraordinary glance he was supposed to possess, to which was attributed his power over people, but I could not find any trace of it or notice anything remarkable about him. The expression of his face was that of a cunning *mougik*, such as one constantly meets with in our country, perfectly well aware of the conditions in which he found himself, and determined to make the best out of them. Everything in him, to begin with his common dress and to end with his long hair and his dirty nails, bore the character of the uncivilised peasant he was.

He seemed to realise, better perhaps than those who surrounded him, that one of his trump cards was precisely this uncouthness, which ought to have been repelling, and that if he had put on different clothes and tried to assimilate the manners of his betters, half of the interest which he excited would have disappeared. I did not stay a long time, and went away thoroughly disappointed, and perhaps even slightly disgusted at the man.

A few months later, in February of the present year, 1916, I was asked again to meet Rasputin at Baron Miklos's house. There I found a numerous and most motley company assembled. There were two members of the *Duma*, Messrs. Karaouloff and Souratchane; General Polivanoff; a great landowner of the government of Woronege, N. P. Alexieieff; Madame Svetchine; the Senator S. P. Bieletsky and other people.

Ladies were in a majority. Rasputin remained talking for a long time with the Deputy Karaouloff in another room than the one in which I found myself. Then he came to join us in the large drawing room, where he kept walking up and down with a young girl on his arm—Mlle. D., a singer by profession—who was entreating him to arrange for her an engagement at the Russian Opera, which he promised her to do "for certain," as he expressed himself.

Every five or ten minutes Rasputin went up to a table on which were standing several decanters with red wine and other spirits, and he poured himself a large glass out of one of them. He swallowed the contents at one gulp, wiping his mouth afterwards with his sleeve or with the back of his hand. During one of these excursions he came up to where I was sitting, and stopped before me exclaiming: "I remember thee. Thou art a gasser, who writes, and writes, and repeats nothing but calumnies."

I asked the "Prophet" why he did not say "you" to me, instead of addressing me with the vulgar appellation of "thou."

"I speak in this way with everybody," he replied. "I have got my own way in talking with people."

I made him a remark concerning some words which he had pronounced badly, adding, "Surely you have learned during the ten years which you have lived in the capital that one does not use the expressions which you have employed. And how do you know that I have written or repeated calumnies. You cannot read yourself, so that everything you hear is from other people, and you cannot feel sure whether they tell you the truth."

"This does not matter," he replied. "Thou hast written that one is stealing, and thou knowest thyself how to do so."

"I do not know how to steal," I answered. "But I have written that one is doing so at present everywhere. This it was necessary to do for the public good."

"Thou hast done wrong; one must only write the truth. Truth is everything," he said.

The conversation was assuming an angry and sharp tone. Rasputin became enraged at my telling him that all he was saying was devoid of common sense, and he began shouting at me, at the top of his. voice. "Be quiet, how darest thou say such things. Be quiet!"

I did not wish to remain quiet, and I began in my turn to shout at the "Prophet," who became absolutely furious when I assured him that I was not a woman whom he could frighten, that I wanted nothing from him, and that he had better leave me alone, or it might be the worse for him.

He then howled at me, screaming as loud as he could: "It is an evil thing for everybody that thou art here!"

51

When in the following April it came to my knowledge that Mr. Sturmer wanted to expel me from the capital, I was surprised to have Baron Miklos come to me one day in the name of Rasputin, who had asked him to tell me that though I was a "proud man," he did not bear me any grudge, that if I wished it, he would take steps to have the order for my expulsion revoked, and that at all events, he begged me not to think that he had taken any part in this whole affair. I categorically refused to avail myself of the help of Rasputin, and there ended the whole matter.

I have reproduced this tale because it seems to me that it helps one to understand the personality of Rasputin, and because it describes to perfection the manner in which he used to treat the people with whom he dealt. Personally, when I interviewed the "Prophet," I had the opportunity to convince myself that the impression which he had produced upon Prince Lvoff was absolutely a correct one, and I made the same remark which the latter had done in regard to the total absence of this magnetic strength which Rasputin was supposed to possess over those with whom he entered into conversation.

The man was a fraud and nothing else. He had been deified by the group of foolish people whom he had persuaded that he was a messenger from Heaven, come to announce to Holy Russia that a new Christ had arisen. But his pretended fascination existed only in the imagination of the persons who asserted its existence. To the impartial observer he appeared what he was—an arrogant and insolent peasant, who, knowing admirably well on which side his bread was buttered, exploited with considerable ability to his personal advantage the stupidity of his neighbours.

I have already related that his house had become a kind of Stock Exchange in which everything could be bought or sold, where all kinds of shady transactions used to take place, and where the most disgusting bargaining for places and appointments was perpetually going on. Gifts innumerable were showered upon him, which he pretended he distributed to the poor, but which in reality he carefully put into his own pocket. This peasant, who when he had arrived in St. Petersburg for the first time, had hardly possessed a shirt to his back, had become a very rich man.

He had bought several houses, gambled in stock shares and other securities, and had contrived to accumulate a banking account which, if one is to believe all that has been related, amounted to several millions. From time to time, however, he used to come out with some munificent offering to some charity or other, with which he threw dust in people's eyes. They thought that it was in this manner that he employed all the money which was showered upon him by his numerous admirers. It was in this way that he built in St. Petersburg, not far from the spot where, by a strange coincidence, his murdered body was afterwards found, a church which was called the Salvation Church, which adjoined a school for girls. There he used to go often.

Whenever he went he was always met by the clergy in charge with great pomp, as if he had been a bishop or some great ecclesiastical dignitary, and was awaited at the door with the cross and holy water. This church was placed under the special protection of the Metropolitan of Petrograd, Pitirim, who often celebrated divine service in it, at which Rasputin always made it a point to be present. But instead of meeting the Metropolitan, as he ought to have done, he was in the habit of arriving after him. Mgr. Pitirim, however, awaited his arrival just as he would have waited for the emperor. Indeed, the submission which the official head of the clergy of the capital affected in regard to Rasputin is one of the most extraordinary episodes in the latter's wonderful career.

In fact, when one reviews all one has heard concerning this personage, one is tempted to ask the question whether his appearance in St. Petersburg had not brought along with it an epidemic of madness among all those who had come in contact with him. It hardly seems possible that bishops, priests, ministers, high dignitaries, statesmen, even, or at least men having the pretension to be considered as such, should have thought it necessary to go and seek the favour of this vulgar, ill-bred, dirty Russian *mougik*, devoid of honesty and of scruples, about whom the most disgraceful stories were being repeated everywhere, and whose presence in the houses where he was a daily visitor used to give rise to the worst kind of gossip.

This gossip was of such a nature that decent persons hesitated before repeating it, let alone believing it. Like an insidious poison, it defiled all whom it touched. One fails to realise by what kind of magic grave men like Mr. Sabler, for instance, who for some time had occupied the highly responsible and delicate function of Procurator of the Holy Synod, one of the most important posts in the whole Russian Empire, could be made so far to forget himself as to prostrate himself before Rasputin in his eagerness to become entitled to the latter's good graces and protection. And that he did so is at least not a matter of doubt, if we are to believe the following letter which the monk Illiodore wrote from his exile on the fifth of May, 1914, to a personage very well known in the political circles of St. Petersburg.

> I swear to you with the word of honour of an honest man that the letter in which I called Sabler and Damansky the instruments of 'Gricha' (Rasputin) contained nothing but the solemn truth, and I repeat it once more, that according to what Rasputin told to me on the twenty-eighth of June, 1911, at 3 o'clock in the afternoon in my little cell, Sabler really kissed the feet of 'Gricha,' who, in relating this story to me, showed me with an expressive pantomime in what way he had done so. I consider as utterly false and as a barefaced lie the declaration of Mr. Sabler that he had never prostrated himself before any one, except before the sacred images.
>
> Respectfully yours,
>
> S. M. Troufanoff,
> formerly the monk Illiodore.

It is difficult to say, of course, how much reliance can be placed on those assertions of Illiodore, and whether Mr. Sabler really thought it necessary to fall on the ground before Rasputin. But out of this letter one can infer that the influence of the latter was considered to be important enough for people to trouble themselves about relating stories of the kind to show it up. Altogether, one may safely conclude, out of the very spare material which so far has come to light in regard to the activity of Rasputin, that we have not yet heard the whole truth about all the circumstances which accompanied his sudden rise and fall, and that there must have been in both events things which perhaps will never come to light.

But all of them point out to some dark intrigue in which he was but one of the pawns, whilst believing himself to be the principal actor. One must not forget that the *czar* himself was at one time liberal in his ideas and opinions, and that it was entirely due to his personal initiative that the Constitution, such as it is, which Russia possessed before his fall was promulgated. This was not done without arousing terrible animosities, provoking awful discontent. From the first hour that its contents were published, there were found persons who began to work against it, and who by their efforts brought about the revolution of the year 1905, with the help of which they hoped to bring back the days of absolute government, when every public functionary was a small *czar* in his own way, and when the caprice of the first police official could send away to distant Siberia innocent people.

This abuse Nicholas II. had tried to put an end to, which was not forgiven by the crew of rapacious crocodiles, who up to that day had administered the affairs of the Russian Empire, and they it was who determined to take their revenge for this noble and disinterested intention of their sovereign.

Rasputin became the instrument of the reactionary party, which he, in his turn, contrived to make instrumental in carrying out his own views and aims. His head had been turned by the unexpected position in which he had found himself placed. It is not surprising that he lost his balance and that he ended by considering himself as being what he had been told by so many different people that he was—a Prophet of the Lord, having the right to say what he liked, to calumniate whom he liked, to make use of whatever means he found at hand, to eliminate from his path any obstacles he might have found intruding upon it. His name became synonymous with that of this ultraconservative party which was leading Russia towards its ruin, and which always contrived to reduce to nothing all the good intentions of the *czar*.

Rasputin was a symbol and a flag at the same time; the symbol of superstition, and the flag of dark reaction. It is impossible to know to this day whether he was not also what everything points to; that is, an agent of the German Government, who had entered into German interests, and who had during the last months of his life been working together with Mr. Sturmer and the latter's private secretary, the famous Manassevitsch Maniuloff, towards a separate peace with the Central Powers, the conclusion of which would have dishonoured forever the *czar*, together with his government, and which would have provoked such discontent in the country that the dynasty might have collapsed under its weight.

There exist at least indications that such a thing was within the limits of possibility, and, if so, those who put an end to the evil career of this dangerous man deserve well from their country, and the leniency which has been shown to them is but the reward for an act of daring which, though unjustifiable from the moral point of view, is nevertheless to be condoned by the circumstance that its patriotic aim was so great that it was worthwhile risking everything, even remorse, in order to accomplish it.

In a certain sense, Rasputin was the curse of Russia. Thanks to him, the purest existences were subjected to a whole series of base attacks and of vile calumnies. Thanks to him, our enemies were given the opportunity to pour out upon us, upon our institutions, our statesmen and even upon our sovereign the poison of their venom, and to represent us to those who do not know us in a light which, thanks be rendered to God, was an absolutely false and untrue one.

Russia was far too great for such things to touch her. That Germany rejoiced at every tale which reached its ears in regard to Rasputin is evident if one reads its newspapers. That it was in understanding and accord, if not directly with him, at least with some of those who were his immediate friends and habitual confidents, has been proved to the satisfaction of all impartial persons. And that he worked continually towards establishing an understanding between the *czar* and the *Kaiser* is another fact of which more than one man in Russia is aware.

Whether he did so intentionally, or whether he was the unconscious instrument of others cleverer and more cultivated than he ever was or would become, is still a point that has not been cleared up to the general satisfaction. But that his so-called influence only existed over certain weak people, and that the *czar* himself never knowingly allowed it to be exercised in matters of state, is a fact about which there can exist no doubt for those who knew the sovereign.

CHAPTER 4

I have quoted the impressions of Prince Lvoff in regard to Rasputin, and have remarked that I have had personally the opportunity to convince myself that they were correct, at least in their broad lines. The interview which I had with Rasputin in the course of the winter of 1913-14 left me with feelings akin to those experienced by the prince. This interview took place under the following circumstances: I had been asked by a big American newspaper to see the "Prophet," whose renown had already spread beyond the Russian frontiers, and who was beginning to be considered as a factor of no mean importance in the conduct of Russian state affairs. This, however, was by no means an easy matter.

For one thing, he was seldom in St. Petersburg. He spent most of his time at Tsarskoie Selo, where his headquarters were the apartments of Mme. W. He used to make only brief and flying visits to the capital, where he possessed several dwellings. One never knew in which one he could be found, as he used to go from one to another, according to his fancy. He gave audiences like a sovereign would have done, and before any one was allowed to enter his presence that person had to be subjected to a course of cross-examination so as to make quite sure that no malicious or evil designs were harboured by him in regard to the "Prophet."

At last, after a succession of unavailing efforts, I chanced to light on a certain Mr. de Bock, with whom Rasputin had business relations, and for whom he procured when the war broke out an important contract connected with the supply of meat for the troops in the field. It was this personage who finally obtained for me the favour of being admitted into the home of Rasputin. The latter was living at the time in a very handsome and expensive flat, in a house situated on the English Prospekt, a rather distant street in St. Petersburg, whose proximity to the quarters of the working population of the capital had appealed to the "Prophet's" tastes.

When I arrived there at about 4 o'clock in the afternoon, I was, first of all, stopped by the hall porter, who wanted me to explain to him where and to whom I was going. Upon hearing that it was to Rasputin he insisted on my taking off my fur coat downstairs, and then examined me most carefully and suspiciously, surveying with special attention the size and volume of my pockets, so as to make sure that I was not carrying any murderous instruments hidden in their depths.

Upstairs the door was opened by an elderly woman with a red kerchief over her head, who, I learned afterward, was one of the "sisters" who followed the "Prophet" everywhere. She asked for my name, and then ushered me into a room, sparely but richly furnished. There some half-dozen people were waiting, in what seemed to me to be extreme impatience, for the door of the next room to open and admit them.

Voices were heard through the door angrily discussing something or other. Among the people present I recognised a lady-in-waiting on the empress, an old general in possession of an important command, two parish priests, three women belonging to the lower classes, one of whom seemed to be in great trouble, and a typical Russian merchant in high boots and dressed in the long caftan which is still worn by some of those who have kept up the traditions of the old school. Then there was a little boy about ten years old, poorly clad, who was crying bitterly. All these people kept silent, but the eager expression on their faces showed that they were all labouring under an intense agitation and emotion. When I entered the apartment a distinct look of disappointment appeared on all their faces. At last the old general approached me, and asked me in more or less polite tones whether I had a special card of admission or not.

"What do you mean?" I inquired.

"Well, you see," he said, "we all who are in this room have got one, but there"—and he pointed with his finger to the adjoining door—"there sit the people who have come here on the chance, just to try whether Gregory Efimitsch will condescend to speak to them. Some have been sitting there since last night," he significantly added. And as he spoke he slightly pushed ajar the door he had mentioned. I could see that a room, if anything smaller than the one we were in, was packed full of persons of different ages and types, all of whom looked tired. They were sitting not only on the few chairs which the apartment contained, but also on the floor.

There were women with children hanging at their breast, military men, priests, monks, common peasants and two policemen. The last named were seated by the window leisurely eating a piece of bread and cold meat, which they were cutting into small slices with a pocket-knife. They had evidently made themselves at home, regardless of consequences or of the feelings of other people. Suddenly we heard another door slam, and a strong step resounded in the hall. A man began to speak in a loud voice. He said: "You just go to see—" and here the name of one of the most influential officials in the Home Office was mentioned, "and you tell him that Gricha has said he was to give you a place, and a good one, too. It does not matter whether there is none vacant, he must find one. There, take this paper, and now go, and don't forget to show it when you come to the Home Office."

The door slammed again, and all remained silent for a few minutes. Then the elderly woman who had admitted me, came into the apartment where we were sitting and beckoned me to follow her. But this proved too much for the feelings of the old general who had accosted me on my entrance, and he pushed himself forward in front of me, exclaiming as he did so:

"I have been here a longer time than she has been," pointing at me with his finger, "and I must get in first."

"You cannot do so," replied the woman; "my orders are to let this lady in first."

"Do you know who I am, woman?" screamed the general at the top of his lungs; he was evidently in a towering passion. "Go at once, and tell Gregory Efimitsch that I must see him at once, I have been waiting here for more than an hour."

"I cannot do so," replied the woman, "I must obey the orders that have been given to me."

"Then I shall do it myself," exclaimed the general, and he rushed toward the door, which he opened, when he was stopped by a whole torrent of invectives coming from the next room.

"How dare you disobey my orders?" cried out an angry voice. "Thou pig and son of a pig, I have said I wish to see this person and no one else! Thou idle creature! Chuck him out of the room, that pig who dares to contradict me, and you come in here!" And the tall figure of Rasputin appeared on the threshold of the room. He rudely pushed aside the general and, seizing my hand, pulled me into another apartment, which seemed to be his dining room.

It was a rather large corner room with three windows, in which stood a quantity of flowers and green plants. A round table occupied the middle, on which was laid a striped white-and-red tablecloth. A *samovar* was standing on it, together with glasses on blue-and-white saucers, slices of lemon, sugar in a silver sugar basin, and quantities of cakes and biscuits. Chairs were placed around it, on one of which Rasputin sat down, facing the tea urn, after having made me a sign to do likewise. I noticed that there was a large writing table in one corner covered with books and papers.

The "Prophet" himself did not at all strike me as being the remarkable individual I had been led to expect. He must have been about forty years old, tall and lean, with a long black beard and hair, falling not quite down to his back, but considerably lower than his ears. The eyes were black, singularly cunning in their expression, but did not produce, at least not on me, the uncanny impression I had been told they generally made on those who saw them for the first time. The hands were the most remarkable thing about the man. They were long and thin, with immense nails, as dirty as dirty could be. He kept moving them in all directions as he spoke, sometimes folding them on his breast and sometimes lifting them high up in the air. He wore the ordinary dress of the Russian peasant, high boots and the *caftan*, which, however, was made of the best and finest dark-blue cloth. What could be seen of his linen was also of the best quality.

After having beckoned to me to sit down, Rasputin poured out some tea in a glass and proceeded to drink it, sipping the beverage slowly out of the saucer into which he poured it out of the glass which he had just filled. Suddenly he pushed the same saucer toward me with the word:

"Drink."

As I did not in the least feel inclined to take his remains, I declined the tempting offer, which made him draw together his black and bushy eyebrows with the remark:

"Better persons than thou art have drunk out of this saucer, but if thou wantest to make a fuss it is no concern of mine."

And then he called out, *"Avdotia! Avdotia!"* The elderly woman who had opened the door for me hastened to come into the room.

"There," said Rasputin, "this person"—pointing toward me with his forefinger—"this person refuses to drink out of the cup of life; take it thou instead."

The woman instantly dropped on her knees and Rasputin proceeded to open her mouth with his fingers and pour down her throat the tea which I had disdained. She then prostrated herself on the ground before him and reverently kissed his feet, remaining in this attitude until he pushed her aside with his heavy boot and said, "There, now thou canst go."

Then he turned to me once more. "Great ladies, some of the greatest in the land, are but too happy to do as this woman has done," he said dryly. "Remember that, daughter."

Then he proceeded at once with the question, "Thou hast wished to see me. What can I do for thee? I am but a poor and humble man, the servant of the Lord, but sometimes it has been my fate to do some good for others. What dost thou require of me?"

I proceeded to explain that I wanted nothing in the matter of worldly goods, but asked this singular personage to be kind enough to tell me for the paper which I represented whether it was true that but for him Russia would have declared war upon Austria the year before.

"Who has told you such a thing?" he inquired

"It is a common saying in St. Petersburg," I replied, "and some people say that you have been right in doing so."

"Right? Of course, I was right," he answered with considerable irritation. "All these silly people who surround our *czar* would like to see him commit stupidities. They only think about themselves and about the profits which they can make. War is a crime, a great crime, the greatest which a nation can commit, and those who declare war are criminals. I only spoke the truth when I told our *czar* that he would be ruined if he allowed himself to be persuaded to go to war. This country is not ready for it. Besides, God forbids war, and if Russia went to war the greatest misfortunes would fall upon her. I only spoke the truth; I always speak the truth, and people believe me."

"But," I remarked, "no one can understand how it is that your opinion always prevails in such grave matters. People think that you must have some strange power over men to make them do what you like."

"And what if I have," he exclaimed angrily. "They are, all of them, pigs—all these people who want to discuss me or my doings. I am but a poor peasant, but God has spoken to me, and He has allowed me to know what it is that He wishes. I can speak with our *czar*. I am not afraid to do so, as they all are. And he knows that he ought to listen to me, else all kind of evil things would befall him. I could crush them all, all these people who want to thwart me. I could crush them in my hand as I do this piece of bread," and while he was speaking he seized a biscuit out of a plate on the table and reduced it to crumbs. "They have tried to send me away, but they will never get rid of me, because God is with me and Gricha shall outlive them all. I have seen too much and I know too much. They are obliged to do what I like, and what I like is for the good of Russia. As for these ministers and generals, and all these big functionaries whom everyone fears in this capital, I do not trouble about them. I can send them all away if I like. The spirit of God is in me and will protect me.

"Thou canst say this to those who have sent thee to see me. Thou canst tell them that the day will come when there will be no one worth anything in our holy Russia except our *czar* and Gricha, the servant of God. Yes, thou canst tell them so, and be sure that thou dost it."

I protested that I should consider this my first duty, but at the same time begged "the servant of God," as he called himself, to explain to me by what means he had acquired the influence which he possessed.

"By telling the truth to people about themselves," he quickly replied. "Thou probably thinkest that all these fine ladies about the court who come to me do not care to be told about their failings. But there it is that thou art mistaken. They feel so disconcerted when they hear me call them by their proper names and remind them that they are but b——s, and the daughters of b——s, that they immediately fall at my feet. A silly lot are these women, and Gricha is not such a fool as one thinks. He knows how they ought to be treated. Wilt thou see how I treat them?"

I said that nothing would give me more pleasure. Rasputin went to the door and called Avdotia.

"Go to the telephone," he said when she came in, "ask the countess to come at once. She must come herself to the telephone, and if a servant replies, say that he must call her immediately, and then tell her that I require her presence here at 12 o'clock tonight; not one minute earlier or later, mind."

The woman went away, and I could hear her talking at the telephone in the next room in an authoritative tone. Soon she returned with the words:

"The countess sends her humble respects to Gregory Efimitsch, and she will be here at midnight as she has been ordered to."

Rasputin turned toward me with a triumphant smile on his coarse cunning countenance.

"Thou canst see, they are losing no time to obey me. Thou dost not know what women are, and how they like to be handled. Wait, and thou shalt see something better. Avdotia," he called again. "Is Marie Ivanovna here?" he asked, when she came in response to his call. "Yes, since three hours," was the reply.

"Call her here."

A young woman of about twenty-five years of age appeared. She was very well dressed in rich furs, and ran up to Rasputin, kneeling before him, and kissing with fervour his dirty hands.

"How long hast thou been here?" he asked.

"About three hours, *Batiouschka*," she answered.

"This is well, thou art to remain here until midnight, and neither to eat or to drink all that time, thou hearest?"

"Yes, *Batiouschka*," was the reply, uttered in timid, frightened tones.

"Now go into the next room, kneel down before the *Ikon*, and wait for me without moving. Thou must not move until I come."

She kissed his hands once more, prostrated herself on the floor before him three times in succession, and then retired with the look of being in a kind of trance during which she could neither know nor understand what was happening to her.

"If thou carest, thou canst follow her, and see whether she obeys me or not," said Rasputin in his usual dry tone.

I declined the invitation, protesting that I had never doubted but that the "Prophet" would be obeyed, adding, however, that though I had understood he could control the fancies and imagination of women gifted with an exalted temperament, yet I was not convinced that his influence could be exerted over unemotional men, and that this was the one point which interested my friends.

"Thou must not be curious," shouted Rasputin. "I am not here to tell thee the reasons for what I choose to do. It should suffice thee to know that I would at once return to Pokrovskoie if ever I thought my services were useless to my country. Russia is governed by fools. Yes, they are all of them fools, these pigs and children of pigs," he repeated with insistence. "But I am not a fool. I know what I want, and if I try to save my country, who can blame me for it?"

"But Gregory Efimitsch," I insisted, "can you not tell me at least whether it is true that some ministers do all that you tell them?"

"Of course, they do," he replied angrily. "They know very well their chairs would not hold them long if they didn't. Thou shalt yet see some surprises before thou diest, daughter," he concluded with a certain melancholy in his accents.

Avdotia entered the room again.

"Gregory Efimitsch," she said, "there is Father John of Ladoga waiting for you."

"Ah! I had forgotten him." Then he turned toward me.

"Listen again," he said; "this is a priest, very poor, who is seeking to be transferred into another parish somewhere in the south. Avdotia, call on the telephone the secretary of the Synod and tell him that I am very much surprised to hear that Father John has not yet been appointed to another parish. Tell him this must be done at once, and that he must have a good one. I require an immediate answer."

The obedient Avdotia went out again, and we could hear her once more talk on the telephone. "The secretary of the Synod presents his humble compliments to you, *Batiouschka*," she said when she returned.

"Who cares for his compliments?" interrupted Rasputin. "Will the man have his parish or not? This is all that I want to know."

"The order for his transfer will be presented for the minister's signature tomorrow," said Avdotia.

"This is right," sighed Rasputin with relief. And then turning to me:

"Art thou satisfied?" he asked, "and hast thou seen enough to tell to thy friends?"

I declared myself entirely satisfied.

"Then go," said Rasputin. "I am busy and cannot I talk to thee any longer. I have so much to do. Everybody comes to me for something, and people seem to think that I am here to get them what they need or require. They believe in Gricha, these poor people, and he likes to help them. But as for the question of war, this is all nonsense. We shall not have war, and if we have, then I shall take good care it will not be for long."

He dismissed me with a nod of his head, and his face assumed quite a shocked look when he found that I was retiring without seeming to notice the hand which he was awkwardly stretching out to me. But I knew that he expected people, as a matter of course, to kiss his dirty fingers, and as I was not at all inclined to do so, I made as if I did not notice his gesture. As I was passing into the next room, I could perceive through a half open door leading into another apartment the young lady whom Rasputin had called Marie Ivanovna. She was prostrated before a sacred image hanging in a corner, with a lamp burning in front of it, with her eyes fixed on Heaven, and quite an illuminated expression on her otherwise plain features. St. Theresa might have looked like that. But seen in the light of our incredulous Twentieth Century, she appeared a worthy subject for Charcot, or some such eminent nerve doctor, and her place ought to have been the hospital of "*La Salpetriere*" rather than the den of the modern Cagliostro, who was making ducks and drakes out of the mighty Russian Empire.

As I was going down the stairs, I met an old man slowly climbing them, with a little girl whom he was half carrying, half dragging along with him. He stopped me with the question:

"Do you happen to know whether the blessed Gregory receives visitors?"

I replied that the "Prophet" was at home, but that I could not say whether he would receive anyone or not.

"It is for this innocent I want to see him," moaned the man. "She is so ill and no doctor can cure her. If only the blessed Gregory would pray over her, I know that she would be well at once. Do you think that he will do so, *Barinia?*" the man added anxiously.

"I am sure he will," I replied, more because I did not know what to say rather than from the conviction that Rasputin would receive this new visitor. I saw the old creature continue his ascent up the staircase, and the whole time he was repeating to the child, "You shall get well, quite well, Mania, the Blessed One shall make you quite well."

On the last steps before the stairs ended on the landing, two men were busy talking. They were both typical Israelites, with hooked nose and crooked fingers. They were discussing most energetically some subject which evidently was absorbing their attention to an uncommon degree, and discussing it in German, too.

"You are quite sure that we can offer him 20 *per cent?*" one was saying.

"Quite sure, the concession is worth a million; the whole thing is to obtain it before the others come on the scene."

"Who are the others?" asked the first of the two men.

"The Russo-Asiatic Bank," replied the second. "You see the whole matter lies in the rapidity with which the thing is made. The only one who can persuade the minister to sign the paper is the old man upstairs," and he pointed out toward Rasputin's apartment. Thereupon the two in their turn started to mount the steps.

My first interview with Rasputin, all the details of which I wrote down in my diary when I got home, gave me some inkling as to the different intrigues which were going on around this remarkable personage. It failed, however, to make me understand by what means he had managed to acquire, if he really acquired, a fact of which I still doubted, the strong influence which he liked to give the impression he exercised. It was quite possible that he had contrived through the magnetic gifts with which he was endowed to subdue to his will the hysterical women, whose bigotry and mystical tendencies he had exalted to the highest pitch possible.

But how could he, a common peasant, without any education, knowledge of the world or of mankind, have imbued ministers and statesmen with such a dread that they found themselves ready to do anything at his bidding and to dispense favours, graces and lucrative appointments to the people whom he called to their attention. There was evidently something absolutely abnormal in the whole thing, and it was the reason for this abnormality that I began to seek.

This search did not prove easy at first, but in time, by talking with persons who saw much of Rasputin and of the motley crew which surrounded him, I contrived to form some opinion as to the cause of his success. It seemed to me that he was the tool of a strong though small party or group of men, desirous of using him as a means to attain their own ends. There is nothing easier in the world than to make or to mar a reputation, and it is sufficient to say everywhere that a person is able to do this or that thing, to instil into the mind of the public at large the conviction that such is the case. This was precisely what occurred with Rasputin.

Count Witte, who was one of the cleverest political men in his generation and perhaps the only real statesman that Russia has known in the last twenty-five years, ever since his downfall had been sighing for the day when he should be recalled to power. He knew very well all that was going on in the Imperial family, and it was easier for him than for anyone else to resort to the right means to introduce an outsider into that very closed circle which surrounded the *czar*.

So long as he had been a minister and had under his control the public exchequer it had been relatively easy for him to obtain friends, or rather tools, that had helped him in his plans and ambitions. When this faculty for persuasion failed him he bethought himself to look elsewhere for an instrument through which he might still achieve the ends he had in mind. He was not the kind of man who stopped before any moral consideration. For him every means was good, provided it would prove effective. When he saw that certain ladies in the entourage of the sovereigns had become imbued with the Rasputin mania, he was quick to decide that this craze might, if properly managed, prove of infinite value to him.

He therefore not only encouraged it as far as was in his power by pretending himself to be impressed by the prophetic powers of the "Blessed Gregory," but he also contrived very cleverly to let the fact of the extraordinary ascendancy which Rasputin was rapidly acquiring over the minds of powerful and influential persons become known. Very soon everybody talked of the latter-day saint who had I suddenly appeared on the horizon of the social life of St. Petersburg, and the fame of his reputation spread abroad like the flames of some great conflagration.

Russia is essentially the land where imperial favourites play a role, and soon the whole country was not only respecting Rasputin, but was trying to make up to him and to obtain, through him, all kinds of favours and material advantages. Together with Count Witte a whole political party was working, without the least consideration for the prestige of the dynasty which it was discrediting, to show up the rulers as associated with the common adventurer and sectarian, who, under other conditions, would undoubtedly have found himself prosecuted by the police authorities for his conduct. They had other thoughts in their heads than the interests of the dynasty, these money-seeking, money-grubbing, ambitious men. They represented nothing beyond the desire to become powerful and wealthy. What they wanted was important posts which would give them the opportunity to indulge in various speculations and more or less fraudulent business undertakings they contemplated.

Russia at the time was beginning to be seized with that frenzy for stock-exchange transactions, share buying and selling, railway concessions and mining enterprises which reached its culminating point before the beginning of the war. Men without any social standing, and with more than shady pasts, were coming forward and acquiring the reputation of being lucky speculators capable in case of necessity of developing into clever statesmen. These men began to seek their inspirations in Berlin, and through the numerous German spies with which St. Petersburg abounded they entered into relations with the German Intelligence Department, whose interests they made their own, because they believed that a war might put an end to the industrial development of the country, and thus interfere with their various speculations.

The French alliance was beginning to bore those who had got out of it all that they had ever wanted; it was time something new should crop up, and the German and Russian Jews, in whose hands the whole industry and commerce of the Russian Empire lay concentrated, began to preach the necessity of an understanding with the great state whose nearest neighbour it was. A rapprochement between the Hohenzollerns and the Romanoffs began to be spoken of openly as a political necessity, and it was then that, thanks to a whole series of intrigues, the *czar* was induced to go himself to Berlin to attend the nuptials of the only daughter of the *Kaiser*, the Brunswick.

This momentous journey to Berlin was undertaken partly on account of the representations of Rasputin to the empress, whose love for peace was very well known. Europe had just gone through the anxiety caused by the Balkan crisis, and it was repeated everywhere in St. Petersburg that a demonstration of some kind had to be made in favour of peace in general and also to prove to the world that the great Powers were determined not to allow quarrels in Serbia, Bulgaria and Greece to trouble the security of the world. The marriage festivities of which Berlin became the theatre at the time seemed a fit opportunity for this demonstration. The bureaucratic circles in the Russian capital and the influence of Rasputin were used to bring about this trip of the *czar*.

Rasputin was thus fast becoming a personage, simply because it suited certain people—the pro-German party, to use the right word at last—to represent him as being important. They pushed things so far that many ministers and persons in high places refused on purpose certain things which were asked of them and which were absolutely easy for them to perform simply because they wished Rasputin to ask for them for those who were weary of always meeting with a *non possumus* in questions for which they required the help of the Administration.

Rasputin's various intermediaries, through whom one had to pass before one could approach him, sold their help for more or less large sums of money, and thus began a period of vulgar *agiotage*, to use the French expression, of which Russia was the stage, and Rasputin, together with the men who used him, the moving spirits. I very nearly said the evil spirits. But of this, more later on.

CHAPTER 5

I must now make one remark which is absolutely necessary in order to enable the foreign readers to understand how the numerous legends which were connected with Rasputin and the influence of the latter on the course of public affairs could come to be accepted by the nation at large. One can seek its principal reason in the tendency which the Russian government has cultivated since immemorial times to forbid the open discussion of certain things and facts. At the time about which I am writing present military censorship did not exist, and there was no war which could have justified the control by the government of the publication by the daily press of the current events of the day.

Yet the censors did not allow any mention of Rasputin to be made in any organ of publicity. Thanks to this senseless interdict, it helped the invention of the most unbelievable tales concerning him and the attitude which he had adopted in regard to state affairs, with which he had begun to occupy himself, much to the dismay of those who had by that time learned to appreciate the fact that the "Prophet" was but the plaything of men far cleverer than himself and 50,000 times more dangerous.

St. Petersburg has always been famed for its gossiping propensities, and in no place in the whole world do the most incomprehensible rumours start and flourish with the rapidity that they do in the Russian capital. What the newspapers are forbidden to mention is told by one person to another, whispered from one ear to another and discussed everywhere, in clubs, drawing rooms, restaurants, in the houses of the proudest aristocrats as well as in the dwellings of the humblest citizens. Nowhere does, or rather, did, because I believe this has become impossible nowadays, the telephone contributes more to relate all kind of gossip concerning both private people and public matters.

Of course, as there existed no possibility of controlling all that was being related under the seal, of secrecy all over St. Petersburg, the most improbable rumours were put in circulation and were carried about not only in the town itself, but in the provinces, where the travellers returning from St. Petersburg were but too glad to repeat with considerable additions all that they had heard in the capital.

The very secrecy which was enjoined by the authorities in regard to Rasputin added to the latter's importance and transformed him into a kind of legendary personage, either too holy or too bad to be mentioned. Soon all kinds of things in which he had had absolutely no part began to be attributed to him, and many persons, earnestly believing him to be all-powerful, took to asking his help not only in the matter of their administrative careers, but also in questions where their private life and private interests were involved.

It happened every day that a man who had a lawsuit of a doubtful character sought out Rasputin, hoping that he might be able to put in a word capable of influencing the judges before whom the case was to be tried. As it was absolutely impossible for anyone to approach him without passing through an intermediary of some kind, it was generally this intermediary who began the regular plundering of the pockets of all the unfortunate petitioners who had hoped to retrieve their fortunes by an appeal to the "Prophet's" protection. This plundering went on as long as the victim had a penny to spare and a hope to live upon.

On the other hand, the liberal parties in the country began to be seriously alarmed at the importance which this uncouth peasant was assuming, and they it was who helped by the anxiety which they openly manifested to set the general public thinking about him more than it ought to have done. In the *Duma,* the name of Rasputin was mentioned with something akin to horror, and allusions without number were made concerning the "Dark Powers," as they were called, who were grasping in their hands the conduct of public affairs. The "Prophet" began to be mentioned as the scourge of Russia long before he had become one. His followers, on the contrary, made no secret of his ever-growing importance, and invented on their side any number of tales absolutely devoid of truth and tending to prove that nothing whatever was done in regard to the management of state affairs without his having been previously consulted.

Who consulted him no one knows, and no one could tell. Certainly, it was not the emperor, who had, when the "Prophet" once or twice had attempted to touch upon this point in his presence, rebuked him most sharply; certainly it was not the empress, who at that time had never yet cared for politics, whether foreign or domestic. It was also not the ministers, and most certainly it was not the leaders of any party in the *Duma*, because all parties there were agreed as to one thing, and that was a thorough detestation of Rasputin and of the whole crew which surrounded him and without which he could not exist. Who consulted him, then? No one knew, and very probably no one cared to know. But the fact that he was consulted was an established one, most probably due to the efforts of those persons in whose interests it lay to represent him as the *deus ex machina* without whom nothing could be done in general, and upon whom everything more or less depended.

It was even related in St. Petersburg that one day, during an audience which he had had with the *czar*, Mr. Rodzianko, the President of the *Duma*, had attempted a remonstrance on the subject of Rasputin for which he had been severely reproved by the sovereign. Personally, I do not believe for one single instant that such an incident ever took place. For one thing, no one, not even Mr. Rodzianko, would have dared to talk to the emperor about such an unsavoury subject as that of the "Prophet," even if he had been endowed with a moral courage far superior to that of the President of the *Duma*.

Then, again, the well-informed were, at the time I am referring to, far too cognisant of what was going on in the way of court intrigues not to understand that all protestations against the constant presence of Rasputin in the vicinity of the Imperial family would have led to nothing, for the simple reason that those upon whom it depended did not and could not even recognise the danger that it presented, because they simply looked upon him as upon a holy man. He soothed the anxieties of the empress in regard to her small son, promising her that the day would come when, thanks to his prayers, the child would outgrow his delicacy. He amused the emperor by talking to him in a rough but bright language, describing bluntly all the incidents that had reached his knowledge generally through the channel of those interested in having them conveyed to the Sovereign in the way that best served their own interests. But Nicholas II. never took him seriously into account, and therefore could hardly have been brought to think that others were doing so, and doing it with a vengeance into the bargain.

Rasputin, however, was of a different opinion, and in his desire that others should share it he liked to boast in public of the things which he had not done and of the words which he had not spoken. He was upon excellent terms with some of the palace servants, in whom he had found comrades and with whom he felt more at his ease than with anyone else. He got them to relate to him all that was going on in the family of the *czar*. He very cleverly made use of this knowledge later on. It is well known in Russia that the emperor himself was watched by the secret police, not only in view of his personal safety, but also because it was to the interest of the police to be thoroughly acquainted with all that he did and with the remarks it pleased him to make.

And the secret police were working hand in hand with Rasputin. Their provocative agents, of which there existed considerable numbers, were everywhere talking about the "Prophet's" influence and ever-growing importance, as well as relating in all the restaurants and public places in the capital wonderful and improbable tales concerning him and his doings. From these they were spread among the public and penetrated to people who otherwise would never have had the possibility of hearing anything about them. Among those who showed themselves the most active and the most eager to talk about Rasputin and about the influence which he was acquiring were persons well known for their German sympathies and others suspected of being German agents in disguise.

At that period, the great aim of the German Foreign Office was to bring about the collapse of the Franco-Russian alliance, and it set itself most cleverly to try to bring it about. Among the persons whom it employed for the purpose was Rasputin, perhaps unknown to himself, but led by men like Count Witte, who had always been pro-German in sympathy and who had almost engaged himself to bring about a rapprochement between the St. Petersburg and the Berlin Court. Working with Witte was Mr. Manassevitsch Maniuloff, one of the most abominable secret agents the world has ever known, who in his unscrupulousness would have done anything he was asked, provided he were paid high enough.

For years, he had been in receipt of German subsidies. By dint of blackmailing he had contrived to maintain himself in the capacity of one of the editors of the *Novoie Vremia*, where he wrote all that was asked of him for a consideration, the extent and nature of which depended upon circumstances. He was also on the staff of the Russian political Intelligence Department, to which he rendered such services as he considered to be advantageous to himself without the least thought of the use these might be to the State which employed him.

Mr. Maniuloff was a spendthrift who never could deny himself any of the good things of life. These are always considered to be expensive ones, and consequently he had expensive tastes. His capacity of police agent had allowed him to blackmail to advantage people against whom he had discovered, or thought he had discovered, something in the way of dangerous political opinions. One of his favourite occupations consisted in going about among these people and hinting to them that unless they showed themselves willing to minister to his numerous wants they might find themselves one day in a very tight corner.

Generally, these tactics proved successful, until he was caught red-handed in Paris, where he had been sent on a special mission, tampering with the funds of which he had control. This accident caused him to be dismissed. But the man knew far too much and had been far too advanced in the confidence of his superiors for them to be able to do without his services, so he was allowed to return to Russia and enrol himself in journalism, thus to make himself useful again. He had a wonderful intelligence and was an excellent worker and talked fluently in most of the European languages. He therefore made his way up the ladder once more, until at last he became the private secretary to Mr. Stunner when the latter was prime minister, an advancement that proved fatal to him because it brought him to prison. But of this I shall speak later on when touching upon the events which culminated in the murder of Rasputin.

Such were the men who virtually controlled every action of the "Prophet," and it is no wonder if guided by them he sometimes contrived to influence never the *czar* himself, but the latter's ministers and officials who had been told, they did not even know by whom, but probably by the loud voice of the public, that to do anything to please Rasputin was to secure for oneself the good graces of the highest people in the land. As time went on the "Prophet" showed himself less and less in public, remaining among a small circle of personal friends whose interest it was to represent him as a kind of Indian idol, unapproachable except to his worshippers.

And in the meanwhile, the ladies who had been the first artisans of Rasputin's favour were still holding religious meetings under his guidance and still seeking inspiration from his teachings. They believed him to be a real saint, refused to admit that he could do anything wrong and refused to accept as true the rumours which went about and which, unfortunately for the "Prophet's" reputation, were but too exact, that he was fond of every kind of riotous living, that he spent his nights in drunken revels and that he gave his best attention to brandy mixed with champagne. His admirers persisted in seeing in him the prophet of the Almighty and believed that they could never be saved unless they conformed to all the directions which it might please him to give them.

The Rasputin craze became more violent than ever during the few months which immediately preceded the war, and it very nearly verged upon complete fanaticism for his personality. Everything that he did was considered to be holy. His insolence and arrogance, displayed with increasing violence every day and hour, were almost incredible. This illiterate peasant dared to send dirty little scraps of paper on which he had scribbled a coarse message to ministers and public men ordering them to do this or that according to his pleasure, and presuming to give them advice, which was never his own, in matters of the utmost public importance.

At first people had laughed at him, but very soon they had discovered that he could revenge himself on them quickly and effectively, and this had led to the general determination not to interfere with him anymore, but to leave him severely alone, no matter what extravagance he might commit or say. And when it came to the extortion of large sums of money, those who were challenged to pay them generally did so with alacrity, as happened in the case of several banks to which Mr. Maniuloff applied for funds, with the help of these illiterate scraps of paper upon which Rasputin had scribbled his desire that the money should be put at the disposal of his *"protégé."*

What I have been writing is fact, which has been proved publicly, and never contradicted by so much as one single word of protestation. It accounts for the hatred with which the "Prophet" came to be viewed. As time went on it was felt that something ought to be attempted against the imposter who had contrived to break through barriers one could have believed to be absolutely impregnable. But no one knew how this was to be done, and at the time I am referring to the idea of a political assassination of Rasputin had not entered into the people's heads. It was a woman who was to bring it before the public in the following circumstances:

During the spring of the year 1914, Rasputin, to the general surprise of everybody, declared to his" friends that he intended to leave the capital and to return for a few months to his native village of Pokrovskoie in Siberia to rest from his labours. Strenuous efforts were made to detain him in Petrograd, but he remained inflexible and rudely thrust aside those who would fain have kept him back. He declared that he was tired and weary of the existence which he had been leading the last year, and that the various annoyances and difficulties that had been put in his way by his numerous enemies had quite sickened him.

Such, at least, was the explanation which he chose to give and to which he stuck. Others, it is true, declared that the real reason for his departure was that he had been given to understand that he would do better to absent himself from St. Petersburg during the time when the visit of the President of the French Republic was expected, as his presence there might prove embarrassing from more than one point of view.

The hint had enraged him, and he had determined to go away for a much longer time than he had been told to do. He had even declared to a few of his closest friends that he was not going to return to the capital any more, but that he would remain in Siberia, where, as he graphically put it, "there was a great deal more money to be made than anywhere else in the world." Whether the above is strictly true or not, I am not in a position to say, but it does not sound improbable. The fact remains that Rasputin left St. Petersburg for Pokrovskoie, where he arrived in the first days of June, 1914, accompanied by the "Sisters," who were his constant companions. He was received with such honours that he might have been the Sovereign himself instead of the simple peasant he was.

A crowd composed of several thousand men and women met him at the gates of the village and threw themselves at his feet imploring his blessing and calling upon him to pray with them, and to show them the real way to God which he was supposed to be the only one in Russia capable of indicating. For a few days, this kind of thing continued, and Rasputin's house was literally besieged by crowds of people who had gathered at Pokrovskoie from all parts of Siberia eager to pay homage to their national hero, for such he was considered to be. Rasputin smiled and chuckled and rubbed his hands, as was his wont in those moments when he allowed his satisfaction at anything to overpower him. If in St. Petersburg he had been considered as a prophet, here in this remote corner of Siberia he was fast becoming a kind of small god at whose shrine a whole nation was worshipping.

This was just the sort of thing to please him and to make him forget any small unpleasantnesses he might have experienced before his departure from the capital.

One morning, it was the 13th of July, 1914, Rasputin was leaving his house on his way to church, whither it was his custom to repair every day. On the threshold of his dwelling a woman was awaiting him. She had her face muffled in a shawl in spite of the warm weather. When she saw him she threw herself on her knees before him, as persons of her kind invariably did when they met him. The "Prophet" stopped and asked her what it was she wanted from him. Her only reply was to plunge into his stomach a large kitchen knife, which she had held the whole, time hidden under her shawl.

Rasputin uttered one cry and sank upon the ground. The crowd which was always following him rushed toward him and lifted him up, while two local policemen who had been set by the authorities to protect and guard him threw themselves upon the woman and seized her violently by both arms. She remained perfectly quiet, declaring that they need not hold her as she had not the slightest intention of running away. She knew very well what she had done, and she had meant to do it for a long time. When asked what had been her motives, she declared that she would speak before the magistrates, and only asked to be protected in the meanwhile against the fury of the mob that was threatening to tear her to pieces in its rage. She did not seem to be in the least disturbed by what she had done and throughout she showed the most extraordinary coolness and self-possession.

Very soon it was ascertained that she was a native of the government of Saratoff, and that her name was Gousieva. When Rasputin had been preaching in Saratoff she was among the women who had been taken in by his speeches, and though married she had left her husband and family to follow the "Prophet." He very soon proceeded to "cleanse her from her sins," according to his favourite expression. We know, of course, what this meant, and Gousieva, who at that time was young and pretty, only shared the fate of so many other women, deluded by the mealy-mouthed utterances of the "new Saviour," that it was only by means of a complete union with himself that they could be saved and their sins forgiven them.

The unfortunate Gousieva had been only one of many. When she had found it out an intense rage had taken hold of her, which had been further enhanced and strengthened by the monk Illiodore, to whom she had related her misfortune. He had already at the time she sought him out become the deadly enemy of his former friend Rasputin. The miserable woman had lost everything—home, children, husband, relatives—on account of her mad infatuation for the deceiver who had made her forget her duties by the fascination which he had exercised over her weak mind. She swore that she would revenge herself and kill the "Prophet," so that at least other women could be saved from the awful fate which had befallen her.

After Rasputin had dismissed her she had been compelled to lead a dreadful kind of existence in order to obtain a piece of bread. At last she had become attacked by an awful disease, which had already eaten away a part of her nose and completely disfigured her face. This, too, she attributed to the "Prophet." In her despair, she decided that as she had nothing to lose the best and only thing left for her to do was to try and rid the world from the awful impostor who had caused so much misery, brought about such abominable misfortunes and occasioned so much distress to such a number of innocent women.

She had followed Rasputin for a long time in St. Petersburg, but had never been able to approach him near enough to execute her design. But when it had come to her knowledge that he was returning to Pokrovskoie she had taken it as an indication that the Almighty would be with her in the deed which she was contemplating, and she, too, started for the distant Siberian village. There she had spent three days waiting for a favourable opportunity until the morning when she had at last succeeded in getting close enough to him to plant in his body the knife which she had carried about with her for more than two years.

This whole story was related by Gousieva with the utmost composure, and without any hesitation at all. She considered Rasputin as the incarnation of the devil, and she had thought it a good deed to put him out of the way of committing any more evil. For the rest, she did not care what was to become of her. As it was she knew that she had not long to live, and with the illness with which she was afflicted existence in itself was not so sweet that she should sacrifice her revenge in order to retain it. She had had no accomplices, and she had consulted no one. In spite of the efforts which were made to induce her to say that she had acted under the directions and the inspiration of Illiodore, she denied it absolutely, adding that had she spoken to him about her intention she knew that he would have dissuaded her from it and that he might even have warned the police so as to frustrate her design.

In the meanwhile, Rasputin had been carried back to his room and telegrams dispatched everywhere for a doctor. The wound, though deep, was not a serious one and it had not attacked any vital organs. The man was in no danger, but his disciples chose to say that it was a miracle of Providence that he had not succumbed at once under the blow which had been dealt at him. The "Prophet," when he had felt himself stabbed, had cried out that someone was to "arrest that b——h who had hit him."

Then he caused several telegrams to be sent to his friends in St. Petersburg in which he described the attempt against his life as the work of the devil, who had inspired the woman Gousieva and induced her to commit her abominable action. He added that at the moment when her weapon had touched him he had seen an angel descend from Heaven, stop her arm, and then put a hand on his wound so as to stop it from bleeding, and that it was only due to this direct intervention of the Almighty that he had escaped with his life. Of course, the story was believed by the credulous people who accepted every one of his words as a manifestation of the will of the Lord, and he became more than ever a saint, to whom the people began to raise altars, and to regard in the light of another Saviour come to redeem mankind from the terrors of sin.

In St. Petersburg, the news of the attempted assassination of Rasputin had produced an immense impression, and had been commented upon in different ways. Some people saw in it an intervention of the secret police, who had been told to get rid in some way or other of a man who was fast becoming a public nuisance and embarrassment for everybody, even for those who had benefited through their acquaintance with him. Others declared that it was a just punishment for his evil deeds, and that the woman Gousieva had not been badly inspired when she had tried to revenge herself on him for the terrible wrong which he had done to her. Everyone was anxious to learn how the news would be received in certain quarters; and among the bevy of feminine worshippers whose existence was wrapped up in that of Rasputin. Public curiosity, however, was not destined to be satisfied, because nothing was heard concerning the feelings of these adepts of his on this remarkable occasion.

The only thing which one learned in regard to the whole affair was that two ladies who figured among his most prominent supporters had started at once for Pokrovskoie, and that a celebrated surgeon from Kazan had also been requested to go to see him regardless of what his journey might cost.

The care that was taken of Rasputin soon restored him to his usual health, and he became at once a martyr. When the first moment of fright—and, being a great coward, he had been thoroughly frightened—I had passed away, he felt rather satisfied at the fuss which was made about him, and more grateful than anything else to the woman Gousieva for having given him such a splendid opportunity to recover some of his popularity, which he had feared might decrease during his absence from St. Petersburg.

The fact that his attempted assassination had brought his name and his person once more prominently before the public pleased him, and his natural cunning made him at once grasp the whole importance of the event and the capital that might be made out of it. He was the first to plead for indulgence for his would-be murderess, perhaps out of fear of the scandal which a trial might produce, a trial during which a lawyer might be found daring enough and enterprising enough to speak openly of the reasons which had driven the accused woman to this act of madness, and to disclose certain episodes in the past existence of the "Prophet" which the latter would not have cared at all to become the property of the public.

On the other hand, the authorities, too, felt that a public trial Should only cause a most painful sensation, by the mention of names which it was of the highest importance to keep outside the question. The culprit herself insisted upon being brought before a jury, declaring that she had sought publicity and that she would not rest until she had it; that, moreover, she did not intend to be cheated out of her revenge or prevented from exposing the man in whom she saw the most flagrant and daring impostor, a creature for whom nothing in the world was sacred and who would not hesitate at anything in order to come to his ends. She insisted on the fact that she would have rendered a public service to the country had she killed him, and that, whatever happened to her personally, the vengeance of God would one day overtake "Gricha" and his wickedness, and that others would be found who would follow the example which she had given to them and not fail as she had failed.

Gousieva told all this to the examining magistrate to whom had been intrusted the preliminary inquest, and she persisted in her allegations, notwithstanding all the efforts and even the threats which were made to her to induce her to retract her first deposition. The authorities found themselves in a dilemma from which they did not know how to extricate themselves, when Rasputin himself came to their rescue.

"The woman is mad," he said. "All that she relates is but the ravings of a madwoman. Lock her up in an asylum, and let us hear nothing more about her!"

This piece of advice was considered to be the best possible under the circumstances, and Gousieva was placed first in a hospital for observation and then a few months later adjudged insane by order. She was removed to a madhouse, no one knows exactly where, and there she probably is locked up to this day unless death in some shape or form has overtaken her and removed her forever out of a world which certainly had never proved a kind one for her.

In the meanwhile, her victim was mending rapidly, and three weeks after his accident he was removed first to Tobolsk and then to St. Petersburg. His disciples were preparing a great reception for him, and he himself was openly talking of all that he would do on his return and of the revenge which he was going to take on the people to whose influence he attributed the "mad" act of the woman who had attacked him.

He made the greatest efforts to connect Illiodore with the attempt of Gousieva, and he was quite furious to see them fail, declaring that when he was once more in the capital he would make it his business to find out whether it was not possible to discover some points of association between the unfrocked monk and the woman whose knife had been raised against him. He further made no secret of his intention to obtain the proofs which he needed, thanks to the intelligence and with the help of his friend Mr. Manassevitsch-Maniuloff. Whether he would have succeeded or not, it is difficult to say, because when Rasputin returned to St. Petersburg and was enabled to visit his friends at Tsarskoie Selo once more, there were other preoccupations which were troubling the public more than anything connected with his individuality. War had broken out with Germany.

Chapter 6

It was perhaps a fortunate thing for Rasputin that he was not in St. Petersburg when Germany attacked us so unexpectedly. It is quite probable that if he had found himself in the capital at the time he would have intrigued in so many ways that he might have put even the sovereign in an embarrassing position, for any hesitations in the decisions of the government would have been attributed to the influence of the "Prophet." At this time of national crisis, if certainly would have been a misfortune if anything had occurred likely to endanger the prestige of the dynasty. But in regard to Rasputin himself, it is likely that his absence delayed the conspiracy which resulted in his death, as he was forgotten for the moment, so intensely was public opinion preoccupied with the grave events that were taking place.

Later on, after the disaster of Tannenberg, the friends of the "Prophet," in order to win back for him some popularity, spread the rumour that he had from his distant Pokrovskoie written to one of his warmest patronesses, Madame W, that he had had a vision during which it had been revealed to him that the Russian armies were to march immediately upon eastern Prussia, where it would be possible to deal a decisive blow at the enemy, and to do so with all their strength. Now this is precisely what was not done, owing to the military misconception of the Russian General Staff, which for political reasons started to proceed to the conquest of Galicia, that could have been delayed with advantage until after the Prussian monster, if not killed, had been at least seriously injured.

The enemies of the Grand Duke Nicholas, of whom there were plenty, seized hold of this rumour, and rallied themselves round Rasputin, declaring that once more God had intervened in favour of Holy Russia, in blessing it with a prophet whose clear glance and visions could be relied upon far better than the strategical combinations of the grand duke that had proved such a complete failure. The grand duke was accused of having despatched two army corps into the Mazurian region without having taken sufficient precautions to insure their safety, and it was said that the only one who had seen clearly the disaster which had overtaken these corps had been Rasputin, and that it had been revealed to him direct from Heaven even before it had taken place.

All this was great nonsense, of course, but nevertheless it did a considerable amount of harm. One must not lose sight of one fact when one judges the whole history of the impostor who for so many years contrived to occupy with his personality the attention of the Russian public, and that is that his sermons and utterances appealed to that mystical side of the Slav character which in all hours of great national crises and misfortunes asserts itself a manner which to the Occidental mind seems quite incomprehensible. It is sufficient to have looked upon the crowds kneeling in the streets of St. Petersburg, and of Moscow, during those eventful August days which saw the breaking out of the catastrophe, to become persuaded of the fact that they reckoned more on God's intervention on their behalf than on the efficacy of any guns or soldiers to insure a victory for the Russian arms.

Rasputin, for a short period, became once more a national hero, at least in the eyes of the select circle that had first brought him prominently before the public, and they began to say among this circle that until one followed his directions and gave oneself up entirely to the service of God in the manner it pleased him to recommend, the campaign that had just begun would never be won. For other people, too, the return of the "Prophet" to Petrograd, as St. Petersburg had been rechristened, was also a boon. All the speculators, army purveyors and persons interested in army contracts awaited him with an impatience which surpassed every description, and they surrounded him at once and laid siege, not so much to his person as to the influence which he was supposed to possess.

There are innumerable anecdotes about this agitated period in the career of Rasputin, each more amusing and each more incredible than the others. I shall here quote a few:

A Danish gentleman had arrived in Petrograd from Copenhagen with a load of medicines and different pharmaceutical products which he wanted to sell to the Red Cross. He brought excellent credentials with him, and he imagined that the business would be a relatively easy one. But to his surprise he found that this was not at all the case. Though the prices which he asked for his goods were not at all high compared with those current in the Russian capital, he could not get rid of them, and he was always put off until the next day.

At last he became quite discouraged and was already thinking of returning home when he met in the lounge of the principal hotel of Petrograd (famed for the financial transactions which were regularly taking place under its roof) a Jew who, seeing him looking worried and annoyed, asked what was the matter. The Dane then related his story, adding that he failed to understand why at a time when the things which he had brought with him were in great demand he could not sell them, though he had lowered his prices to a point below which it was quite impossible for him to go.

The Jew looked at him for some minutes, then asked him whether he would feel inclined, if he could help him to dispose of his wares at a profit, to give a large commission in exchange. The Dane of course (assented, and the Jew took him the next day to Rasputin, to whom he told a long story of which the seller of the articles in question understood nothing at all, but which culminated in the "Prophet" scribbling something in pencil on a dirty scrap of paper, and handing it to his visitors. The same afternoon the two men went to the head offices of the Red Cross, accompanied by another gentleman, who introduced himself as Rasputin's secretary.

To the intense surprise of the Dane, the medicines which he had been trying uselessly to sell for three weeks were at once accepted on the producing of the "Prophet's" note, and sold at such an enormous profit that he remained absolutely astounded. The contract was signed there and then, and a cheque handed to the happy seller. His two companions then accompanied him to the bank, where he handed over to them their share in the transaction, Rasputin's representative taking the lion's share of course, but whether for his master or for himself has never been ascertained.

Another example is still more typical. There existed in Petrograd a German who had lived there for years, and who had acquired considerable property, among other things several houses in Petrograd, bringing him a large income. Very soon after the breaking out of the war the properties belong ng to the enemy were sequestrated, and German subjects sent away from the capital to live out the war in some northern government. The same fate overtook our friend. But he was a man of resources, and he immediately proceeded to pay a visit to Mr. Manassevitsch-Maniuloff. The latter was about the last man capable of allowing such a wonderful chance to escape him.

How he managed he did not say, and the German never cared to learn, but he was allowed not only to remain in Petrograd, but also to sell his houses to a personage occupying such a very important administrative position that no one cared or dared to inquire of him whether he paid into the bank, as he ought to have done, the price of his acquisitions, or whether he gave it in the shape of a cheque on a foreign bank to the seller. And to crown the whole matter, the German in question was allowed to leave Russia with all due honours, and received the position of official buyer of different military goods for the Russian government in Scandinavia. He soon managed to indemnify himself to the full for the loss he had incurred in parting from his property for a mere song, and in paying the three hundred thousand *rubles* commission which Mr. Manassevitsch-Maniuloff and Rasputin had together obtained from him.

Such things were of daily occurrence, known to the general public, and of course commented upon in terms which were anything but favourable to the "Prophet." The latter, however, did not mind and seemed absolutely convinced of immunity in regard to the different transactions in which he indulged and which increased in importance every day. He began to give his special attention to the interesting matter of army contracts, and there he found a very rich field to explore. All the different agents and intermediaries who constituted such a notable element in Petrograd crowded around him, offering him their services, or imploring his help in all kinds of shady business, put of which no one with the exception of Rasputin himself got a single penny.

Thanks to him, bad cartridges were delivered to the army; rotten meat, or meat at a fabulous price, was sold for its wants, and not only sold once, but several times over. No matter how strange this last assertion may sound, it is absolutely true. If at the beginning of the war people were afraid to indulge in that kind of sport, they became adepts at it later on, and the only art which was practised in regard to it consisted in bribing an official not to put the government stamp on the goods which were delivered to the Red Cross or to the Commissariat Department, an omission which allowed them to be returned to those who had already once disposed of them, and thus become the object of a new transaction, perhaps even more profitable than the first.

In regard to important matters, Rasputin did not disdain occasionally to play the spy. I remember a curious instance which during the first five or six weeks of the war greatly amused those who became aware of it. The whole incident is most characteristic of the business methods then in vogue in Russia, which are at present dying out fast, thanks to the co-operation of the English and French authorities with the Russians in all questions connected with army contracts.

When war was declared, the military administration proceeded to requisition numerous things which it required in the way of war material. Among others were sand bags for the trenches. Now there happened to be a Jew in Petrograd who had about 50,000 of them. He did not care to declare them as he ought to have done, knowing very well that he was not in a position to obtain from the Commissariat Department the price which he wanted. He therefore sold them to another Jew, who gave him a certain sum on account, stipulating that he would take the delivery of the goods in the course of the next week or so. But in the meanwhile, prices went down, and the unlucky buyer found that he had indeed made about as bad a bargain as possible. While he was thus lamenting his bad luck, he happened to meet one of the secretaries of Rasputin to whom he related his misfortune.

"Is this troubling you?" exclaimed the latter. "This is nothing, and we shall soon set it all right." He took him to the "Prophet," where the trio came to the following arrangement: The Jew was to go forthwith to the Commissariat Department and declare that he had so many thousand sand bags to sell. Rasputin was to speak in his favour and to do his best to obtain the highest prices possible. Rasputin's secretary proceeded then to denounce the first Jew, who was the real owner of the bags, as having neglected to declare their existence.

Immediately a requisition was made in the latter's store, where the bags of course were found. Then the Jew who had given an account of them interfered, and said that they were his property, and that he had fulfilled all the formalities required by the law in regard to them. He forthwith proceeded to take possession of the bags, laughing in the face of their real owner whom he defied to claim the balance still due to him, well knowing that the unfortunate victim could do nothing, because if he had tried to complain he would inevitably have been condemned to pay a heavy fine and to be imprisoned.

Then again there was a story of railway trucks in which the "Prophet" also was mixed up in some unaccountable way. Some Jews, protected no one knows to this day by whom or in what way, had obtained some contracts from the government for different goods which were to be delivered to the army, together with the necessary numbers of railway trucks to carry them to the front. They immediately proceeded to sell these contracts at a fair price, though not an exaggerated one, to other people, but with the clause that these other people were to take upon themselves the care of forwarding the goods to their destination. And they kept for their own use and benefit the trucks which had been allotted to them, hiring them afterward to whoever wanted to have them for as much money as they could get.

One Jew, a certain Mr. Bernstein, thus obtained control over more than 500 trucks, out of which he drew during six months an income amounting to something like 250,000 *rubles* a month. And this occurred while everybody was complaining of the impossibility of forwarding anything anywhere, owing to the total lack of railway material. It is related that in this little business, too, Rasputin was mixed up, and that without him the military contracts which the heroes of the anecdote I have just related obtained would never have been granted.

These stories, scandalous though they were, are well known. There were others of which it is hardly possible to speak in a language fit for a drawing room. Such, for instance, is the sad case of a young girl, the daughter of a rich merchant in Moscow, who travelled all the way to Petrograd, to see the "Prophet" and implore his prayers for her *fiancé* who was at the front. Rasputin received her, and forthwith proceeded to tell her that the young man for whom she felt so anxious was doomed and could be saved only if she consented to unite herself with him, Rasputin, and to be cleansed by him of all her sins. The poor child, frightened out of her wits and fascinated by the terror which the dreadful creature inspired in his victims, allowed him to do what he liked with her. But she afterward became mad, on hearing that in spite of her sacrifices her lover had fallen at Tannenburg, during the terrible battle which took place in that locality.

All these things were whispered from ear to ear with horror and disgust, but they did not harm in the least the impostor who was pursuing his career of wickedness, deceit and crime. As time went on, he got more and more insolent, more and more overbearing, so that at last even some of his former protectors found that he was going rather too far, and he was no longer received at Tsarskoie Selo with the same kindness that had been shown to him previously.

He did not care for this, nor did those with whom he was working care either. They were all unscrupulous, daring people, determined to make hay while the sun was shining, and careless as to what others might think of them. Count Witte, who saw further and understood better than most of the public the hopeless muddle into which the administration had fallen, felt sure that sooner or later the country would demand an explanation for the many mistakes and errors which had been committed, and that a change in the government was bound to take place. He fully meant this change to affect his own prospects in so far that it would put him again at the head of affairs, and he was helping Rasputin as hard and as well as he could to discredit the Cabinet then in power, and to show it up as being thoroughly incapable of managing the country at this moment of grave crisis.

It was about that time that the Massayedoff incident took place, about which such a lot has been written, and which deserves a passing mention in this record. Massayedoff was a colonel who had already given some reasons to be talked about for misdeeds of a more or less grave nature. General Rennenkampf, when he had received the command of the Kovno Army Corps, had energetically protested against his appointment on his staff, but headquarters ignored his representations and maintained the colonel in his functions.

After the disaster of Tannenberg and the loss of two Russian army corps in the swamps of the Mazurian region, it was discovered that some spying of a grave nature had been going on and that the principal spy was Colonel Massayedoff, who had kept the enemy informed of the movements of the Russian troops. He was tried and condemned to death, which sentence was duly executed. Together with him several individuals compromised in the same affair, mostly Jews connected with questions of army purveyance, were also hanged.

Among these last was a man called Friedmann, who had been one of the parasites who were perpetually crowding around Rasputin. The latter, however, when asked to interfere in his favour had refused to do so, but whether this was due to the desire to get rid of a compromising accomplice or the dread of being mixed up himself in a dangerous story, it is difficult to say or to guess. But others talked, if the "Prophet" himself remained silent, and soon it began to be whispered that he was also, if not exactly a German agent, at least a partisan of a separate peace with Germany.

There certainly exist indications that such was the case. In spite of the strong character upon which Rasputin prided himself, it is hardly possible that he could have escaped the influence of the people who were constantly hanging about him, and who were all partial to Germany. This was due to the fact that they hoped, if the latter Power triumphed and vanquished the Russians, to obtain from the German Government substantial rewards for their fidelity, in! the shape of some kind of army contracts, for the time that the Prussian troops remained in occupation of some Russian provinces.

It is quite remarkable that while the nation in general was all for the continuation of the war, and would have considered it a shame to listen to peace proposals without consent of its Allies, commercial and industrial people were always talking about peace to whomever would listen. And Rasputin had now more to do with that class of individuals than with the nation.

It was at that time that he suddenly imagined himself to be endowed with perspicacity in regard to military matters, and that he attempted to criticise the operations at the front, and especially the leadership of the Grand Duke Nicholas, whom he hated with all the ferocity for which his character had become famous. He was known to be absolutely without any mercy for those whom he disliked. He disliked none more than the grand duke, who had, on one occasion when the "Prophet" had tried to discuss with him the conduct of the campaign and even volunteered to arrive at headquarters, declared that if he ever ventured to put in an appearance there he would have him hanged immediately from the first tree he could find.

Rasputin was prudent, and moreover he knew that Nicolas Nicolaievitsch was a man who always kept his word, so he thought it wise to leave a wide berth between him and the irascible commander-in-chief. But he applied himself with considerable perseverance to undermine the position of the latter, and especially to render him unpopular among the people, accusing him openly of mismanagement in regard to military matters and of want of foresight in his strategical dispositions.

In the beginning this did not succeed, partly because the staff did not allow any news of importance to leak out from the front and partly because the country believed so firmly in a victory over the Prussians that it was very hard to shake its confidence in the grand duke's abilities. The early successes of the first Galician campaign had strengthened this confidence, and no one in Petrograd during the first months of the year 1915 ever gave a thought to the possibility of our troops being compelled to retreat before the enemy, and no one foresaw the fall of Warsaw and of the other fortresses on the western frontier.

Rasputin, however, knew more than the public at large. He had his spies everywhere, who faithfully reported to him everything that was occurring in the army. He was well aware that the army was suffering from an almost complete lack of ammunition, and that it would never be able to hold against any offensive combined with artillery attacks on the part of the enemy. This knowledge, which he carefully refrained from sharing with anyone, enabled him to indulge in prophesies of a more or less tragic nature, the sense of which was that God was punishing Russia for its sins, and that with an unbeliever like the commander-in-chief at the head of its armies it was surely marching towards a defeat which would be sent by God as a warning never to forget the paths of Providence, and never to disdain the advice of the one prophet that He had sent in His mercy to save Russia from all the calamities which were threatening her.

He used to speak in that way everywhere and to everybody, even at Tsarskoie Selo, not to the emperor and empress, of course, but to all those persons surrounding them who were favourably inclined toward himself and likely to spread abroad the prophecies which he kept pouring into their ears.

But, in spite of all this, he was not quite so successful as he had hoped, because owing to the ignorance which prevailed as to the real state of things in the army, few people believed him, and fewer still would own that they did so. Once more Rasputin's star was beginning to wane, and even the empress began to think him very wearisome with his perpetual forebodings concerning misfortunes which seemed to be far away from the limits of possibility.

Then suddenly things changed. Mackensen began his march forward, and the grand duke, with his heart full of rage and despair, was compelled, owing to the mistakes, the negligence and the crimes of others, to make the best out of a very bad job, and to try at least to save the army confided to his care. Even if he had to sacrifice towns and fortresses, he had declared he would never, and under no conditions whatever, surrender to the enemy. The great retreat began, and proved to be one of the most glorious pages in the history of Russian warfare, a deed the gallantry of which will live in the military annals of the world as almost as grand a one as the famous retreat of Xenophon and his 10,000 warriors.

Russia appreciated its importance; the world admired it; the *czar*, though he may have shed bitter tears over its necessity, felt grateful for the talent which was displayed in such a terrible emergency; but people in Petrograd began looking for those upon whom they could fix the responsibility for this awful disappointment which had overtaken them. This was the moment for which Rasputin had been waiting with the patience of the serpent watching for its prey, and of which he hastened to make use with the infernal cunning he usually displayed in all the evil deeds with which he was familiar.

The secret police agents, who were working with him, and thanks to whom he had been enabled to make the enormous profits that had added so many millions to his fortune since the war had started, began to spread the rumour that the grand duke was plotting against the *czar*, and wanted to usurp the latter's throne and crown, out of fear of being called upon to render an account of his activity during the nine months of the campaign. Though it was quite evident that the responsibility for the lamentable want of organisation which had culminated in the momentary defeat of the Russian troops lay upon the War Office and the Artillery and Commissariat Departments, and though the War Minister, General Soukhomlinoff, had been dismissed in disgrace before being sent to the fortress of St. Peter and St. Paul to await there his trial; though strenuous efforts had been made to punish those to whose carelessness this mass of misfortunes had been due, yet Rasputin and his friends applied themselves to the task of representing the grand duke as being more guilty than anyone else, and of having on purpose kept secret the real state of things, out of fear that he would be called upon, if he revealed the truth, to surrender his command.

There was not one word of truth in these accusations, because Nicholas Nicholaievitsch had, on the contrary, worked harder than anyone to repair the blunders of others, and had never shared the blind confidence in victory which so many people who knew nothing about the real condition of affairs professed to nurse. He had done all that it was humanly possible to do, in order to save a situation which had been doomed from the first day that it had begun to develop. If he had failed, this had been in no way his fault, but that of circumstances and of fate which had proved too strong for him.

The public, however, thought differently, and Rasputin's numerous supporters helped it to come to the conclusion that the grand duke ought to be deprived of his command by some means or other. This, however, was not such an easy thing to do, because the emperor had a sincere esteem and respect for his uncle, and understood better than all those who criticised the latter the extent of the difficulties against which he had had to fight. He refused to listen to those who tried to shake his confidence in the commander-in-chief.

He might have gone on for a long time doing so had not Rasputin succeeded in winning over to his point of view several high ecclesiastical dignitaries, who took it upon themselves to speak to the sovereign of the desire and wishes of the nation to see him assume himself the supreme command over his armies. They assured him that it was quite certain that the armies would fight ever so much better under the personal leadership of their *czar* than under any other commander-in-chief, no matter how high might be his military reputation, or how elevated might be his rank. This was quite a new point of view, and Nicholas II. had to examine it with attention, the more so as the empress, too, had been won over to the idea, and was pressing him to give to his subjects this satisfaction for which they craved.

The military situation was then recognised, even by the most optimistically inclined people, to be very serious, and it was generally felt that something had to be done to excite the enthusiasm of the troops, which had lately begun to wane. The assumption by the *czar* of the supreme command seemed to present itself almost in the light of an absolute necessity. Perhaps from some points of view Rasputin was not so very wrong to urge it, as it most certainly produced a salutary effect on the whole situation. But it is to be doubted whether the "Prophet" had ever looked at it in that light. It is far more likely that his only aim had been the displacing of the Grand Duke Nicholas, who had begun to look too closely into all that was going on around Rasputin, and to watch the different intrigues in which the latter was taking part with an attention that did not promise anything good for him, or for the further development of his career as an adventurer.

When the grand duke had been appointed Viceroy of the Caucasus, and had left for his new residence, Rasputin breathed freely once more. For one thing, this incident had given him a greater confidence in his own strength than he had even possessed before. Now that he had been able to remove the commander-in-chief of the Russian armies from his post, it seemed to him that it would be a relatively easy thing to push forward, and to appoint to the most important functions in the State people indoctrinated with his view and ready to help him in keeping undisturbed and unchallenged the position into which he had glided so naturally, and as now appeared to him, so simply—a position which he was absolutely determined not to lose.

With a prime minister at his command, he would become the real master of Russia, and the *czar* himself would be compelled to take him into account, a thing which up to then he had refused to do, much to the distress of the "Prophet." Though he repeated everywhere, and to whomsoever wished to listen to him, that he could do all he liked at Tsarskoie Selo, he knew very well in his inmost heart that such was not the case, and that in the Imperial Palace Rasputin was nothing but Rasputin, an ignorant peasant, endowed sometimes with gifts of second sight and always with religious fervour, but a peasant all the same, with whom one might pray, but whom one would never dream of appointing to any responsible position.

The knowledge that such was the case, and that his so-called influence existed mostly in the imagination of the people who spoke about it, worried Rasputin. Though he dictated to ministers his will, though he decided together with them more than one important matter, yet he felt that there was a flaw in the edifice of his fortune, and that this flaw consisted in the fact that the sovereign did not share the feeling of reverence with which the Russian nation, as the "Prophet" flattered himself was the case, experienced for his person and for his teachings.

This was what tormented him, and he spent the whole time thinking how it might become possible to put in the place of Mr. Goremykine another prime minister more ready to enter into his views, and to follow his advice in regard to matters of state. This the then President of Council, in spite of his deference for Rasputin, had refused to do, preferring to discuss the affairs of the government alone with the emperor, without any interference of the former.

Rasputin spoke of his wishes to some of his confidants, and even mentioned the subject to several of the high-born ladies who formed the great bulk of his "*clientele.*" These entered into his views with alacrity, the more so as he developed them in a pathetic tone, which appealed to their feelings of "patriotism." They would have given much to be able to help him, but they did not very well know how this was to be done. This was due to the sad fact that there seemed to be no one available.

The unexpected and sudden death of Count Witte, which had occurred in the meanwhile, removed the only person whom they could suggest as a candidate for the functions of prime minister. All those whose names might have been mentioned as fit individuals for the post, such as Mr. Krivoscheine for instance, were people who would, with a greater energy even than Mr. Goremykine had ever displayed, oppose any interference of Rasputin into the conduct of the government. Their perplexity might have lasted a long time if Providence, in the shape of Mr. Manassevitsch-Maniuloff, had not interfered in their favour, and had the latter not suggested the advisability of entering into negotiations with Mr. Sturmer.

Chapter 7

Mr. Sturmer was not a novice in politics and he was known to be a reactionary of the deepest dye. It is likely that even Rasputin's friends would never have given a thought to the possibility of his becoming prime minister if Count Witte had still been in the land of the living. With the latter's death, the sort of coalition or secret society that had hoped through the occult influence of the "Prophet" to rise to power had lost its best head. There was no one to take his place, officially at least, because with the best will in the world it was impossible to suggest as a candidate for a ministerial portfolio Mr. Manassevitsch-Maniuloff. The past record of this man did not permit him to play any role but that of the Père Joseph of a minister who was not a Richelieu. And though the secret position of principal adviser to a personage of the importance of Rasputin had its advantages, it nevertheless precluded the possibility of becoming a candidate for the place of a statesman.

The next best thing, therefore, was to find someone who would be willing to become consciously what the "Prophet" was unconsciously, the instrument of the vile crew whose ambition was to make money by all means out of the terrible situation into which the country was plunged. These unscrupulous people all felt that they would never again in the whole course of their life have another such opportunity of becoming rich beyond the dreams of avarice, and they were not the kind of people to allow it to escape them.

Every effort was therefore put forward to bring Mr. Sturmer to the notice of the emperor, and to the attention of all those capable of suggesting to the latter the choice of this functionary to replace Mr. Goremykine, who had openly declared that he could not any longer go on fighting against the subterranean forces which were slowly but surely working against him, md making his position more unbearable every day. The candidate who would have been the most welcome to public opinion was Mr. Krivoscheine, but he was the last man whom Rasputin's friends would have cared to put forward.

On the other hand, Mr. Sturmer, for personal reasons into which it is useless to enter here, when approached by Manassevitsch-Mani-uloff, had not hesitated a single moment in promising to indorse the purposes of the small group of persons who had made up their minds to become the real rulers of the State. As soon as he had declared his willingness to join with them in the future an energetic campaign was started in his favour, not in the press nor in the *Duma*, nor even among the public, but in the immediate vicinity of the sovereign, a campaign in which some of the highest authorities in the Greek Church were enrolled, and in which the empress herself was persuaded by some of her personal friends to take part.

The expected then occurred. The *czar* was finally persuaded that in Mr. Sturmer he would find a faithful servant, which in a certain sense he did, and also a minister determined to govern according to the old principles of autocracy with an utter disregard for the liberal parties, as well as for the *Duma*. The *Duma* had not spared the government during the whole summer, and its activity had been viewed with dismay by certain members. Yet the country was glad to find that at last there existed among its representatives, men courageous enough to say what they thought, and to try to save Russia from the abyss into which it was felt that she was falling through the influence not so much of Rasputin himself as of those who surrounded him and who used him for their own ends.

This campaign succeeded and Mr. Sturmer was appointed. His selection caused an outcry of indignation throughout the whole country, and distressed its best friends for more than one reason. But even among the functionaries of the ministry, which had to accept him as its chief, there were found some rebellious spirits, among whom was the then Minister of the Interior, Mr. Chvostoff, who made up their minds that it was at last high time to get rid of Rasputin in some manner or other. He was also a reactionary, like Mr. Sturmer, and even a furious one. When he was still a deputy in the *Duma* he had been one of the leaders of the faction of the right and before that time had made for himself the reputation of being an ultraconservative in all the different administrative posts which he had occupied.

Among others, he had been governor at Nijni Novgorod for a short period. He belonged to the number of persons who held the opinion that Rasputin ought to be removed. But whether he was really a party to the extraordinary story I am going to relate is a matter about which I shall abstain from expressing an opinion.

The fact is that about the beginning of the year 1916 people were startled by hearing of a new conspiracy against Rasputin, in which it was rumoured that the Minister of the Interior himself was a party. Things stood thus: A secret agent of the Russian police called Rgevsky, a man about as unscrupulous as Manassevitsch-Maniuloff but not so clever, who had already figured more than once in occasions when the need for a provocative agent had been felt, arrived in Christiania, in Norway, where the unfrocked monk Illiodore was living, and sought him out. His journey had been undertaken without the knowledge of the chief of the secret police, Mr. Bieletsky, but on the express orders of Mr. Chvostoff, the Minister of the Interior.

Bieletsky, however, had suspected that some underhand game was going on, and had caused Rgevsky to be watched. When the latter had crossed the frontier at Torneo, he had been thoroughly searched and examined by special orders received from Petrograd, without, however, anything suspicious being found on him. When he was questioned as to the reasons for his journey abroad he had, in order to be allowed to proceed, to own that it was undertaken by command of the Minister of the Interior.

On his return from abroad Rgevsky was at once arrested under the pretext of having blackmailed another police agent. Furious at what he considered to have been a breach of faith, he contrived to apprise

Rasputin of the position in which he found himself placed, and revealed to him that the object of his mission had been to see and speak with Illiodore to try to persuade the latter to organise a conspiracy with the help of the many followers he still had in Russia. The object of this plot was to be the murder of the "Prophet." Illiodore had been considered ever since his quarrel with Rasputin one of the latter's worst enemies, and it was felt that he would enter with alacrity into the plot which it was proposed to engineer. But to the stupefaction of the persons who had thus applied to him in the hope of finding in him the instrument which they required, Illiodore went over to the enemy. On the advice of Rgevsky he telegraphed to Rasputin, asking the latter to send someone whom he could trust to Norway, and telling him that he would deliver into the hands of that person the proofs of the plot that was being hatched against his, Rasputin's, life.

Mr. Chvostoff, when taken to task for the affair, of course, denied it in its entirety. He declared that he had given quite different instructions to Rgevsky, and that he had sent the policeman to Norway to buy the memoirs of Illiodore, which he had heard the latter was about to publish abroad. But at the same time Chvostoff made no secret of his feelings of repugnance to Rasputin, and declared that he considered him a most dangerous and mischievous man, whose presence at Petrograd was exceedingly harmful for the prestige of the dynasty, as well as for the welfare of the State in the grave circumstances in which the country was finding itself placed.

According to Mr. Chvostoff, Rasputin was surrounded with individuals of a most suspicious character, who spent their time in concocting any amount of shady affairs and transactions, and who had organised a regular plundering of the public exchequer. He did not dare to do anything directly against the "Prophet," but he tried to get at him through the arrest of several of his adepts and friends. He caused the houses of a considerable number of these to be thoroughly searched for compromising documents. Among other places searched was the flat of a Mr. Dobrovolsky, who held the position of a school inspector. This search gave abundant evidence by which he might have been incriminated in more than one dirty transaction. But he was not immediately arrested and contrived to make his escape. Another of the Rasputin crew, a certain Simanovitsch, was arrested at the very moment when he returned to his home in the private automobile of Mr. Stunner, one of whose familiar friends he happened to be.

At the request of the "Prophet" an inquest into the denunciation of Rgevsky was ordered by Mr. Sturmer, and a certain Mr. Gourland, whose name had often been mentioned as that of a rising secret agent, was entrusted with it. But Manassevitsch-Maniuloff contrived to oust him and to get himself appointed in his place.

At the same time, it was decided to send someone to Norway to interview Illiodore, and to try thus to come to the bottom of the whole business. A certain General Spiridovitsch, who had already more than once been entrusted with missions of a delicate character which he had always accomplished to the satisfaction of those who had employed him, was selected for the task. The general had several interviews with Mr. Chvostoff, but they all came to nothing, and he did not go abroad as it had been rumoured that he would do. At last both the Minister of the Interior and the chief of the secret police, Mr. Bieletsky, had to resign their functions, and Rasputin found himself delivered from two of his most dangerous enemies.

The next question which arose was that of the appointment of Chvostoff's successor. The post which he had vacated was such a difficult and responsible one that several persons who were sounded as to their readiness to accept it refused the offer in a most categorical manner. The story which I have just related died at last a natural death. Rgevsky disappeared, no one knew where, but the difficulties out of which it had arisen were still there. They could hardly be set aside by any minister, unless some radical measures were adopted, such as the exile of Rasputin, a thing which no one dared to propose, and which no one would have dared to enforce even if someone else had proposed it.

After the resignation, or rather the dismissal, of Mr. Chvostoff, his post was finally offered, by the advice of Rasputin and at the suggestion of Manassevitsch-Maniuloff, to Mr. Protopopoff, a rich landowner of the Government of Simbirsk, who for some time had occupied the position of vice president of the *Duma* of the Empire.

Just before his appointment to what is the most important and responsible function in the whole Russian Empire, there was much talk of an interview which he had had at Stockholm with Mr. Warberg, a representative of the German Government, during which the conditions at which a separate peace might come to be concluded between Russia and the Central Empires had been discussed. Later on, when this meeting, which had been arranged through the good offices of a Jew, Mr. Maliniak, became the subject of general knowledge in Stockholm, and details concerning it had found their way into the Russian press, Mr. Protopopoff was violently attacked by the liberal parties in the *Duma*, which accused him of treason, and refused even to listen to the clumsy explanations which he attempted to give of the affair.

It was then generally believed that the political career of this gentleman was at an end, and it was assumed that he would have to resign his vice presidency in the House. Certainly no one ever thought that he would suddenly develop into a minister. And yet, this is the very thing which happened, thanks to the Rasputin crew, which persuaded Mr. Sturmer to present Mr. Protopopoff to the emperor as the best candidate for the place vacated by Mr. Chvostoff. In the meanwhile, Manassevitsch-Maniuloff, who had been the moving spirit in this whole intrigue, had been appointed private secretary to Mr. Sturmer, and at his instigation there began dissipation of public funds such as Russia had never seen before, and such as, let us hope, she will never see again.

There are many more things than I could possibly relate in regard to the incidents of which I have given the outline here, but these could hardly be published at present. The only thing which I can do is to try to make my readers understand the general position as it presented itself before the murder of Rasputin by quoting some speeches which were delivered in the *Duma* as far back as the year 1912. They were reproduced in the Russian Liberal organ, the *Retsch*, on the day following the assassination of the "Prophet." The Russian censor offered no opposition to this republication.

The first of these speeches was made by Mr. Goutschkoff, one of the most enlightened men in the whole of the Russian Empire, whose liberal opinions and sound political views had won for him the respect of all parties, even those who were opposed to them. The occasion upon which it was pronounced was that of the discussion of the budget of the Holy Synod, a discussion during which for the first time the personality of Rasputin, together with his activity, was publicly denounced as one of the greatest sources of danger that had ever threatened the country as well as the dynasty.

Mr. Goutschkoff said in this memorable address:—

You all know, what a terrible drama Russia is living through at present. With sorrow in our hearts and with terror in our souls we have followed its developments, and we are dreading its consequences. Standing in the very heart of this drama we see a mysterious, enigmatical, tragi-comical figure, who seems

96

to have come out of the dark ages, which we believed had passed away forever, into the full light of the twentieth century. Perhaps this figure is that of a sectarian of the worst kind who is trying to popularise amongst us his mystical rites: perhaps it is that of an adventurer seeking to hide under the cloak of religious fanaticism and superstition his numerous swindles. By what means has this individual succeeded in rising to such a prominent position and in acquiring such an influence which even the dignitaries of our church, together with the highest functionaries in our State, acknowledge and which they seek to propitiate?

If we had had to do with only this one figure which had made its way on the field of religious superstition and which has thriven, thanks to an exalted spirit of mysticism, a state of mind which, though not perhaps bordering on insanity, is yet not quite normal, then we should have said nothing. We might have regretted the fact; we might even have wept over it, but we would not have spoken about it. But unfortunately, this figure is not standing alone. Behind it there is a whole crew, strong and varied, unscrupulous and grasping, which is taking advantage of its position and of the talents of persuasion which it may possess.

Amongst this crew there are to be found journalists in want of copy, shady business men, adventurers of every kind and sort. It is they who are the moving spirits in all this sad history, it is they who inspire it, they who tell it what it is to do. They constitute a kind of commercial enterprise, and they understand how to play their game in the most clever manner.

Before such a spectacle it is our duty to cry out as loud as we can that one ought to beware of all those people, and that the church—our church, and the country—our country, find themselves in imminent danger, because no revolution and no anti-Christian propaganda have ever done them more harm than the events which are daily taking place under our eyes for the last twelve months.

Two years later, in 1914, a few weeks before the breaking out of the present war, another deputy, this time a clergyman, Father Filonenko, spoke about Rasputin in the *Duma*, and did so in the following strong terms:

As a faithful and devoted son of our Holy Orthodox Church, I consider it my painful duty to mention once more what has already been discussed here, by so many orators better than myself, and to recur to a subject which is at present talked of at the corner of every street, in every town and in every village, no matter how distant and how far from any civilised centre in our vast Empire. We find ourselves compelled to look upon this unexplainable influence of a common adventurer, belonging to the worst type of those sectarians, whom until now we have known by the name of *Khlystys*, and despised accordingly. We are obliged to reckon with this influence of a man upon whom all the sane elements in our society look with contempt.

On that same day another deputy belonging to the group of Ultra-Conservatives, Prince Mansyreff, also spoke about Rasputin, with perhaps even more energy than any one had ever done before in the *Duma*. Said the prince:—

The adventure of Illiodore ended in ridicule, but we have now in his place another adventurer, with the personality of whom are connected the most nefarious and disgusting rumours, the most unnatural and contemptible crimes. It is useless to mention his name; everyone knows who he is, and of whom I am talking. He has been let loose on our society to acquire some influence over it, by men even more shameless than he is himself; he has been used to terrorise all those who have dared to express their opinions against the currents which prevail at present in our administrative circles.

This adventurer, whenever he travels and whenever he arrives in St. Petersburg, is met at the railway station by the highest dignitaries of the church; before him pray, as they would do to God, unfortunate hysterical ladies of the highest social circles. This individual, who only seeks the satisfaction of the lowest instinct of a low nature, has introduced himself into the very heart of our country and of our society, and we find and feel everywhere his disgusting and filthy influence.

A few days after this memorable sitting of the *Duma* the government issued instructions to the press never to mention Rasputin's name or to speak of any subject connected with him in the newspapers. As soon as this became known the *Octobrists* put down on the order of the day in the *Duma* an interpellation on the matter, and Mr.

Goutschkoff in moving it exclaimed:—

> Dark and dangerous days have arrived, and the conscience of
> the Russian nation has been deeply moved by the events of
> the last few months, and is protesting against the appearance
> amongst us of symptoms proving that we are returning to the
> darkest periods of the middle ages. It has cried out that things
> are going wrong in our State, and that danger threatens our
> most holy national ideals.

Prince Lvoff seconded the motion, and asked the government to
explain who was this:—

> Strange personality who had been taken under the special pro-
> tection of the administration, who was considered as too sacred
> to be subjected to the criticism of the press, and who had been
> put upon such a pedestal that no one was allowed to touch or
> even to approach him.

I would not have quoted these speeches but for the fact that they
all bore on the same point, the one that I have tried to make clear to
the mind of my readers. This point is that the danger which Rasputin
undoubtedly personified in Russian society at large did not proceed
from his own personality, but from the character of the men who
surrounded him, who had made out of him their tool and who were
trying through him to rule Russia and to push it into the arms of
Germany. There is no doubt that Germany had been carefully following all the phases of the drama which culminated in the assassination
of the "Prophet" and had been helping by her subsidies the underhand
and mysterious work of men like Mr. Manassevitsch-Maniuloff and
his satellites, and like Mr. Sturmer.

Sturmer believed quite earnestly that he would secure immortal-
ity for his name and for his work if he contrived to conclude a peace
which everyone knew that Russia required, but which no one except
himself and the adventurers to whom he owed his elevation thought
of making except in concert with Russia's Allies, and only after Germany had been compelled to accept the conditions of her adversaries.

The whole Rasputin affair was nothing but a German intrigue
which aimed at discrediting the dynasty and perhaps even at overthrowing the sovereign from his throne.

Thanks to the infernal cunning of the people who were its leaders,
the Imperial circle and even some of the Imperial family were repre-

sented as being entirely under the "Prophet's" influence. And thanks to the solitary existence which the emperor and empress were leading, and to the small number of people who were allowed to see them, these rumours gained ground, for the simple reason that there existed no one capable of contradicting them or of pointing out their absurdity. Calumnies as stupid as they were degrading to the authors of them were set in circulation, and the revolutionary movement which Germany had been fomenting grew stronger and stronger every day, until it reached the lower classes. These classes by a kind of miracle were also kept very well informed as to everything that was connected with Rasputin or with the subterranean work performed by his party, a work which tended to only make the House of Romanoff unpopular, and to represent it as incapable of taking to heart the interest of the country over which it reigned.

If we consider who were the people at the side of the "Prophet," and who inspired all his actions as well as his utterances we find police agents, adventurers who had been sometimes in prison, and sometimes in exile; functionaries eager to obtain some fat sinecure in which they might do nothing and earn a great deal; stock exchange speculators of doubtful morality and still more doubtful honesty; women of low character and army purveyors, mixed up with an innumerable number of spies. Most of these last were in the German service and were working for all that they were worth to bring about some palace conspiracy or some popular movement capable of removing from his throne a *czar* whose honesty and straightforwardness of character precluded the possibility of Russia betraying the trust which her Allies had put in her.

Yet this was precisely what these people wanted, and what they had made up their minds to force through, thanks to the indignation which the various stories which were being repeated every day concerning Rasputin and the favour which he enjoyed was arousing all over Russia. The emperor, of course, knew nothing of all this; the empress even less. There was no one to tell them the truth, and they would have been more surprised than anyone else had they suspected the ocean of lies which had been told concerning themselves, and concerning the kindness with which they had treated a man whom they considered as being half saint and half mad, but of whom they had never thought in their wildest dreams of making their chief adviser.

In this extraordinary history, there is also another point which must be noticed. When the first deceptions produced by the disasters of the beginning of the campaign had thrown public opinion into a state of mind which was bordering well-nigh upon despair, and before it had had time to recover from the shock of the fall of Warsaw and the line of fortresses upon which they had relied to protect the western frontier, people had begun to seek for the cause of the great disillusion they had been called upon to experience. It was very quickly discovered, partly through the revelations that had been made in the *Duma*, that the real reason for all the sad things which had happened lay in the systematic plundering of the public exchequer, that had been going on for such a long time and which even the experiences of the Japanese war had not cured.

When the fierce battle against Germany began in grim earnest, the first thought of the emperor had been to try to put an end to these depredations that had compromised the prestige and the good name of Russia abroad as well as at home. Great severity was shown to the many adventurers who had enriched themselves at the expense of the nation. When it had come to the fabrication of the necessary ammunition required by the army, then the help of Russia's Allies—England and France—had been sought. Thanks to the efforts of these two Powers, something like order was re-established in the vast machine of the War Office. The fabrication of shells of a size that could not fit any gun was stopped. The army at the front got clothes and food of which it had been in want at the beginning of the campaign. Ammunition was despatched where it was required, and not in the contrary direction as often had been the case before.

The Allies helped Russia to the best of their ability, and Russia, at least the sane and honest part of Russian society, felt grateful to them for their co-operation in the work of their common defence against a foe which it had become necessary to defeat so thoroughly that civilisation could no longer be endangered by its existence and activity.

But the people who surrounded Rasputin and with whom he was working were not grateful for the labour of love which Great Britain and France had assumed. They began to complain of the so-called interference of foreign elements with the details of the Russian administration. Some went even so far as to say that Russia was becoming an English colony.

All the plunderers, all the thieves who had had their own way for so many months, perceiving that they would no longer have the opportunities which they had enjoyed before to add to their ill-gotten gains, tried by all means in their power to discredit the sovereign whose firmness they had found in their way. They joined all the pro-Germans of whom, alas, there existed but too many in the country, in an effort to bring about a peace, the shame of which would have been quite indifferent to them.

It is not at all wonderful if those shameless adventurers started the conspiracy for the success of which they required the moral influence of Rasputin and the authority of his person. It was, after all, such an easy matter to say that in such and such a case he had been acting in conformity with the Imperial will. No one could disprove the truth of the assertion, and in that way the emperor was made responsible for all the unavowable things which were going on. He was sup-posed to have given his sanction to all these things simply because it had pleased, not even Rasputin himself, but individuals like Mr. Manassevitsch-Maniuloff, to declare that they had been done with his knowledge and approval.

Can one feel surprised if in the presence of this artificial atmos-phere, and still more artificial position, an intense feeling of disgust took hold of real patriots, and made them contemplate seriously the possibility of trying at least to unmask Rasputin and his crew and bring to the ears of the *czar* all the different rumours which were in circulation concerning the "Prophet" and what was going on around him? Men of experience and of weight seriously thought how this could be done. They made no secret of the fact, unfortunately for themselves as well as for the success of their plans.

What was going on very soon came to the knowledge of Ma-nassevitsch-Maniuloff and made him more frantic than he had ever been to overthrow what he called "foreign influences" in Russia. He applied himself with renewed energy to bring about, by fair means or foul, the conclusion of a peace on which depended his whole future destiny. And he might perhaps have succeeded if circumstances had not turned against him and put an end to his machinations, at least for a time.

Mr. Sturmer was but a tool in the hands of this artful, clever private secretary whom he had been persuaded, or rather compelled, to take. Manassevitsch-Maniuloff had managed to get hold of him and to keep him securely bound to his own policy. He was the man who had con-trived to put him into the position of authority which he enjoyed, and Mr. Sturmer, whatever may have been his other defects, had a grateful nature. Besides, Maniuloff amused him, and took an immense amount of trouble off his hands. He could rely on his never doing anything stupid, even when he did something very dishonest.

Mr. Sturmer was absorbed in great political combinations and was looking toward a long term of office. He felt absolutely safe in the situation which he occupied, where at any moment he liked he could speak with the *czar* and explain to him what he thought to be most advantageous to the interests of his party, or the events of the day as they followed in quick succession.

Alas for this security! An unexpected incident was to destroy it in the most ruthless manner. Rasputin, together with Mr. Maniuloff, went too far in the system of blackmailing which they had been practising with such skill for so many long months. For once they found their master in the person of one of the directors of a large banking establishment in Petrograd, who, upon being threatened with all kinds of unpleasantness unless he consented to pay a large sum of money, did not protest as others had done before him in similar cases, but gave it immediately, first having taken the numbers of the banknotes which he had handed over to Mr. Maniuloff. He went with these numbers to the military authorities and lodged with them a formal complaint against the blackmailers.

The result was as immediate as it was unexpected. The general staff had been waiting a long time for just such an opportunity to proceed against Rasputin and the members of his crew. That very same night, in obedience to orders received from the military commander of Petrograd, Mr. Manassevitsch Maniuloff's house was searched from top to bottom, and he himself conveyed to prison, without even having been allowed to acquaint his chief, Mr. Stunner, with what had happened to him.

Chapter 8

The arrest of the prime minister's private secretary produced, as may well be imagined, an immense sensation in Petrograd and intense consternation among the friends of Rasputin. They were thus deprived of the one strong ally capable of guiding their steps in the best direction possible under the circumstances, and, moreover, of the one who was possessed of information which no one else could possibly get at. Mr. Sturmer himself was more than dismayed at this step taken by the military authorities without consulting him and resented it as a personal affront. He tried to interfere in the matter and went so far as to demand as his right the liberation of Manassevitsch Maniuloff. But his intervention, instead of helping the person in whose favour it had been displayed, gave on the contrary the signal for a series of attacks against Mr. Sturmer, attacks of which the most important was the speech made by Mr. Miliukoff in the *Duma*, where he publicly accused the prime minister of being in league with Germany and of working in favour of a separate peace with that country.

Of course, the remarks of the leader of the opposition in the chamber were not allowed to be published, but so many persons had heard them and so many others had heard of them that the contents of the address of Mr. Miliukoff very soon became public property. No one had ever cared for Mr. Sturmer, whose leanings had always been for autocracy. While governor of Tver he had distinguished himself by the zeal which he displayed in putting down every manifestation of public opinion in his government.

In addition, he had been connected with various matters where bribery played a prominent part, a fact which had not helped him to win any popularity in the province which he had administered. His only merits lay in his ability to speak excellent French and in his having very pronounced English sympathies. These sympathies, however, by some kind of unexplainable miracle, died out immediately after his assumption of office. He at once fell under the influence of a certain party that clamoured for the removal of foreigners from the administrative and political life of Russia. He was not clever, though he had a very high idea of his own intelligence and knowledge.

Though he had never carried his knowledge beyond a thorough grasp of the precedence that ought to be awarded to distinguished guests at a dinner party (which he had acquired while he was master of the ceremonies at the Imperial Court), yet he was convinced of his capacity to fill the most important offices of the Russian State. These he looked upon with the eyes of a farmer in the presence of his best milking cow. He was not a courtier, but a flatterer by nature, and an essentially accommodating one, too. There was no danger of his ever turning his back on persons who he had reasons to think were in possession of the favour of personages in high places. And he had a wonderful faculty for toadying wherever he expected that it might prove useful to his career.

For some years, he had vegetated in a kind of semi-disgrace and fretted over his inactivity. When he found himself able once more to make a display of his administrative talents he took himself and these talents quite seriously and imagined that perhaps he could become the saviour of Russia, but surely a very rich man. This last idea had been suggested to him by Mr. Manassevitsch-Maniuloff, who in conversations with him had imbued Mr. Sturmer with the conviction that it would be a proof of careless neglect oi his part if he did not make the most of the many opportunities his important position as prime minister put in his way, and did not assure the prosperity of his old age, when he had at his disposal all possible sources of information out of which he might make a profit. Mr. Sturmer was no saint, and the weaknesses of the flesh had always appealed to him. There is nothing wonderful in the fact that he listened with attention, and even with satisfaction, to the confidences which were poured into his ear by his private secretary, of whose talents he had a most exalted opinion.

When his *fidus Achates* was arrested, and thrown into a more or less dark dungeon, Mr. Sturmer was so dismayed that he allowed himself to be drawn into the mistake of identifying himself with the prisoner and claiming his liberty as a right. It is related that when the object of his solicitude heard of the various steps undertaken by the prime minister on his behalf he gave vent to words of impatience at what he considered an imprudence likely to cost a good deal to the guilty ones, he had exclaimed:—

Sturmer ought to have known that a man like myself does not allow himself to be arrested without having taken the precaution to be able to impose on those who had ventured to do so the necessity of liberating him.

The fact was that Manassevitsch-Maniuloff had put to profit the months when, in his capacity as private secretary to the prime minister, he had access to all the archives and secret papers of the Ministry of the Interior. He had taken copies of more than one important document, the divulging of which might have put the Russian Government in an embarrassing position. Some persons even said that his zeal had carried him so far as to make him appropriate to himself the originals of these documents, leaving only a worthless copy in their place. True or not, it is certain that the spirit of foresight that had always distinguished him had induced him to take certain precautions against any possible mishap capable of interfering with his career. He was able to regard his imprisonment philosophically. This was more than Mr. Stunner could do.

The latter had reason to fear that during the police search of the flat occupied by Mr. Manassevitsch-Maniuloff some compromising letters had been discovered. This fear did not add to his happiness or to his equanimity. Besides, he was not strong enough to resist the attacks which, dating from that day, were poured upon his head. In spite of the assurances which Rasputin was continually giving him that he had nothing to fear, he did not share the confidence of the "Prophet."

He had good reasons for this fear. In the *Duma*, in the Petrograd drawing rooms, in the army and among the public, all had grown tired of Mr. Sturmer, and all spoke of nothing else but of the necessity of compelling him to resign his post. Among the different reproaches which were addressed to him was that of being an enemy of England and of trying to work against the Russo-English alliance. It was very well known that his relations with Sir George Buchanan, the British Ambassador, were not cordial. Sir George, in spite of all that the pro-Germans liked to say about him, was a popular personage in Russia, that is, among the sane portion of Russian society, which had hailed with joy the initiative that he had taken in the great work of reorganisation of the Russian administration.

Thanks to the English officers who had arrived in Russia with the aim of bringing some kind of order out of the chaos that had prevailed not only in the War Office, but in every other branch of the government, the military position of the Empire had considerably improved, and the great work of national defence had been at last put upon a sound basis. As a man occupying a very important position in Petrograd wrote to me during the course of last summer:

> There are some people here who say that Russia is fast becoming an English colony, but I reply to them that she might certainly do worse, if by that word is meant the introduction of the English spirit of order and of English honesty in our country.

This was the opinion of a sincere Russian patriot. There is no doubt that it was shared "by all the best elements of the nation, who had recognised that in the crisis through which their Fatherland was going only one idea ought to dominate everything, and that was the necessity of imposing upon Germany a peace that would at last give to the world the assurance that it would never be called upon again to undergo another such catastrophe as the one under which it was struggling. Mr. Sturmer, however, was of a quite different opinion. This was well known everywhere, especially in parliamentary circles. Mr. Miliukoff made himself the echo of the popular voice when he delivered his famous indictment of the prime minister.

The latter retorted by issuing against the leader of the Opposition a writ for libel, and applied himself with renewed energy to the task of getting out of prison the man who had been the prime mover in the dark and sinister intrigue of which Rasputin was the principal figure. At last he succeeded, and Manassevitsch-Maniuloff was released on bail. Among all the papers which had been confiscated at his home not one incriminating document had been found, and the only thing against him that could be proved was the blackmailing scheme against the bank whose director had had him arrested.

He threatened, in case he should be brought to trial, to make certain revelations absolutely damaging for more than one highly placed personage, and he contrived to inspire a great terror even among those most eager to have him condemned for his numerous extortions and other shameful deeds. As soon as he was at liberty he set Rasputin to working in his favour, and made the latter display an activity that at last exasperated the public against the "Prophet" to such an extent that the first thought of organising a conspiracy to remove him was started, and very soon became quite a familiar one with more than one person.

To be quite exact, this thought had already existed for some time. About a year after the beginning of the war some enterprising individuals in Petrograd tried to get rid of the "Prophet" by entangling him in some disgraceful escapade which would have made it necessary for him to leave Petrograd. In accordance with this plan he was invited one night to supper at some fashionable music hall, of which there exist so many in the Russian capital. Bohemian singers were called in and an unlimited amount of champagne provided.

Rasputin, who was rather fond of such adventures when he was not obliged to pay for their cost in *rubles* and *copecs*, accepted with alacrity. He soon became quite drunk. Then, at the invitation of one of the guests, he proceeded to show them the manner in which the *Khlistys*, the religious sect to which he belonged, danced around the lighted fire, which was an indispensable feature of their meetings. As he was dancing, or rather turning round and round a table that had been put in the middle of the room, he took off some of his clothes, just as his followers used to do when they were holding one of their assemblies in real earnest.

Some of the assistants seized hold of the opportunity and hid the garments of which he had divested himself, then called in the police, requiring them to draw up a report of what had taken place. On the next day, this report was taken to a high authority, in the hope that it would have a damaging effect on the reputation of Rasputin. The result, however, was quite different from that which had been expected, for the person who had brought the report to the authority in question instead of being believed was treated as a libeller and himself compelled to retire from public life. After this it was generally recognised that nothing in the world would be strong enough to bring about the downfall of the "Prophet."

In the meanwhile, the efforts of the Opposition party in the *Duma* had succeeded to the extent of forcing Mr. Sturmer to resign as prime minister; but he had influence enough to secure his appointment as High Chancellor of the Imperial Court, one of the most important positions in Russia. He did not fall into disgrace, but remained the power behind the throne whose existence, though not officially recognised, yet was everywhere acknowledged. He had not been dismissed, he had simply gone away—a very different thing altogether in the realm of the *czar*. Though no longer a minister, he was still a personage to be considered as capable of an infinitude of good or of harm, according as it might please him to exert his influence.

His successor, Mr. Trepoff, an upright and fairly able man, did not long retain the office he had accepted much against his will. With him departed one of the most popular ministers Russia had known for a long time, Count Paul Ignatieff, the able son of an able father. He had for something like two years held the portfolio of Public Instruction to the general satisfaction of the public and had come to the conclusion that it was useless to go on fighting against dark powers which were getting the upper hand everywhere.

The resignation of these two statesmen was preceded by one of the most scandalous incidents in Russian modern history, the trial of Mr. Manassevitsch-Maniuloff. This had been put off from day to day for a considerable length of time until at last it became impossible to secure further delay. The culprit had taken good care, as I have already indicated, to put in safety documents of a most incriminating nature, implicating many persons whom the authorities could not afford to see mixed up in the dirty business connected with the numerous sins of Mr. Sturmer's private secretary. When the latter was questioned by the examining magistrate in regard to that last transaction which had brought him into court, he declared that he had acted in accordance with the instructions which he had received from his chief and that it was not he himself, but the prime minister who had received the money which the bank that had lodged a complaint against him had been induced to pay in order to be spared certain annoyances with which it had been threatened. He had insisted upon this version of the affair and warned the magistrate that his counsel would develop it in all the details before the jury.

In the meanwhile, Rasputin was moving heaven and earth to get the trial postponed and to get the charges against the prisoner quashed by the Chamber of Cassation. He had long conferences with several ladies having free entrance into the Imperial Palace and he put forward, among other arguments, the one which had certain points in its favour: that it would be detrimental to the public interest to have the scandal of such a trial commented upon by the press of the whole of Europe at a time when Russia was struggling against a formidable foe, always ready to catch hold of anything that would discredit it or its institutions.

For a time, it seemed as if the efforts of the "Prophet" would be crowned with success. Then one fine day opposite currents became powerful and Mr. Maniuloff was sent before a jury in spite of his protestations and his threats of revenge upon those who had taken upon themselves the responsibility of subjecting him to that annoyance.

On the fifteenth of December, the day appointed for the trial, the halls and corridors of the law courts of Petrograd were filled with an inquisitive crowd struggling to get access to the room where it was to take place. The spectators waited a long time, watching curiously the impassive face of the hero of the day, who had quietly entered the hall and taken his place in the criminal dock. About 12 o'clock the judges, together with the public prosecutor, made their entrance, when to the general surprise the latter rose and said that, owing to the absence of several important witnesses for the prosecution, he moved an adjournment of the proceedings until an indefinite time. What had happened, what had brought about such an extraordinary change? This was the question which one could hear everywhere after the court had risen and the assembly dispersed. Comments without number followed upon this decision, which no one would have thought possible a few hours before.

In spite of the severe censorship over the press, the principal Liberal organs of the capital published short commentaries which revealed the feeling of intense indignation that prevailed in every class of society. The words "Shame, shame!" were heard on all sides. It is not at all wonderful that they found an echo among some determined spirits who resolved at last to free Russia from the scourge of Rasputin, whose hand was again seen in the whole disgraceful affair.

This, however, was not at all an easy matter, considering the fact that the "Prophet" had become very careful and that his followers had him watched wherever he went for fear of an attack which they strongly suspected was being contemplated. The house where he lived, 64 Gorokhovaja Street, was always surrounded by policemen and se- cret agents, who examined every person who entered or went out of it. Rasputin himself had also grown suspicious, even of persons with whom up to that time he had been upon friendly terms, and he avoid- ed the numerous invitations that began once more to be showered upon him. He spoke again of returning to Siberia, which was always with him a sign that he did not feel himself at ease in the capital.

I had an opportunity to observe this restlessness the second time that I met him at the house of that Mr. De Bock whom I have already mentioned, when he declared to us that he was sick of Petrograd and of the many intrigues which were going on there. But that was before the war, and it seems that after it began the ideas of Rasputin changed and that he was always saying that he considered it his duty to remain beside his friends at this hour of national peril. The fact that his feel- ings had changed on the last point proves that he was aware of the danger in which he stood, and of which it is likely that he had been warned by the numerous spies who were but too ready to keep him well informed of all that was to his interest to know.

One thing seems certain, and that is the activity which he began to display during the last weeks and days of his evil life in favour of the conclusion of a peace, which he now said Russia ought to make if she wished to escape from further sin, as he termed it.

Why his feelings had undergone such a change it is impossible to say, but one may make a pretty near guess. One of the principal motives which actuated him undoubtedly was the idea that existed among a certain circle of persons that if peace were made with Ger- many, the English and French officials working with Russian officials in perfecting the defence of the fatherland, and whose presence al- ready had prevented so many malversations, would depart. This would leave once more a free field for the rapacity of all the civil and mili- tary functionaries of the War Office and Commissariat Departments, who could make a new harvest of *rubles* as a result of the unavoidable expenses which the liquidation of the war would necessarily entail.

There were, however, some persons who, seeing the dangers in the path in which this nefarious individual was leading Russia, decided that, as nothing else could bring about his removal, it had to be effected by violent means. I do not seek to excuse them, far less to take their part. Murder remains murder, but if ever an assassination had an excuse, this was the slaying of Rasputin, which also implied the destruction of the crew of unscrupulous people of which he was the tool. There was something of self-sacrifice in the conspiracy to which he fell a victim, something of an intense love of the Fatherland in the spirit that armed the hand of the man whose pistol sent him into eternity.

One may condemn the deed and yet excuse its motive. Though I am not trying to do so, yet I shall not be the one to cry out for vengeance against the over-excited young people who risked everything in the world to deliver their country from evil.

Of the details of the murder we know very little, and even the travellers who have gone abroad since it was committed could only speak vaguely about the circumstances that attended it. It is certain, however, that there was a deeply laid and well organised plot to kill the "Prophet," that about a dozen persons, some of them belonging to the best and to the highest social circles, were concerned in it, and that at last lots were drawn to select the man who was to execute the victim.

Among those persons were members of the Conservative faction of the *Duma*, some officers of several guard regiments, and even ladies of the smartest set of Petrograd. That something was known concerning this plot in governmental circles can be seen from the fact that the Minister of the Interior, Mr. Protopopoff, who had always been one of the most ardent disciples of Rasputin and who had been working with him for the conclusion of a peace which both considered to be useful to their personal interests, hearing that he was going to have supper at the house of Prince Youssoupoff, sent there the Prefect of Petrograd, General Balk, with instructions to watch over the "Prophet." When the *prefect* appeared upon the scene, he was politely asked by the master of the house to withdraw, as his presence was not required.

Young Prince Youssoupoff, who, by the way, is well known in London, was the husband of the Princess Irene of Russia, the first cousin of the *czar*. By virtue of his position he could be whatever he liked, even to dismiss curtly the principal police official of the capital. At the supper which he gave on the night when Rasputin was killed about a dozen people belonging to the best circle of Petrograd society were present. What passed during the meal and how the murder itself was committed is not known even now, though several versions of the crime are given.

Some say that it was done during the meal, and that the pretext for it was the conduct of Rasputin toward one of the ladies present at the table. Other people relate that they waited until the "Prophet" was on the point of departing, and that as he was putting on his overcoat the young man who had drawn the lot designating him for the deed shot him with his revolver at the foot of the stairs. The body was then wrapped up in a blanket and put into the automobile of a very high personage, which was waiting. in the garden of the house where the event took place, and driven to the Neva, where it was dropped under the ice. It seems that after this had been accomplished one of the conspirators went to Tsarskoie Selo and informed the *czar* of what had taken place, as well as of his own share in the deed.

In the meanwhile, the authorities had become suspicious. At 3 o'clock in the night screams had been heard by a policeman on duty at the corner of the street in which was situated the house of Prince Youssoupoff. He also noticed several persons coming out of the house, not by the usual entrance, but by the garden, which had a door leading into another street. After this, an automobile was seen driving out of that same garden, an altogether strange circumstance. This automobile was seen by another policeman about one hour later in the islands which surround Petrograd, driving close to the Neva and not on the usual road.

The next day the garden of Prince Youssoupoff was searched by Secret Service agents, who found some traces of blood on the snow, but the servants of the prince declared that it was that of a dog that had been shot the day before. No one dared say or do anything more against the supposed murderers, especially as the body of their victim had not yet been found. The river was dragged, but it was not until twenty-four hours after the event that the dead man was discovered under the ice in a frozen condition, with the features so completely battered that they could be recognised only with difficulty.

The curious thing is that, though it was known exactly where the body had been dropped, it could not be found at once, having been carried away by the current further than had been expected. This gave rise to all kind of rumours, and the friends of Rasputin tried to spread the news that he had escaped and was hiding away somewhere from his persecutors. The tale, however, could not be kept up for any length of time, as the whole capital with an unheard-of rapidity became aware that the most detested man in the whole of Russia had at last met with the fate which he so richly deserved.

The joy of the public could not be suppressed, notwithstanding the fear of the police. In all the theatres and public places the national anthem was sung with an immense enthusiasm. No one regretted what had happened, and the people suspected of having had a hand in the murder received messages of congratulation from every quarter. In fact, they became at once national heroes. The murder so far has remained unpunished, and it is more than likely that no one will be brought to account for it.

As for the body of Rasputin, it was at first kept in the hospital where it had been taken after its recovery from under the ice. The police received orders not to allow it to be seen by the crowds, which it was feared would flock in numbers to have a last look at their "saint," the "Blessed Gregory," as he was called. But to the general surprise these crowds did not manifest any curiosity to view the mortal remains of the man about whom so much fuss had been made in his lifetime, but after whose death the whole Russian world seemed to breathe more freely than it had been able to do for the last ten years or so. Among the clergy satisfaction was openly expressed, and it was only a few hysterical women who were found to weep over the end of the career of one of the wickedest men who had ever lived.

The question most discussed in connection with the death of this sinister adventurer was whether he was to be allowed a Christian burial. He had been, after all, but a sectarian, a heretic, the follower of a creed which was not only reproved by the orthodox church, but also prosecuted by the law of the land. The synod was called upon to pronounce itself on the subject when the advice of the Metropolitan Pitirim of Petrograd, one of the personal friends of Rasputin, at last prevailed, and he was buried with the rites of Holy Church.

Some of the ladies who had been the first cause of his having obtained the importance which grew to be attached to his strange figure did not wait, however, for the permission of the ecclesiastical authorities, and a few hours after the body had been discovered Madame W., one of the most hysterical among the many women followers of Rasputin, caused solemn prayers to be celebrated in her apartments for the repose of his soul. She went to fetch his two daughters, girls of sixteen and fourteen years of age, who were living with him at Petrograd, taking them to her house and declaring that she would henceforward consider and treat them as her own children.

But apart from this small group of blind admirers no one regretted him, not even the crew of parasites that had surrounded him and exploited him. By one of those strange anomalies, such as can only take place in Russia, Mr. Manassevitsch-Maniuloff, who had been the indirect cause of his death, was appointed, together with other secret police agents, to investigate the details connected with the murder of his former friend and patron. Of course, the inquest led to nothing. No one had any wish to see it end otherwise than in oblivion. Every political party in Russia was agreed in thinking that with the disappearance of this dangerous man the dynasty had won a battle just as important for the safety of its future existence as would have been a victory on the battlefield against a foreign foe. The names of the murderers, though pronounced nowhere, were blessed by all sincere Russian patriots, who cried out when they heard that Rasputin was no more, "Thank God that this adventurer is dead and long live the *czar!*"

Chapter 9

Rasputin, taken individually, did not deserve any notice. He was never in possession of the influence which was attributed to him, and his voice was never preponderant in the councils of the *czar*. It served the interests of those whose tool he had become to spread the notion that he had acquired it, and that, thanks to the religious enthusiasm which he had contrived to arouse among a certain small circle of influential men and women, he had installed himself in the confidence of his Sovereign. Unfortunately for Russia, these people not only had accomplices in their evil deeds, but also had the means to spread their opinions among the public and the ability to make these opinions penetrate into all the different classes of the nation.

They discredited the Imperial family; they discredited the government of the day; they discredited the monarch, until it became at last a political, and I shall even say a national, necessity to suppress them, together with the adventurer whom they had put forward and thanks to whom they had been able to play unmolested for so many years the most nefarious of games.

Unfortunately, the slaying of Rasputin did not destroy the persons who had used him. It did not put an end to the many abuses which had brought Russia to the sad state of chaos in which it found itself at the moment of its great trial. The man himself was but an ensign, and the loss of an ensign does not mean that the regiment that carried it about has shared its fate.

Rasputin was the last representative of the old regime. His appearance on the horizon of Russian social life was but the last flicker of a detestable past. During his time of favour and of success the two forces that struggled for supremacy in the land of his birth fought their last battle, in which he was the stake. We must rejoice that it was not the force which he was supposed to incarnate in his enigmatical and mysterious person that remained master of the field. Whether he would have been killed under different circumstances is a question to which it would be very difficult to find a reply.

Most probably the spirit of mysticism which lies at the bottom of the Slav character would have prevented even his worst enemies, let alone his simple adversaries, from trying to remove him from the position into which he had been thrust. They would most likely have shrugged their shoulder and waited for that intervention of St. Nicolas, who, according to Russian traditions, always arrives at the right moment, to put straight everything that has gone wrong.

The peril in which Russia found herself placed gave energy even to those to whom that quality had hitherto been unknown, and it was felt everywhere that, together with the Fatherland, the *czar* ought to be saved from a danger of which, perhaps, he did not himself realise the real importance. Rasputin, and especially Rasputin's followers, had worked as hard as they could to make Russia's Allies, and especially England, unpopular with the Russian nation. He paid with his life for the attempt, and one can only rejoice that such was the case. As things stand at present, it is principally toward Great Britain and America that Russia must look for its salvation.

What I am writing today has been my earnest and deep conviction for long years, and I have preached it not only since the beginning of this war in all the books and articles which I have written, but also long before anyone ever thought or suspected that the day would come when the English Union Jack and the Stars and Stripes would float beside the Russian flag and the French Tricolour on the same battlefields, united against one common enemy. I have always considered that in human life, as well as in the existence of nations, it is essential to recognise the superiority of others where this superiority exists, and that true civilisation consists in assimilating to oneself with gratitude the virtues of other nations, whose example one ought to follow instead of trying to ridicule.

Russia, with all its vast resources and with its immense territory, would do well to imitate England and the United States in their immense work of culture and to call the latter countries to her help in developing her own national existence on proper and useful bases. In doing so she would not abase herself; she would only prove that she was great enough to admire the greatness of others.

It is certain that if Anglo-Saxon influence had been so dominant in Russia in the past as it is to be hoped it will remain in the future, we should not have seen occur in Petrograd incidents like those connected with the career of Rasputin. We should not have witnessed all these perpetual changes of ministers, over which Germany has rejoiced with such evident relish. We should not have heard people defy the authority of the *czar*, as unfortunately has been the case.

We former monarchists, who have been brought up in the old traditions of loyalty to bygone days, have often been accused by this crew of adventurers of harbouring revolutionary ideas. They have reproached us with the spirit of criticism that has sometimes induced and prompted us to speak out what we thought and to lay blame where blame was due; to criticise where criticism was almost a national necessity. Time shall prove whether we have been mistaken.

It seems to me, however, that as English ideals and English respect for individual liberty and individual opinions become more and more familiar to Russians and penetrate into the Russian mind, the public, will acknowledge that we have not been so very wrong when we have raised our voices against the importance which individuals such as Rasputin have been allowed to take in our society and in our governmental circles, and against this corrupt system of administration, which, thanks to its crawling, flattering propensities, caused our people to kneel at his feet with the idea that by doing so they were pleasing the higher authorities, who most of the time knew nothing about the developments for which this intrigue was responsible.

Russia has still something oriental about her, and in some respects she resembles the Greek empire which fell under the blows dealt at it by the power of Islam. It needs new life and new blood in its veins. It requires the support of this strong, earnest British civilisation, which is, perhaps, the most beautiful the world has ever known.

I have always been accused of being too pro-English in my ideas and opinions. If being pro-English means the wish to see my country freed from the abuses, the existence of which has prevented her from developing herself on the road of a progress embodied in the respect of the individual, together with the institutions that rule him, such as Great Britain has known for so many centuries, then I will willingly confess it, I am pro-English. I feel sure that all good Russians share my feelings. We have had enough of the German *Kultur* and of German intrigues. They it is that have brought my beloved Fatherland to the brink of ruin. The whole sad incident of Rasputin's rise and fall has been the result of German interference, and it would never have assumed the proportions to which it rose if the German press had not exaggerated it and German spies spoken about it, not only abroad, but also in Russia itself.

When thinking about this story, which savours in some of its details of superstitions of the Middle Ages, one must always remember what I said at the beginning of this sketch of the career of a man whom circumstances and the hatred of our enemies transformed into a kind of monster devouring all that it touched. This fact is that Russia is still the land of many surprises, because of its tendency toward mysticism, always so strong in all the Slav races.

Before Rasputin appeared there had been other sectarians who had drawn thousands of men and women around them and who had inspired crowds with feelings of fanaticism in no wise different from the ones which the modern "Prophet," as some called him, the modern Cagliostro, as others had nicknamed him, had evoked in the breasts of the simple-minded people whose confidence he had abused and whose spirit of superstition he had impressed. But these had remained strictly in the field of religion and had not meddled with any other questions. They had grouped around them only persons convinced of the truth of their teachings, while Rasputin had gathered about him men determined to use him for the benefit of their money-seeking, money-grubbing schemes; men who saw in the misfortunes that had fallen upon their Fatherland only the possibility to enrich themselves at her expense.

They would not have sacrificed the smallest things for her welfare; far less would they have given up the chance to add to the ill-gotten gains they were daily accumulating. Without those persons, the whole story of Rasputin would have ended in ridicule. Thanks to them and to their rapacity, it finished in blood.

It was, after all, the aristocracy that finally got rid of Rasputin, perhaps to the great relief of many persons who out of weakness, or let us say kindness, had hesitated before taking the strong measure of sending him away where it would have been difficult for him to do any more mischief. And it is doubtful whether his removal anywhere than to a place whence there existed no possibility for him to return would have stopped the evil which the very mention of his name alone was sufficient to cause. Credulous persons exist everywhere and will always exist; timorous ones also abound in the world.

Even if Rasputin had been exiled it would have been relatively easy for those who reaped such a rich harvest out of the blood and the tears of the whole Russian nation to attribute to him powers which he did not possess, to threaten with his vengeance the persons who might refuse to lend themselves to their dirty schemes. He would have been a perpetual menace suspended over the heads of those who would have tried to rebel against the directions issued by the enterprising scoundrels who abused the prestige which his so-called holiness had won for a man who in other times and in another country, would not have arrested for a single moment the attention of any one, let alone the crowds.

Rasputin is dead! Let us hope that his former supporters have lost, together with him, their audacity and their power of doing mischief. But to say that he was ever a paramount strength in Russian politics is an error which I have tried to correct as far as lay within my power. Rasputin's story is simpler than many persons think, and perhaps the best explanation that can be given of it is to be found in the Book of Esther in the Bible, a careful perusal of which is recommended to those who are interested in the character of Rasputin.

Part 2 The Great Revolution

CHAPTER 1

On the 15th day of May, 1896, Moscow was celebrating the Coronation of the czar Nicholas II. of Russia. In the large courtyard inside the Kremlin, an immense crowd was gathered, awaiting the moment when the sovereign together with his consort would come out of the Cathedral of the Assumption, to make the customary round of the different shrines and churches, which according to the ancient custom, they had to visit after they had assumed the old Crown of the Russian Autocrats.

Among this crowd, there were persons who remembered having witnessed the same kind of ceremony thirteen years before, when Alexander III. had been standing in his son's place. What a splendid apparition it had been that of this *czar*, gigantic in stature, whose quiet and strong features seemed in their placidity to be a true personification of the might of that Empire at the head of which he stood. One had hoped at that time, that he would preside over the destinies of his realm for long years to come, and no one had given a thought to the possibility that he would so soon be lying in his coffin.

Now it was with mixed feelings of pity, combined with a sympathy which already was no longer so strong as it had been when he had ascended the throne, that all were awaiting the new Monarch, who had become in his turn the chief of the old House of Romanoff, so that when the golden gates of the Assumption were thrown open to give passage to the procession which was escorting Nicholas II. all the heads of the numerous people gathered in honour of the occasion, under the shade of the ancient belfry of Ivan Weliky, turned with an anxious curiosity towards the Sovereign about to show himself for the first time before his people, in the full pomp of his Imperial dignity.

What did one see? A young man thin and slim, who seemed to be entirely crushed under the weight of the massive crown which was reposing on his head, and of the heavy robe of cloth of gold, lined with ermine, which was thrown upon his shoulders. He was tottering as he walked along, and his pale, tired face, together with his uncertain steps, bore no resemblance whatever to the firm and superb countenance of his father thirteen years before. As he reached the door of the Church of the Holy Archangels, one noticed that he suddenly stopped, as if unable to proceed any further, completely worn out by the fatigue of the long ceremony that had come to an end a few moments before, and the hand which was holding the sceptre, enriched with precious stones, which the Metropolitan of Moscow had just handed to him, dropped down at his side, whilst the symbol of might and of power which it was holding, escaped from its grasp.

Chamberlains and lords in waiting hastened to pick it up, and the crowd never noticed what had occurred, but those who had witnessed the incident, were deeply impressed by it, and different rumours began to circulate in regard to it, rumours which would have it that it was a bad omen, whilst persons well up in the study of history, and especially in that of foreign countries tried to find an analogy between it, and the remark made by Louis XVI. on the day of his coronation at Rheims, when he had complained that his crown was hurting him, and felt too heavy for his head.

A few days later there happened another event, which reminded one of a similar coincidence between the life of the unfortunate king whose head was to fall on the scaffold of the Champs Elysées, and that of Nicholas II. It occurred during the popular feast which is always given in Moscow after the coronation of a *czar*. A crowd amounting to several thousands of men and women, some say three hundred thousand, had gathered together on a field known by the name of Khodinka Plain, in the immediate neighbourhood of the town, to be present at it, when suddenly a panic which was never accounted for nor explained, seized this multitude, and about twenty thousand human creatures were crushed to death in the short space of a few minutes.

The emotion produced by this disaster among all the different classes of society was very deep and terrible. The only person who accepted it with calm and even with indifference, if the reader will forgive me for this expression, was the *czar* himself, who, however, and this is a justice which I must render to him, only heard much later the whole extent of the disaster, but who at the same time, did not try to learn anything definite about it, on the day when it took place, and who, under the direct influence of his consort, gave directions to reply to the French Ambassador, the Comte de Montebello, who had enquired whether he ought to postpone the ball he was giving that same night, that "he did not see any necessity for doing so."

This answer became known at once, and it traced between the monarch and his subjects one of these white lines which in a tennis ground marks the antagonistic camps, and out of two players makes two enemies ... and this line went on getting wider and wider as time went on. It still existed when Nicholas II. abdicated, but it had then become an abyss.

In general, there is nothing sadder in the world than a misunderstanding between two people both possessed of good intentions towards each other. It is something worse than a discussion, worse than a quarrel, and even worse than hatred, because it is the only thing which sound reasoning cannot conquer, and which is bound to go on aggravating itself from day to day. How much worse therefore is a thing of the kind when it has established itself between a nation and those who rule it. The great, the supreme misfortune of Nicholas II. consisted in the fact that he never could understand his people or their wants, whilst Russia on the other hand was, through circumstances independent of its will, brought to distrust the real feelings harboured by the *czar* in regard to its welfare, and to indulge in comparisons which certainly were not to his advantage, between him and the sovereign to whom he had succeeded, who had possessed the full confidence of his subjects.

This fatality which has dogged all the footsteps of the emperor who abdicated a year ago, from the very first moment that he had ascended his throne, can be partly attributed to the defective education which he had received, together with the deplorable weakness of his character; and partly to the state of absolute subjection in which he had been kept first by his father, during the whole time of the latter's life, and later on by his wife, together with the complete ignorance in which he remained in regard to the wants, the aspirations, needs and character of his people. He was a despot by temperament, perhaps because he had never seen anything else but despotism around him, and perhaps because he had got a mistaken idea in regard to the duties which devolved upon him.

He had always been told that he ought to uphold intact the principle of autocracy, thanks to which his predecessors had maintained themselves upon the throne. He had seen Alexander III. adopt him with these principles with success, and he had forgotten, or rather he had never known, that in order to be a successful autocrat, one must neither prove oneself a tyrant, nor an oppressor of people's consciences and opinions. His first steps as a sovereign had hurt all the feelings of loyalty of his subjects.

Among the many addresses of congratulation that had been presented to him on the occasion of his marriage and of his accession to the throne, there had been one from the Zemstvo or local assembly of the government of Tver, a town which was known to be very liberal in its opinions, in which was expressed the hope that the Monarch would try to govern his people with the help and with the co-operation of these same Zemstvos or local assemblies, the aim of which was the improvement of the local conditions of existence of the population of the different governments or provinces of the Russian Empire.

There was absolutely nothing that was revolutionary in this address. Unfortunately, there happened to be in the vicinity of the young empress a person whose influence had always been perniciously exercised, whenever it had manifested itself: the Princess Galitzyne, her Mistress of the Robes. Out of a feeling of personal dislike, or rather hatred, against one of the signatories of this document, which, on account of the consequences that followed upon its composition, became historical, Princess Galitzyne explained to the sovereign at the head of whose household she stood, that this appeal in favour of a liberal system of government ought to be discouraged, if not crushed, at once.

Alexandra Feodorovna was then beginning to acquire the absolute power over her consort's mind, which she was never to lose in the future, and she spoke to him of the matter suggested by the princess, on the very day that different deputations, coming from all parts of Russia to express their good wishes to the young Imperial couple, were about to be received by them in the Winter Palace.

Nicholas II. has never in his whole life had an opinion of his own, but he has shown himself enthusiastic for all those that have been suggested to him. He promised his wife "to say something," which would put into their proper place the people daring enough to dream of anything likely to diminish his own power or prerogatives. He forgot, however, one thing, perhaps the most important one, and that was that these persons he was about to see, were not at all those who had signed the unlucky address, of which it would have been far better for everybody to forget the text as soon as possible. The result of this first intervention of the empress in affairs of State which did not concern her is but too well known.

The *czar* instead of thanking the people who had come to lay at his feet the expression of their loyalty, declared to them that they ought never to "indulge in any senseless 'dreams.'" The words were repeated everywhere, and ran from mouth to mouth in the whole of Russia. They inflicted on the young popularity of Nicholas II. a blow from the effects of which it never recovered.

This was the prologue of the tragedy which came to an end, if it has done so, with the signature of the Manifesto of Pskov. After this rise of the curtain was to begin a drama, all the different acts of which appear to us shrouded in bloody clouds.

One questions at present whether this drama could have had a different end from the one which we are witnessing, or whether the historical evolution that has been accomplished in the course of the last few months in Russia could have been avoided, or at least otherwise directed. Personally, I believe it to have been unavoidable, but it could have unfurled itself with dignity, if the crown had consented to concessions which would have taken nothing away from its greatness or importance, but which would on the contrary have lent to it a new lustre.

In any case, it would have been possible for autocracy to die, or better still, to live otherwise. No matter what reproaches could have been addressed to the Romanoffs in the past, no matter the injustices and the cruelties they had committed in the course of their family history, there is one thing which cannot be taken away from them, and that is that they have all of them been strong and courageous men, incapable of trembling before the attacks of any enemies, however powerful, or before the fury of a revolted mob. Nicholas II. was the first one among them who proved himself unable to inspire either love or hatred in his subjects, and for whom they held nothing but contempt, because they very quickly grasped the fact that he would never be able to give to himself or to others an account of the position he stood in, or to realise the tragedy of his own fate.

People who knew him well have wondered whether he ever understood what his duty really meant. I think, however, from the personal knowledge which I have of his character, that in a certain way he wished to do what was right, but I doubt whether he knew the responsibilities of his position, and the fact that he ought to put the

THE FIRST BOLSHEVIKI CABINET

interests of the State before those of his own family. For him his wife and children held the first place, and were the first objects of his consideration. This would have been a virtue in a private person, but it could easily assume the proportions of a crime in a sovereign.

His father had left to him a splendid inheritance, which he might have kept intact with a little care, and very small trouble. Before the Japanese war, it might have been still possible for him to rule his country autocratically, though not despotically; but after Moukhden and Tschousima, and especially after the revolution which followed upon these two catastrophes, and which would have been hardly possible, had they not occurred, the thing became more difficult, if not impossible, because the Russian nation had begun to wonder at the causes that had brought about these terrible disasters, the consequences of which had been the loss of Russian prestige in the Far East, and even in Europe.

It would, however, still have been possible to save something out of the former form of government, if a serious and honest appeal had been made to the nation to help to consolidate its strength, and if an attempt had been made to modify it according to the exigencies of the times and of the moment. But after the famous day which saw rivers of blood flow in the streets of St. Petersburg, and the wholesale slaying of thousands of innocent workmen, whose only crime had consisted in wishing to lay their grievances before their *czar*, every attempt to keep up the old order of things was bound to fail.

Something else had to be tried to save the dynasty together with the country, but not the granting of a so-called Constitution, which it had been determined beforehand to leave a dead letter. If on the occasion, I have just referred to, Nicholas II. had found sufficient courage to meet his people face to face, and to speak with them as his great grandfather had done on an occasion far more critical even than the ones which prevailed in 1905, it is likely that the divorce which finally separated him from his subjects would never have taken place. But he went to Tsarskoie Selo as soon as he heard there was likely to be trouble in his capital, forgetting everything else but his own personal safety, which, by the way, had never been seriously threatened.

He proved himself to be a coward, and cowardice is the last thing which a nation forgives in those who rule it. The *czar* lost in consequence of his conduct every prestige he had left. And he also lost the respect of Russia, owing to the shameless corruption which established itself everywhere during his reign, when at last everything under the sun could be bought or sold in the country, to begin with, a court appointment, and to end with, the highest functions in the State. The emperor was unable to refuse anything to those whom he liked, and he never grasped this essential fact, that when one gives too easily and without discernment, it inevitably follows that one also allows people to take what perhaps one would never have granted, had one thought about it.

Alexander III. had been just as generous as his son showed himself to be later on. But his generosity was only exercised in regard to what belonged to him personally, whilst no one was more careful than this sovereign of the public exchequer. He had seen what corruption meant during his own father's reign, when abuses had also prevailed, which though in no way comparable to those that established themselves towards the close of the one which has come to an end a year ago, were still sufficiently grave and serious to cause anxiety to a Monarch eager and anxious for the welfare of his State.

He therefore had applied himself to put an end to them, and knowing as he did, admirably well the character of the Russian nation, he took up morally the famous stick of Peter the Great, with which he dealt at times most severe blows to those whom he believed to be in need of them. The result of this system made itself felt within a very short time, and when Alexander III. died, the old custom of taking bribes, which had been formerly so prevalent in Russia, had nearly died out, or at least existed upon such a small scale that it could no longer do any harm.

But under Nicholas II. the old evil was revived, and finding no obstacle in its path, it soon assumed most unheard of proportions, and became at last a regular institution. Soon everything in the vast Empire of the *czars* was put up at public auction, everything could be purchased or sold, and everything became buyable, provided a sufficient price was offered for it. The emperor knew nothing, and saw nothing, and no one dared to tell him anything, whilst many unscrupulous persons found it to their advantage to profit by the changes that had taken place to enrich themselves quickly and with very little trouble. The whole country was seized with a perfect fever of speculation, and with the frantic desire to win millions as rapidly as possible.

When I say the whole country, this is not quite exact, because it was not the country, but only some people in it, who, thanks to the position which they occupied, or to their relations in influential circles, found themselves able to take a part in this general plundering. The Japanese war which was to have such a sad end, was entirely brought about through certain concessions being granted by the Russian Government on the River Yalou which never belonged to the Russian State, to a number of persons who hoped to transform them into shareholders' companies, and to make money out of them. They had bribed officials who persuaded the emperor to sign the decree which was presented to him, of which he failed to see the importance or the meaning, or the strange light in which it put him, to distribute thus what he did not possess, and what had still to be taken away from the Japanese Government before it could be disposed of.

This war, one cannot sufficiently repeat it, was brought about willingly and knowingly, by people who saw in it an opportunity to enrich themselves at the expense of their fatherland, thanks to the ammunitions and provisions they would be able to deliver for the use of the army in the field, and which that army never got at all. The system of an organised plundering which in the present war has had such mournful and such tragical consequences, was then inaugurated with a success that went far beyond the most sanguine expectations of those who indulged in it. Huge fortunes were made in the space of a few months whilst our troops were in want of everything, and enduring cold, hunger and thirst. The *czar* remained in utter ignorance of all that was being done in his name. He never suspected anything. But his people never forgave him for this indifference to its fate. One sees it today, (1918).

One wonders what was in the mind of this sovereign, who having ascended the throne amidst so many sympathies, had contrived to lose them within the space of a few months! Did he ever realise the importance of the ocean of unpopularity which was submerging him slowly, and the waves of which were rising higher and higher, with each day that passed? One would like to know it now, when one tries to go back to the sources of the tragedy to which he has fallen a victim.

Or was his character so shallow and so careless, that he only looked at the outside of things, and could not appreciate their real depth? He was of a very reticent nature and disposition, and rarely confided in any one, not even in his wife, whose inspiration and advice he was nevertheless to follow so blindly. And the tastes for solitude which he was to develop so strongly later on soon brought him to lead a kind of existence that can be compared only to that of the *Mikado* of Japan, before the reforms that were to change everything in that country.

That he was surrounded by flatterers goes without saying, but he could nevertheless have manifested some desire to learn the truth, and not have been so continually busy with the exclusive wish to maintain his own authority, which in spite of his efforts to the contrary, no one in the whole of Russia either respected or feared. All the concessions which politically were squeezed out of him, came too late, or else were accepted by him at the wrong time. Even when he seemed in the eyes of the public to be following the advice which was given to him by disinterested and honest persons, he tried in an underhand way to counteract the efficacy of the measures he had himself ordered to be taken, and whenever he resigned himself to the inevitable, he did not understand the reason why he was so doing.

With it all he was in some respects an intelligent man. He cared for good reading, for arts, for music, for all the things which help to make out of life a pleasant thing for irresponsible individuals. He was fond of study, very painstaking, but ignorant, and doing all that was required of him, in an almost automatic manner; kind, it is true, but incapable of coming to any serious resolution or determination of his own accord; devoid of political sense, occasionally most obstinate, and, unfortunately for him as well as for his country and dynasty, he had the misfortune in all the circumstances when a sacrifice of some fraction of his Imperial prerogatives came into question, not to be able to understand either his people or the times he was living in, and to have no thought for anything else but the safety of his own family, forgetting utterly that his country and its welfare ought to have come before them.

When he resigned himself to grant that shadow of a constitution, the advent of which was hailed with such enthusiasm by the whole of Russia, he might still, had he liked, have regained some part at least, of his lost popularity. His personal prestige, or rather that of the position he stood in, was still so great among the nation, that it would have felt gratitude toward him, for every favour he would have chosen to confer upon it, if only he had not taken back all that he had given, almost immediately after he had awarded it. It is quite certain that the first *Duma* committed many errors, but it should have been remembered that no human achievement can reach perfection at once; and the excitement and effervescence that had followed upon the opening of the first Russian Parliament ought to have been allowed to cool down, and been given sufficient time to make an honest trial of its rights and privileges.

At the period I am referring to, and this notwithstanding all that was said to the contrary, a revolution like the one which took place the other day, would have been an impossible thing, because the Sovereign could still rely upon the army, and it would have been better for him had he always leant upon it rather than upon the low crowd of state functionaries with which he was exclusively surrounded and out of which his wife had picked her favourites. He might have checked the then rising tide of radicalism with which he found himself unable to cope later on, and in the strength of which he was to remain to the end mistaken, because he dreaded it when it was not dangerous, and imagined that he had subdued it, at the very moment when it had become, thanks to his own errors, and to his own faults, sufficiently strong to carry him away on its waves.

Such a thorough weakness of character was bound to bring about the most serious consequences, and these did not fail to produce themselves. If Nicholas II. had had beside him a wife able to lead him, to advise him, to open his eyes which perhaps he did not quite close, but which he was never to succeed in keeping sufficiently open, and to show him not only the perils which surrounded him (these she never forgot to point out to him in an exaggerated manner), but also to bring to his notice his duties towards his subjects, he might have become a sovereign like any other, neither better nor worse, insignificant perhaps, but never really dangerous for his country or for his dynasty.

Even if that wife he was so devoted to had wished not to identify herself with State affairs, had kept outside them, and not surrounded herself with people lost to every sense of shame, he might have come out of the numerous difficulties with which he found himself confronted, if not exactly to his honour and credit, at least without losing too much of his prestige. But Alexandra Feodorovna was the fatal and dissolving element which destroyed, thanks to her attitude and conduct, every scrap of respect for the sovereign, and who inspired in the whole of the nation the desire to get rid of an authority in which it believed no longer, and in which it saw only an obstacle in the way of its development and of its historical evolution.

The empress understood even less than her husband the state of mind of his subjects; she raised between him and them a barrier which nothing could destroy, because it was made out of the contempt which they both inspired in the whole of Russia. There is one curious thing contrasting with the facility with which Nicholas II. accepted the opinions of others, and with his total absence of personal initiative; and that is the persistence with which he maintained himself during the whole time that his reign lasted, in one line of conduct which never varied in regard to the determination to govern his country in a despotic sense, and which was the more singular that he never knew the meaning of real authority. He always kept listening to those who represented to him that the first duty of a Russian Emperor consisted in keeping up the prestige of the police before the mass of the citizens.

Under no reign in Russia, if we except the dark period of the Opritschnikys under Ivan the Terrible, did the police play such an important part in public life, or become guilty of more abuses and of more malversations of every kind. I will not mention here the horrors which took place during and after the revolution of 1905, when no one felt secure against an anonymous denunciation, the consequences of which might be that one saw oneself exiled in Siberia, simply because one had not sufficiently bribed the police officer in charge of the district where one lived; but later on, even after things had calmed down, the might of what was called the Okhrana, remained just as formidable as it had been before.

Literally no one could feel safe under this so-called liberal *czar*, whilst under the reign of his father everybody possessed of a good and clear conscience could rest peacefully in the certitude that neither the security of his domicile or his personal safety would ever be threatened or infringed upon by the caprice of this secret power called by the vague name of "administration." But after all was he really liberal, this *czar* who had so little known or understood how to endear himself to his subjects, or did he merely say that such was the case, in order to dissimulate despotic leanings which were the more dangerous that they exercised themselves without any judgment or without any justification for their explosion?

A considerable number of persons have wondered about it, and have found themselves unable to solve this riddle. To hear him speak, one would have thought that such was the case, whilst it was hardly possible to talk with him for any length of time, without finding him a sympathetic, kind personality, curious mixture of totally different elements in a character that was chiefly remarkable for its weakness. One could like him, one could even admire some of the qualities which he undoubtedly possessed, but it was utterly impossible to respect in him the monarch, or to esteem the man, so strange did his conduct sometimes appear, a conduct which finally dragged him into an abyss, together with his family and with his dynasty.

Physically, he had a sad and kind face, affectionate and clear blue eyes, a charming voice, much affability in his manners; a wonderfully bright smile, reminding one of his mother's, a most cordial manner of shaking hands that went straight to the heart and made one suspect a lot of things which in reality did not exist; a rapid and quick walk, a certain hesitation in his speech, and in the expression of his face at times; such was the man.

Morally, he was possessed of honesty of purpose to such an extent that he could realise its absence in others; he had no will of any kind, but a good deal of obstinacy; principles which were always forgotten when they interposed themselves between his personal welfare and his duty; no sense of responsibility, but a very exalted opinion of his own rights, and especially of his might; the conviction that autocracy ought to be maintained at any cost, and simultaneously the sincere desire, during a short while, to govern according to the change of system to which he had been compelled to submit, more by the force of things and of events, than through his personal opinions; absolutely no consciousness of the great events with which he found himself mixed up, or of the wants of the country over which he ruled; no conception of the aims he ought to have had in view; no real sympathy for his people, but a vague wish to help them; an unacknowledged dread of finding himself thrown into any intimate contact with the mob, combined with the hope that this feeling would not be noticed by the public at large; far too much confidence in incapable advisers; an exaggerated mistrust of the persons courageous enough to tell him the truth, an absolute incapacity to resist bad influences; sometimes considerable dignity, and often useless haughtiness; a good deal of superstition combined with religion; a deep conviction that his own person was something so sacred that though it might come to be attacked and criticised, yet nobody would be daring enough to lay a sacrilegious hand upon it; a complete incapability of making any distinction between his friends and his foes, and such a persuasive manner that no one could ever contradict or resist him, so that the Revolution in which he lost his crown must have surprised him to the extent of paralysing all his faculties of realising its importance and its extent; such was the sovereign.

Chapter 2

By the side of this monarch in whom his subjects at last lost every vestige of confidence, there stood a sinister figure, the bad genius of a reign that would most probably have been far more peaceful if it had not been there: the figure of his wife, the Empress Alexandra Feodorovna, "the German," as she had been called even long before the present war broke out. It was undoubtedly to her that were due, at least to a considerable extent, the various misfortunes which have assailed the unfortunate Nicholas II., and it was also she, who, in the brief space of a few short years, discredited him together with the throne to which he had raised her. It was she who destroyed all the prestige which the Monarchy had retained in Russia, until the day when she tarnished it. She was another Marie Antoinette, without any of the qualities, or the courage that had distinguished the latter, who had become the object of the hatred and furious dislike of her subjects, more on account of the vices which were attributed to her, than of those which she really possessed.

In regard to the consort of the Czar Nicholas II., it was just the contrary that occurred, because the general public never became aware of all the strange details concerning the private life of this princess, who compromised by her conduct the inheritance of her son, together with the crown which she herself wore. On her arrival in Russia she had been met with expressions of great sympathy, and it would have been relatively easy for her to make herself liked everywhere and by everybody, because the peculiar circumstances which had accompanied her marriage had won for her a sincere popularity all over Russia. At the time she arrived there, as the bride of the future sovereign, there existed in the country a strong current of Anglomania, which disappeared later on, to revive again during the last year or two.

The princess who came to Livadia from Darmstadt was the granddaughter of Queen Victoria of Great Britain, by whom she had been partly brought up, a fact which spoke in her favour because it was supposed that her education would have developed in her liberal opinions, love for freedom, and the desire to make herself liked as well as respected by her future subjects, who received her with the more enthusiasm that they all hoped she would influence in the right direction her husband, whose weakness of character was already at that time known by those who had had the opportunity of becoming acquainted with him. One felt therefore inclined to forgive her any small mistake she might be led into committing during those first days which followed upon her arrival in her new Fatherland.

One pitied this young bride, whose marriage was to follow so soon the funeral of the monarch whose untimely death was lamented so deeply by the whole of Russia, and one felt quite disposed, at least

132

among the upper classes of St. Petersburg society, as well as in court circles, to show oneself indulgent in regard to the almost inevitable errors into which she might fall, at the beginning of her career as an empress. This feeling was so strong that during the first months which followed upon her marriage, the popularity of her mother-in-law, who had been so sincerely loved before, suffered as a consequence of this general wish to make an idol of Alexandra Feodorovna. The eyes of everybody were turned towards the new star that had arisen on the horizon of the Russian capital.

Amidst this general concert of praise which arose on all sides in honour of the newly wedded Empress, there were a few persons who, having had the opportunity to listen to some discordant notes, kept aloof and waited for what the future would bring. At the time of the death of Alexander III., a man belonging to the prominent circles of Russian society, who had been for a long period of years upon terms of personal friendship with the German Royal Family, happened to be in Berlin, and during a visit which he paid to the Empress Frederick, the aunt of the future wife of the new *czar*, he told her how many hopes were set in Russia upon her young niece. He was very much surprised to hear the empress express herself with a certain scepticism in regard to the bride, and finally say that she felt afraid the Princess Alix, as she was still called at the time, would not understand how to make herself beloved by her subjects, or how to win their hearts.

Seeing the astonishment provoked by her remark, she added that the character of the girl about to wear the crown of the Romanoffs, was an exceptionally haughty and proud one, and that as in addition to this defect she was possessed of an unusual amount of vanity, she would most probably have her head turned by the grandeur of her position, and would put forward, in place of the intelligence which she did not possess, an exaggerated feeling of her own importance. The gentleman to whom I have referred returned therefore to Russia with fewer illusions concerning Alexandra Feodorovna than the generality of his compatriots indulged in.

I must give the latter their due, they did not keep these illusions for any length of time, because from the very beginning of her married life the new *czarina* contrived to wound the feelings and the susceptibilities of all those with whom she was thrown into contact. She had absolutely no tact, and she fancied that if she allowed herself to be amiable in regard to anyone, she would do something which was below her dignity. She applied herself to treat everybody from the height of her unassailable position, and she took good care never to say one word that might be interpreted in the light of a kindness or amiability towards the people who were being presented to her, so that though they tried hard to attribute her utter want of politeness to a timidity which in reality did not exist, yet they felt offended at it.

Russian society had been used to something vastly different, and to a certain familiarity in its relations with its sovereigns. The mother of Nicholas II., the Empress Marie, had been worshipped for the incomparable charm of her manners, and the simple kindness with which she received all those who were introduced to her, asking them to sit down beside her, and talking with them in a charming chatty way, full of sweet and unassuming dignity. Her daughter-in-law abolished these morning receptions which had brought the sovereign into close intercourse with so many different people.

She received the ladies who had asked to be presented to her, standing, surrounded by her court, with two pages behind her holding her train, and she merely stretched out her hand to be kissed by those whom she condescended to admit into her august presence, without speaking one single word to them. Of course, the people whom she treated with such rudeness felt hurt at it, and it began to be said among the public that the empress was not at all amiable, and people abstained from seeking her presence or appearing at court, unless it was absolutely necessary to do so, leaving thus the field free to people devoid of self-respect, to whom one impoliteness more or less did not matter.

The balls at the Winter Palace, which formerly had been such brilliant ones, became dull and monotonous. The smile of the Empress Marie was no longer there to enliven them. At last the *czarina* left off giving any, and no one missed them, or felt the worse for their absence. One felt rather relieved than otherwise not to be compelled any longer to appear in the presence of the empress.

As time went on, an abyss was formed which divided the consort of Nicholas II. from her subjects, whose feelings manifested themselves quite openly on the day of the solemn entry of the Imperial Family into Moscow, on the eve of the coronation of the new sovereigns. The golden carriage that contained the dowager empress was followed all along its way by the cheers of the population of the ancient capital, whilst a tragic silence prevailed during the passage of the coach in which sat her daughter-in-law. The contrast was such a striking one that it was everywhere noticed and commented upon.

This latent animosity, the first signs of which manifested themselves on this memorable occasion, became even more acute after the catastrophe of Khodinka. Russia did not forgive its empress for having danced the whole of the night that had followed upon it, and for having given no sign of regret at a disaster that had cost the life of more than twenty thousand people, who had perished in the most awful manner possible. The divorce between her and her subjects was accomplished definitely after that day, and without any hope of a future reconciliation coming to annul its effects.

This unpopularity, and let us say the word, this hatred of which she became the object, did not remain unknown to the empress, who either noticed it herself, or else was enlightened on the point by her German relatives, with whom she had remained upon most intimate and affectionate terms. She attributed it at first to the fact that she had not during many years given a son to her husband and an heir to the Russian throne, but later on she was compelled to acknowledge that the dislike which she inspired was due to other causes which were dependant on her own self.

The discovery angered and soured her, and made her nasty and ill natured. She tried to avenge herself by the assumption of an authority in the exercise of which she found a certain pleasure, because it procured her at least the illusion of an absolute power, allowing her, if the wish for it happened to cross her mind, to crush all those who were bold enough to criticise any of her actions or her general demeanour. Her character was obstinate without being firm. She believed herself in all earnestness to be the equal of her husband, and did not think of herself at all as his first subject, so that, instead of giving to others the example of deference towards their Sovereign, she applied herself to lower him down to her own level, to diminish his importance, and to show quite openly that she did not in the very least respect either him or the throne which he occupied.

One heard a number of anecdotes on the subject, among others one to the effect that during a regimental feast, at which the Imperial Family was present, the empress, who had arrived a little in advance of the *czar*, did not rise from her seat when he entered the riding school in which the guests were assembled to receive him. This want of deference was commented upon in unfavourable terms, and caused such a scandal that Alexandra Feodorovna was taken to task for it by her mother-in-law, with the only result that she impertinently told the latter to mind her own business and to hold her tongue. The dowager empress did not allow her to repeat such a remark, and withdrew herself almost entirely from the court, much to the regret of all her admirers.

All these things were perhaps not important ones, at least from other points of view than the purely social one, but they constituted this drop of water, which by its constant and continual dripping ends in attacking the solidity of the hardest granite. Very soon it became a subject of general knowledge that no one cared for the empress, and one came to the conclusion that this initial want of sympathy would easily become very real and implacable hatred.

The woman who had become the object of it, instead of trying to fight against the general dislike which she inspired, did absolutely nothing to try to persuade her subjects that she was not the detestable being she had been represented to be, but that she cared for their welfare, in spite of her cold appearance. The haughty and mistaken pride which was one of the chief features in her strange character, led her to retire within herself and to try to avoid seeing the people, who by that time had grown to meet her whenever she appeared in public, with angry and unpleasant expressions in their faces.

The Imperial Court under her rule was quickly transformed from the brilliant assemblage it had been into a desert—a solitude no one cared to disturb. The empress amused herself chiefly in turning tables and in evoking spirits from the other world, in company with mediums of a low kind who abused the confidence that she so unwisely and unnecessarily placed in them, and predicted for her (as it was to their interest to do) a happy and prosperous future.

Then came the war with Japan, together with the disasters which attended it, a war that shook most' seriously the prestige of the throne of the Romanoffs. It brought to light all the defects, the disorder, and the inefficiency of the War Office; it enlightened the nation as to the real worth of the people who were standing at the head of its government, and it sounded the first knell of the Revolution which was at last accomplished. This war afforded another pretext to the public for attacking the personality of the empress, who according to the rumours which circulated at the time, had only looked upon it from the joyous and glorious side, and never noticed its earnest and sad one.

It is a fact that neither disasters like those of Moukhden and Tschousima, nor even the revolutionary movement that broke out in consequence of them, affected her equanimity. She remained absolutely cold in presence of these grave events and was absorbed in the joy of the new maternity, which just at that time was granted to her—the birth of the long expected and hoped for heir to the Russian throne, which occurred in the very midst of the Japanese campaign. This event certainly did not contrive to make her more popular among her subjects, whilst on the other hand it increased considerably her importance, so that after the appearance in the world of the son she had so ardently wished for, she began to display more independence in her conduct than had been formerly the case, and to discuss more eagerly, and more authoritatively than she had ever been able to do before, matters of State which her position as the mother of the future sovereign gave her almost a right to know, and to interfere with.

She brought forward her own opinions and judgments, which never once proved in accord with the real needs of the Russian people. The empress was neither good, kind, nor compassionate. Her nature was cold, hard and imperious, and she had never been accessible to the divine feeling which is called pity for other people's woes. She would have signed a death warrant with the greatest coolness and indifference, and more than once her husband decided, thanks to her intervention, to confirm those submitted to his consideration. This last fact became known, and, as may be imagined, it did not procure her any sympathy among her subjects.

It was about that time, that is just before the birth of the heir to the throne, and whilst the war with Japan was being fought, that people began to spread dark rumours concerning the private life of Alexandra Feodorovna. A most extraordinary friendship which she contracted with a lady whose reputation left very much to be desired, and who had been divorced from her husband under circumstances that had given rise to much talk, Madame Wyroubieva, was severely criticised. The empress remained deaf to all the hints which were conveyed to her on the subject. She kept the lady in question beside her, gave her rooms in the Imperial Palace, and took her about with her wherever she went, without minding in the least the impression which this bravado of public opinion produced everywhere.

Another friendship for a certain Colonel Orloff, an officer in her own regiment of lancers, also gave rise to considerable gossip, which increased in intensity when after the death of the latter, who committed suicide under rather mysterious circumstances, the empress repaired every afternoon to the churchyard where he was buried, prayed and laid flowers upon his grave. One wondered why she did such strange things, and of course persons were at once found to explain

137

THE BOLSHEVIKI HEADQUARTERS IN PETROGRAD

her motives in a manner which was the reverse of charitable.

The emperor knew and saw all that was going on, but said nothing. His wife by that time had acquired over his mind quite an extraordinary influence, and either he did not dare to make any remarks as to the originality which she displayed in her conduct, or else he imagined that her position put her so much above criticism that it was useless to interfere with what she might feel inclined to do in the matter of eccentricity. A legend soon established itself in regard to Alexandra Feodorovna. She was said to suffer from a nervous affection, which obliged her at times to keep to her own apartments, and not to appear in public. People tried, thanks to this pretext, to explain her absence on different occasions when her position would have required her to show herself to her subjects.

But the truth of the matter was that the empress did not wish to see anybody, outside the small circle of people before whom she need not constrain herself to be amiable or pleasant; and that utterly forgetful of the duties entailed upon her by her high rank and great position, she wanted only to live according to her personal tastes, surrounded by flatterers or by people resigned beforehand to accept and bow down before her numerous caprices, and to fulfil with a blind obedience all the commands it might please her to issue to them.

She mixed openly in public affairs, and began to play a leading part in the conduct of the State. Her husband never dared to refuse her anything, and the empress attempted to lead the destinies of Russia in the sense which she had the most at heart, that is in one corresponding to the interests of her own native country. She had remained entirely German in her tastes and opinions, and her English education had had absolutely no influence on her character. Thanks to an active correspondence which she kept up with her brother, the Grand Duke of Hesse, she was able to acquaint the Emperor William II. with a good many things that he would never have learned without her.

This is the more curious, if one takes into account the fact that during the first years which had followed upon her marriage, and especially after the different journeys which she had made in France, Alexandra Feodorovna had expressed great sympathy and admiration for everything that was French, perhaps on account of the great enthusiasm with which she had been received by the French population. But later on, thanks to the influence of the unscrupulous people into whose hands she fell, her ideas became transformed, and she boldly tried to fight against the French leanings of her husband, and to lead him towards an alliance with Germany, in which she thought that she saw the advantage, and even the safety of her throne, and of the son she loved above everything else in the world.

All these facts could not long remain unknown, and soon the public began to discuss them, together with the story of the different intrigues of which the palace of Tsarskoie Selo became the centre. Thanks to the friends whom she had chosen for herself, the antechamber of the empress was transformed into a kind of annex to the Stock Exchange, where all sorts of people, honest or dishonest, used to meet, in order to obtain through her intercession more or less extravagant, if not dangerous, favours.

Thanks to Madame Wyroubieva, there were introduced into the intimacy of the *czarina* certain members of the orthodox clergy recommendable only by their love for money and for lucrative employments, or rich dioceses and monasteries. The empress together with her sister, the Grand Duchess Elisabeth, who after the murder of her husband had become a nun and the superior of a cloister which she had founded in Moscow, and to whom one might have applied with success the remark of Marie Antoinette in regard to her aunt Madame Louise of France, "she is the most intriguing little Carmelite in the whole of the kingdom," tried to mix themselves up in every important matter in the State, and to lead it according to their own lights and aims, making use of the emperor as of an instrument of their own private ambitions and desires. They were both fierce reactionaries, who from the first day that Nicholas II. had promulgated the Constitution of the 17th of October, had tried to persuade him to recall it.

It was thanks to the initiative of the empress that the first *Duma* was dissolved, and that the government began to exercise considerable pressure over the elections in order to prevent the candidates whom it believed it could not trust from being chosen by their constituents. One minister after another of those whom the *czar* appointed in rapid succession, resigned their functions, until at last it was an acknowledged fact in Russia that no honest trial of constitutional government could or would be attempted so long as Alexandra Feodorovna would be there to counteract its existence. When the Revolution broke out in the year 1905, and especially at the time of the disturbances which took place in Moscow, it was the empress who excited her husband to adopt rigorous measures in order to crush it, measures which led to nothing, and which only made Nicholas II. a little more unpopular than he already was among his subjects.

It was related, whether true or not I cannot say, that when the famous Semenovsky Regiment was sent to Moscow to reduce into submission the insurrection which had broken out there, Alexandra Feodorovna had desired to say goodbye to the officers before their departure, and that the only recommendation which she had made to them had been not to show any mercy to the insurgents. She had read without understanding it in the very least, the history of the French Revolution in 1789, and one had often heard her say that to show any weakness or compassion in times of danger was equivalent to signing one's own death warrant.

Her friends were nearly all of them men and women with a bad reputation, and amidst the circle of her own immediate family she had only contrived to make herself enemies, thanks to her influence, and to her petty personal spite, the young Grand Duke Cyril, the son of the Grand Duke Vladimir, was deprived of his titles and dignities and exiled from Russia for having dared to marry his first cousin, the divorced wife of the empress's brother, the Grand Duke of Hesse, the Princess Victoria Melita of Edinburgh.

This punishment, however, was promptly cancelled, thanks to the numerous protests which followed upon it from all quarters, but the two people concerned never forgave the empress her attitude in re-gard to their union, and we saw an echo of this hostility the other day when the Grand Duke Cyril on the outbreak of the Revolution tried to play the part of Philippe Egalité in the Romanoff family, and went with his regiment to put himself at the disposal of the new govern-ment appointed by the *Duma*.

The only brother of Nicholas II., the Grand Duke Michael Alex-androvitsch, saw the influence of the empress exercised against him in a manner which was even more odious, because she contrived to deprive him of the control not only of his fortune, but also of his per-sonal liberty to manage his estates. With her mother-in-law, the Dow-ager Empress Marie, Alexandra Feodorovna showed herself absolutely abominable in her disdain, haughtiness and pride. With the persons composing her court and household, she was unpleasant and bitter. Even in regard to her own daughters she proved herself heartless, and she never once during the twenty-three years which followed her arrival in Russia until the day of her downfall, tried to do any good around her or induce her husband to accomplish one of those actions full of generosity and mercy which unite a nation with its sovereign, and make their hearts beat together for some noble cause or other.

Then again there occurred the Rasputin incident. I have discussed it at length in the first part of this book, and shall therefore not enter here into a second description of the career of this strange personage, this low Cagliostro of a reign that did not deserve to have any great nobleman or even gentleman for its favourite. The only thing which I want to point out to the reader, is the responsibility which devolves upon the empress in this disagreeable story, which more perhaps than anything else hastened the fall of the old Romanoff monarchy. Whether she was really persuaded of the holy character of the sinister adventurer who had contrived so cleverly to exploit her credulity, or whether there was in this curious infatuation for an unworthy object a question of hypnotism, combined with the extravagance of a badly balanced mind and imagination, it is difficult to say, especially when one has not followed otherwise than by hearsay the different incidents of this almost unbelievable tragedy.

It is probable that the mystery, such as it was, will never be quite explained, but one may reasonably suppose that the perpetual invocations to spirits of another world, which Alexandra Feodorovna had practised for so many years, have had a good deal to do with the obstinacy with which she insisted upon imposing this personage upon all those who surrounded her, and with which she allowed him to interfere with the details of her family life, a thing which went so far that one day the governess of the young grand duchesses, Mademoiselle Toutscheff, a most distinguished lady, went to seek the emperor, and told him that she could no longer be responsible for the education of his daughters if Rasputin was allowed to enter their apartments at every hour of the day and night.

The only reply which was made by Nicholas II. to this communication was that the empress ought not to be crossed, on account of the state of her nerves. He seemed to approve of everything that was going on in his house, and, this is the point which has always seemed so incomprehensible in his character, he even appeared to view with a certain pleasure the admittance into the intimacy of his home life of this uncivilised and uncouth creature called Rasputin, whose hand Alexandra Feodorovna bent down to kiss with a reverence that she had never before in the course of her whole life shown to anyone else, not excepting Queen Victoria of England, whom she had tried to snub during the official visit which she had paid to her after her marriage.

The complete indifference of the *czar* as to what was going on around him and under his own roof, combined with his weakness of character and his unreasonable love for his wife, did not add to the feelings of respect that his subjects ought to have entertained for him. In a very short time extraordinary rumours began to circulate concerning all that was supposed to take place at Tsarskoie Selo, rumours which, disseminated as they were among the population of Petrograd, contributed in no small degree to the promptitude with which it rallied itself to the cause of the Revolution that put an end to the reign of Nicholas II. It was related amongst other things that the Commander-in-Chief of the Army, the Grand Duke Nicholas, had one day told his Imperial nephew that if he did not lock up Alexandra Feodorovna in a convent, he would come himself at the head of his troops, to carry her away, and confine her within the walls of the monastery of Novodievitvchy.

True or not, the story was repeated everywhere, and it procured for the grand duke a considerable number of friends and sympathisers. Soon after this it was related that the empress was in connivance with the numerous people who had made it their business to plunder the national exchequer, and that she looked with indulgence upon the malversations from which profited the partisans and the accomplices, for one could hardly call them by another name, of Rasputin. She began to be hated even more ferociously than had been the case before, and at last the police had to let Nicholas II. know that his consort would do better not to show herself too often in public, because an attempt against her life might easily come to be made, under the influence of all the stories which one heard right and left concerning her private conduct and her affection for a being who was accused by the whole nation of being fatal to Russia's prosperity at home and good renown abroad.

The *czar* listened to all this, as he was to listen later on to the remonstrances of his own family, but he did not act on all that he had been told. He continued to see Rasputin, partly because, according to the tales of those who were in the secret of what really went on in that strange Imperial household, the frank way of speaking of this uncouth peasant amused him and pleased him, being something so totally different from the language which he was accustomed to hear. But contrary to what was generally believed, he did not discuss with him matters of State, any more than did the empress. It is to be hoped that this last assertion is correct, and that Rasputin in regard to Nicholas II. only played the part sustained by Chicot at the court of Henri III. of France, that of the king's jester, capable occasionally of telling

143

some truths to his master.

But during the last months which preceded the removal of this sinister figure from the horizon of Tsarskoie Selo, no one in Russia would believe in such a version, seeing that this Jester could dispose according to his pleasure of all the high places in the State, that he had created ministers, functionaries of paramount importance, church dignitaries, and that whoever addressed himself to him generally got what he wanted, whilst it was his friends who were controlling the government of the vast empire of the *czars*. One did not realise that this had become possible only because all persons endowed with the slightest independence of character, had gradually become estranged from their sovereign, and had come to the decision to abandon him to his fate, disgusted as they were by his weakness in regard to his wife, and being moreover unwilling to accept the responsibility of duties which they were not allowed to fulfil according to the dictates of their conscience.

One after another the ministers, who at the beginning of the reign of Nicholas II. had helped him to rule Russia, had been dismissed by him, or retired of their own accord, and their places had been taken by simple subaltern functionaries, preoccupied only with that one single thought of remaining as long as possible in possession of the places which they had been called upon by a caprice of destiny to occupy, and for which they knew at heart that they were not fit. Everybody who had a sense of decency left, had fled from Tsarskoie Selo, not caring to enter into conflict with the mysterious and subterranean powers, which, to repeat the words used by Professor Paul Miliukoff in his famous speech in the *Duma* a few days before the Revolution, alone decided the most important questions in the State.

The whole country was disgusted at the conduct of those who ruled it, and this disgust was soon to change into an absolute contempt. The unpopularity of the empress had extended itself to the person of the *czar* himself, whom one was beginning to render responsible for the different things going on under his roof and to accuse of seeing, without any emotion, the Imperial prestige and honour sullied, and this autocracy for which he cared so much dishonoured. This unfortunate emperor did not find anywhere a support. His mother had been estranged from him; his whole family had turned against him, after numerous and useless attempts to open his eyes as to the dangers which surrounded him and the position in which he stood before his subjects.

144

THE BOLSHEVIKI GENERAL STAFF

His brother had been systematically kept away from him by the empress, who did not care to have in her vicinity a man in whom she saw an eventual pretender to the throne of her son. His sisters tried to remove themselves as far from his as possible. He was longing for disinterested affections, and there is therefore nothing wonderful or surprising that he sought them from the wife whom fate had associated with his existence, whom in spite of everything he continued to love tenderly, and whose nefarious influence was to lead him to his destruction.

And she, this woman who alone stands responsible for all this ruin that has overtaken her consort, and his dynasty, did she ever understand the terrible responsibility that she had assumed? Did she ever try to be for her husband the faithful companion whom he required, and on whom he might have leant in the hour of danger and of peril? Did she attempt to develop in him those strong and virile qualities a sovereign conscious of his might requires to be able to handle it wisely? Did she ever enter into the needs of her people, or identify herself with the interests of the nation whose empress she happened to be? Alas! Alas! history has already replied to those questions, and it is history which tells us that, thanks to Alexandra Feodorovna, the inheritance bequeathed by Peter the Great to his posterity has been squandered and lost.

If there has ever existed a woman who has proved fatal to all those with whom her lot has been thrown, it is this little Hessian princess, whom fate or chance associated with one of the greatest political crises of which Russian history will keep the record and the remembrance, and for whose tears no one will find any pity, even when her sorrows will need it most.

CHAPTER 3

In one of her letters addressed to her daughter Marie Antoinette, the Empress Marie Therese wrote:

> I am glad to hear that you have decided to re-establish the old etiquette and representation of Versailles. However tiresome it may be, its inconveniences are still far less than those which arise out of its absence. A court must learn to know well its sovereigns.

These words of a woman who knew better than any other queen had ever known how to uphold the prestige of her crown, ought to have been remembered by the Czar Nicholas II., because it is an un-doubted fact that the custom which was established during his reign to keep the emperor and his family isolated from the nation over which he ruled, had a good deal to do with the change that estab-lished itself gradually in the ideas of the people, as well as in the minds of the aristocracy, in regard to the reigning house.

One forgot that there existed in Russia an emperor, and one only remembered the manifold abuses which were the consequence of the detestable government to which the nation was subjected. All the per-sonal ties that might have bound the monarch with those who could in an emergency have defended him against danger, had been snapped asunder by that monarch himself. St. Petersburg, which formerly (I have now in mind only the upper classes) had converged towards the sun represented by the Imperial Palace and its inhabitants, learned how to do without it, and it was no longer considered to be an hon-our to have relations, no matter of what nature, with any member of the House of Romanoff.

The Imperial Family, in imitation of the conduct pursued by its chief, seemed as if it wished to efface itself and to lead the existence of common mortals, which it did not succeed in doing, because it had been brought up too far from the world in general, represented by that portion of humanity which suffers and which works in silence, to be able to enter into its interests, and to make them its own. On the other hand, that same family gave the first signal of rebellion against the system represented by the masters of the Palace of Tsarskoie Selo, whom it applied itself to discredit with an energy which was the more tenacious that it would have liked to be in their place.

The Grand Duchess Vladimir, especially, together with her two sons, who had never cared for the head of their dynasty, were the first ones to greet in their house all the discontented people who abound-ed in the Russian capital, and to deplore in their presence the scandal occasioned by the strange conduct of the empress. The Revolution which was to come later on was prepared silently in the palaces of the very persons who ought to have fought against it, as well as in the homes of those old servants of the monarchy, who would have wished to save it from the disaster, which they saw but too well, was fast over-taking it, but who had to own themselves powerless to do so, and had to acknowledge with sorrow and with shame that it was discrediting itself a little more with each day that was passing.

The nation, on its side, was preparing itself for the impending struggle. The systematic manner in which the labour party in Russia organised itself in view of the approaching Revolution, has never been sufficiently known or appreciated abroad. It has constituted for those who have followed the slow evolution which was the consequence of the premature revolutionary movement that had failed in 1905, one of the most interesting political problems of the twentieth century.

I have lived in Russia during the years which have immediately preceded the war, and I have been in personal relations with some of the leaders of this party. I can therefore write about it from the point of view of a witness eager to watch the slow transformation, which out of a party essentially violent in its view and aspirations had produced a political faction, sufficiently ripened and saddened by the unsuccesses of its first fight not to seek elsewhere than in a too rapid solution the end of the difficulties under which it had been condemned to develop itself. It was quite sufficient to have witnessed the manifestations that used to take place each first of May, to come to the conclusion that the workman who was walking the streets, singing and carrying revolutionary flags, in 1906, was quite a different man from the one who indulged in manifestations of the like kind in 1913 and 1914.

The general strike which preceded the war by a few weeks upon which the Germans founded so many useless hopes was, notwithstanding its revolutionary character, rather an expression of opinion on the part of a powerful and perfectly well organised party than a rebellion against authority. The workman had at last realised that he had got the future for him, provided he did not allow his natural impatience to carry him too far, and that he could resist the temptation to proceed too quickly with the plans which he had formed. He had also realised another thing, and that was that neither the liberals nor the *octobrists*, nor the party called that of the cadets, nor even the revolutionary socialists, were strong enough to constitute a government, and that all the plans they were continually talking about, would only end in speeches more or less empty and devoid of practical common sense.

The workman applied himself to avoid mistakes, which perhaps he had noticed before he had quite grasped their importance. He understood on the other hand perfectly well the fact that the immense industrial movement, which had developed itself during the years that had followed immediately upon the war with Japan, was bound to increase still further in importance, and that the future belonged to those who would be able to profit by it, to guide it, and to direct it in the sense of a great and general reform of the different abuses which had corrupted all the higher classes of the nation.

The number of factories which suddenly arose everywhere, the speculation that followed upon the rise in the value of all kinds of industrial securities, and the knowledge that the workman very quickly acquired as to the different means thanks to which the fortunes of so many people come, no one knew from whence, had been edified, gave him a strength which became the more formidable that he was compelled to remain silent in presence of so many spectacles that revolted his sense of integrity. In regard to this particular point, the impossibility to hold public meetings proved a blessing in disguise for the development of the activity of the Labour Party, because it allowed it to proceed in secret to a propaganda that became the more dangerous for the security of the government in that there existed no one able to point out to those among whom it flourished its perilous, and even to a certain extent, its disastrous sides.

Under the very eyes of the police, the mass of the workmen employed in the different factories scattered all over Petrograd, prepared itself for the mission which it felt but too well was bound sooner or later to devolve upon it; so that whenever it allowed its voice to be heard, it was always with prudence, and even with a certain amount of cautious wisdom that prevented the general public and the authorities noticing how strong and powerful it was getting, and what a wonderful instrument it would prove later on, in the hands of those who in the meanwhile were leading it in secret, until the day when, thanks to their help, it would be able in its turn to lead others.

It must here be remarked that the Russian Government of that time never understood the wants of the labour party. It is sufficient to recall the terrible drama which was enacted in the Lena gold fields of Siberia, when the troops, called to the help of the owners of the works, fired on the mass of workmen who were simply asking for some legitimate improvements in their conditions of existence, to come to the conclusion that, according to the words of Hamlet, "*there was something rotten in that state of Denmark.*" Only, neither the government nor the upper classes of society, who were all of them, or nearly all, in the dependence of a few lucky speculators in stocks and shares, nor these speculators themselves, whose number was getting larger and larger every day in St. Petersburg, cared to remember that such was the fact.

During the years which immediately preceded the great war, the whole of Russia had become one vast Stock Exchange, the securities of which were quoted at every street corner, where the only things that had any value, were those which could be turned into a shareholder's company. The Emperor Alexander III. had tried, during the whole time of his reign, to improve agriculture in his land, and he had tried to bind together the different social classes of the nation, by a common love for their native soil.

It had been told at that time that he had been wrong in looking upon Russia exclusively from the agricultural point of view, but in presence of the things which have happened recently, one may wonder whether after all he had not been right, because it is quite certain that the change of system that had followed upon his death, and the exclusive protection which to the detriment of everything else, industry was awarded, during the twenty-two years of Nicholas II.'s administration, and especially during the time that Mr. Kokovtsoff remained at the Treasury, darkened the judgment of the people who under different circumstances, and if they had made less money, would have probably noticed the progress made by socialism, and the growing influence of the labour party over its adherents, who from the outset had been determined to break this might of capital which was of no good to the country, and simply added to the importance of lucky speculators.

As for the emperor, he had ceased to count for anything in Russia, after the failure of the so-called Constitutional government, which he had inaugurated rather out of caprice than because he had become convinced that it was indispensable to the welfare of Russia to see it ruled by a responsible cabinet. At the time I am referring to, it was an acknowledged fact in the whole of Russia that it was governed by some mysterious and dark powers which in secret were proceeding to any amount of malversations, most harmful for the prosperity of the nation, as well as for its prestige in Europe. The one general feeling which prevailed everywhere was one of immense lassitude at a state of things one knew but too well could not last, but which no one yet felt strong enough to try to ameliorate, change, or overturn. If the war had not broken out, it is likely that this condition, which hovered between a dream and a nightmare, might have gone on for a long time, because though the public realised perfectly well that the throne, as well as the man who occupied it, represented only a dead thing, yet it appeared still so immense that no one dared to touch it, but continued looking upon it, with the same eyes one would have done had it remained the great one it had been formerly.

The war broke out and awakened the nation out of the state of *marasm* into which it had fallen. During the first weeks which followed upon its declaration there took place in Russia an explosion of enthusiasm such as had never been witnessed before. It did not, however, last any appreciable length of time, and collapsed together with the news of the reverses that attended the Polish campaign.

Nowhere were these reverses felt more than amidst the ranks of the labour party, which, as a direct consequence of them, acquired all at once an importance it had hardly dared to hope it could win so soon. Factories became the principal organ of the national defence, and the word "ammunition" was transformed into the flag under which all those who were dissatisfied with the government then in power enrolled themselves as well as the people who longed for the end of an order of things the faults and mistakes of which were known in Russia long before they came to be recognised abroad.

The workman suddenly became the individual to whom was awarded the greatest importance, there where the question of the salvation of the Fatherland came to be raised. He was the one to whom everybody said aloud what he had been himself aware of long before, that it was from him, and from his efforts, that depended victory over the enemy who had audaciously invaded Russian territory.

This workman (this must never be lost sight of) was intimately connected with the army in which he had served, with the army that had far more confidence in him, and in his knowledge and efforts, than in the incapable government that had sent it to be slaughtered without providing it with any means to fight its foes. The workman became thus conscious of his extreme importance, and he aspired to be awarded the place in society which he imagined that he had the right to pretend to. He raised his voice, and insisted upon its being listened to. Perhaps Nicholas II. would still be in possession of his throne had he had sufficient common sense to do so.

There were at this juncture people who tried to make the sovereign understand that it was not enough for him to have assumed the supreme command over his troops in order to win back the popularity he had so completely lost, and that he would do well, in the interest of his dynasty as well as in his own, to show himself more frequently to the population of Petrograd, and to try to get into direct touch with it otherwise than through his official visits to the factories where ammunition was prepared for the army; visits during which he

SOLDIER AND SAILOR CITIZEN'S *DUMA*

was escorted with great pomp and ceremony by his usual cortege of attendants and in the course of which he had never found one single word of encouragement to say to those who were toiling for the welfare of the Fatherland.

The emperor failed to grasp the wisdom of this piece of advice, nor did he realise the importance of another one, which proceeded from the few friends he had still left to him, the advice to call together a national and responsible ministry, composed of men chosen among the representatives of the country in the *Duma*, and in possession of the confidence of the latter. He understood even less the necessity, recognised everywhere outside the gates of his palace, to try and raise the prestige of the crown, by getting rid of the compromising personalities, whose presence at his side dishonoured him as a man, and discredited him as a sovereign. He did not see, and perhaps no one dared to point out to him, the shameless money speculations which were taking place everywhere in Russia, and even under his own roof; the bargaining of everything that there was to sell or to buy in the country; honours, dignities, distinctions, places, and the Fatherland itself, by a gang of shameless adventurers, who had found the protection which they needed to carry on their plunder within the walls of the Imperial residence.

He believed what his wife kept repeating to him, that once he had declared such was not the case, no one would dare to think that he consulted Rasputin or the metropolitan Pitirim in regard to State affairs, and he simply laughed at those who pretended that he was doing so. He was blind until the end. He is perhaps blind still, and it is quite possible that he will persist in remaining so until the day when his revolted subjects will come and claim his life, after having compelled him to surrender his throne. Unconscious creature, unable to notice the dangers amidst which he had been living, or the abyss that was already swallowing him up.

It is when considering this point that one feels tempted to ask what would have become of Nicholas II. had he had beside him one of these intelligent women, endowed with a strong character, and understanding the nature of her duties as a wife, as a mother and a sovereign. It is likely that if he had found such a help he might have prevented or at least have contrived to give a different shape to the crisis through which Russia had to pass. The war was an unavoidable misfortune, owing to the firm determination of Germany to provoke it, no matter in what way, or under what pretext, but it would have been possible to conduct it differently than was the case.

One could also have been prepared for it, and one ought to have realised that the old and superannuated system of government so utterly rotten, where everything was left in the hands of corrupt functionaries, who had never learned anything out of the book of history, for whom the intellectual development of nations meant nothing at all, and who did not look beyond their personal advantages in all the great crises which might come to shake the equanimity of the country, that this system had served its time, and was bound to collapse under the weight of the universal contempt. But Nicholas II. called together a *Duma* which he had determined beforehand to deprive of every initiative, and of the liberty to say what it wished concerning the needs of the country that had entrusted it with the defence of its interests.

He made many fine promises which he never intended to keep, and when he spoke about the necessity of bringing about a close union between the *czar* and the representatives of his people, he never wished to give to the latter the possibility to approach him, or to lay their grievances at his feet. Had there been in Russia an empress worthy of the name, and competent to fill the position she occupied, she would have told her husband that the duty of them both consisted in remaining loyal towards their subjects. She would have exposed her person, and risked her life if necessary, in the accomplishment of the task which had been allotted to her by Providence. She would have spent her time otherwise than in the practices of a piety that was nothing else but superstition mingled with erotic tendencies.

What did Alexandra Feodorovna do during those solemn hours of a supreme crisis? I do not wish to be hard on her now that misfortune has overtaken her, but the truth must be told, and it is necessary to point out that her principal preoccupation during the months which preceded the Revolution consisted in defending Rasputin against the attacks directed against him from all sides, and in isolating the emperor from all the people capable of enlightening him in regard to the conduct and the character of the sinister personage whom her imagination had transformed into a saint, and to whose presence at her side she attributed a miraculous power, capable of protecting her and her family, against every kind of danger.

Under his influence and thanks to the impulse which he gave to her activity, she applied herself to persuade the *czar* to conclude a separate peace with Germany, working upon the humanitarian feelings of Nicholas II., and repeating constantly to him that he owed it to his subjects to put an end to a useless effusion of blood, and not to go on with a perfectly hopeless struggle. If the Revolution had not taken place it is most probable that a separate peace would have been signed between Russia and Germany during the course of the next few months, and it is also likely that if this intention of the empress had not transpired outside the gates of her palace the Revolution would not have broken out when it did, because all the different political parties in the *Duma* were agreed as to the advisability of putting it off so long as the enemy was in occupation of a part of the country.

But Alexandra Feodorovna poured the last drops into a glass which was ready to overflow, and the hatred which the Russian nation bore her found at last its justification in the general opinion which suddenly exploded like a barrel of powder in the whole of the country, that she also was a traitor, who had been won over to the German cause, and who was ready to give up into the hands of the adversary against whom one had been fighting for so many long and anxious months of a struggle during which so much blood had flown, this Russia that had offered her the Imperial diadem, which she had found nothing better to do than to sully with the mud of the dirty roads whither her steps had taken her.

Here I must make a pause, and try to analyse the real part played in the drama by the unfortunate sovereign on the head of whom so many curses have been showered. I do not believe that it was in order to hand over to her own native country, the one which had become hers by marriage, that Alexandra Feodorovna lent herself to the intrigue in which it is unfortunately an uncontested fact that she took an active share. It seems to me, so far as I can judge of things which did not take place in my presence, that her intentions were sincere according to her lights.

She was not an intelligent woman by any means, and what she possessed in the way of intellect had disappeared in a vanity and haughtiness of which it is hardly possible to form an adequate idea. She cared only for her crown, and for autocratic power over her subjects, and under the influence of those who represented to her that the least concession to the spirit of the times was bound to further the cause of a revolution which she abhorred, she had awarded her protection to this reactionary party represented by men like Sturmer, Protopopoff, and others of the same kind. She had preached to her husband whenever she had had the opportunity for doing so, the necessity to stand firm, and never to sacrifice one fraction of the principle of absolute power over his subjects. She had pointed out to him on every possible occasion the example of Louis XVI., who had been beheaded, because he had not had sufficient courage to resist to the pressure exercised over him by the revolutionary elements in the French monarchy.

She did not grasp in the very least that times were different, that ideas as well as men had changed, and that a sovereign who in a moment of danger does not seek help from his people, or try together with them to find a solution to the difficulties of a threatening situation, courts an inevitable ruin. The empress has, without any doubt being allowed as to this point, been the direct cause of the misfortunes as well as of the fall of her husband, and probably when history will be called upon to judge her, it will show itself even more severe in regard to her and to her conduct than her contemporaries have been, because she has certainly done more to destroy the respect of Russia for the throne to which she had been raised than the most violent revolutionary attacks that were ever directed against it. Instead of trying to bring her consort nearer to the nation at whose head he stood, she only inspired him with suspicions and even with dislike for this nation, or at least for the best among its representatives.

There happened circumstances when the empress interfered directly in the affairs of the State, and persuaded the *czar* to do what she required of him; as, for instance, the exile in Siberia, this Siberia whither she was to be sent herself, and the arbitrary arrest of several leaders of the labour party, whom, under some futile pretext or other, the government threw into prison a few weeks before the outbreak of the Revolution, in spite of the indignant protestations made by the *Duma* on the subject. It was also Alexandra Feodorovna, who, on the advice of the metropolitan Pitirim, a creature of Rasputin, who had caused him to be appointed to the See of Petrograd, the most important one in the Empire, persuaded the emperor to follow the advice of the minister Protopopoff to prorogue the *Duma*, and to arm the police with machine guns, in view of a possible revolt of the inhabitants of the capital against the government, a fatal and most imprudent measure, if there ever was one, which decided the fate of the Romanoff dynasty.

In this last occurrence, it was less out of fear of the debates that might take place in the *Duma*, than because he wanted to have his hands untied in regard to the conclusion of peace for which he had been working ever since he had been called to the ministry of the interior, that Protopopoff induced his sovereign to resort to a measure absolutely devoid of common sense, and the only effect of which could be to add fuel to a fire that had been smouldering for months, if not years. It proved fatal for everybody, and it is still a question whether it was not to be more fatal for Russia than anything else which Nicholas II. had ever done, because it has thrown her into an era of revolution and of trouble, for which she was neither prepared nor ripe.

At that time, I am writing about, the members of the Imperial family together with the aristocracy were beginning to get more and more alarmed at the manner in which events were unfolding themselves, and were wondering as to what could be done to put an end to the influence of the Empress and of her favourites. One of the oldest, and the only surviving personal friend of the late Czar Alexander III., Count Vorontzoff Dachkoff, when he visited the emperor to take leave of him, on his resignation of the functions of Viceroy of the Caucasus, had tried to remonstrate with him on the subject, and to point out to him the necessity of getting rid of Rasputin and of the followers of the latter.

He had known Nicholas II. as a child, and he could therefore talk with him more familiarly than anyone else in Russia: "I must tell you the truth," he said. "Do you know that, thanks to your Rasputin, you are going to your ruin and endangering the throne of your son?"

The old soldier, who had served under four sovereigns, became quite eloquent in his speech. The *czar* listened to him in silence, and at last exclaimed almost with a sob: "Why did God lay upon me such a heavy burden?"

After Count Vorontzoff, the Dowager Empress Marie Feodorovna tried to do something to save her son. She had left Petrograd months before, not caring to live in the vicinity of her daughter-in-law, whom she disliked as much as did the other members of the Imperial family. When Nicholas II. visited Kieff in October, 1916, where his mother was residing, the latter had a long conversation with him, in which she pointed out to him the peril which threatened him and the dynasty, unless he decided upon an energetic step, and removed from her side the favourites of his wife. But even Marie Feodorovna was powerless in presence of the dark and occult powers that held her son in their trammels, and nothing followed upon her remonstrances or her adjurations that he might consider the dangers with which he was surrounded, and try at least to conjure them.

After this interference of the widow of Alexander III., some of the members of the cabinet who were not of the same opinions as Messrs. Sturmer and Protopopoff, attempted to reason with their sovereign, among others Count Ignatieff and Mr. Bark, but they were also not listened to, and the former at last handed in his resignation which was accepted with alacrity, Alexandra Feodorovna not trying even to hide the extreme satisfaction she felt at its having taken place.

Count Ignatieff had been the most popular minister of public instruction Russia had ever known, and his departure was looked upon in the light of a national misfortune, adding to the dislike with which the empress was viewed everywhere. Mr. Bark did not feel himself at liberty to abandon the department of finances of which he had the charge at the very moment when a new loan was being floated, but he avoided seeing the consort of his sovereign, and only appeared at Tsarskoie Selo, when he could not help doing so.

On the 1st of November, 1916, one of the cousins of the *czar*, the Grand Duke Nicholas Michaylovitsch, who was perhaps the cleverest member of the Imperial family, a man wonderfully well learned, and who had acquired the reputation of an excellent historian, thanks to the remarkable studies which he had published on the life and times of Alexander I., and the Napoleonic wars, made another effort to shake the influence of Rasputin, Protopopoff and the empress. He asked the *czar* to receive him, and during a long and heated conversation which he had with the latter, he read to him a letter which he had prepared beforehand, in which were exposed not only the political, but also the private reasons, which made it an imperative necessity to remove Rasputin from Tsarskoie Selo.

As the grand duke told his friends later on, there were in this letter some passages that might have wounded Nicholas II. in his feelings as a husband, not only as a sovereign. But the *czar* did not reply one single word, only went to fetch the empress, and in his turn read to her the incriminating epistle. When he reached the passage in which remarks were made concerning her, Alexandra Feodorovna rose up in a passion, and snatching the document out of her husband's hands, she tore it up into a thousand small pieces. In the course of this memorable conversation, the grand duke asked the emperor whether he knew that the appointment of Protopopoff was the work of Rasputin, with whom the former had become acquainted at the house of one of their common friends, a certain Badmaieff.

"Yes," replied the *czar*, "I know it."

"And you find this a matter of course," exclaimed his cousin.

FOREIGN MINISTER LEON TROTZKY

Nicholas II. replied nothing.

In spite of the angry tone which the discussion had assumed, the emperor remained perfectly civil to the grand duke. The latter afterwards remarked that he had been more than surprised to meet with such utter indifference, and at the same time such kindness, in appearance at least, from his cousin. It seemed as if nothing that he could say could move the *czar*, who, during the most heated moments of this interview, handed the matches to his kinsman, when he noticed that the cigarette of the latter had gone out. At last the grand duke exclaimed: "You have got Cossacks here, and a great deal of room in your gardens. You can have me killed and buried without anyone being the wiser for it. But I must tell you the truth, and say to you that you are going to your ruin."

The *czar* continued to be silent, and his cousin had to take his leave, without having been able to obtain one single word from him by which he might have guessed whether he had been believed or not.

The confessor of the Imperial family, Father Schabelsky, was induced to interfere in his turn, and to warn the emperor of the ever-increasing unpopularity of his consort, advising him at the same time to send her somewhere for the benefit of her health, until the storm had abated which everybody except the few people who surrounded the sovereign saw was on its way. His advice also was disregarded. A lady belonging to the highest social circles, whose family had always been upon terms of intimacy with that of Nicholas II., the Princess Vassiltschikoff, bethought herself to write to the empress, and to entreat her to save the country and the dynasty, and to induce her husband to call together a responsible ministry, in possession of the confidence of the *Duma* and of the nation.

The only reply which she received was an order commanding her to leave the capital immediately for her country seat, with a prohibition to return to it again. Alexandra Feodorovna remained the only person the *czar* would listen to, and Alexandra Feodorovna was but the mouthpiece of people like Rasputin, Sturmer, and Protopopoff, who kept telling to her that she must not yield, and that the only thing capable of restoring peace to Russia was to subdue the rebellious spirits who dared talk about the necessity of making concessions to public opinion, coupled with the firm determination to crush, even by force, any manifestations which might be made in that direction.

Acting upon this advice, the empress assumed a power which had never belonged to any consort of a sovereign before. In the absence of Nicholas II. at the front, it was she who gave out orders, not only to the different ministers, but also to the troops composing the garrison of Petrograd; she had people arrested according to her fancy, she caused the houses of others that had displeased her to be searched by the numerous police agents whom she had at her disposal, ready to execute any of her caprices; she showed herself the absolute master in her consort's dominions, and she held everybody, including himself, in a firm grasp, which (this must be added) was more the grasp of Rasputin and Protopopoff, than her own.

It was evident that such a state of things could not go on indefinitely. There were still some persons left who hoped to be able to save the dynasty by removing its principal enemy, the unscrupulous peasant who had tarnished its prestige. A plot, into which entered different persons belonging to the highest aristocracy of the land as well as some members of the Imperial family, was arranged, and culminated, as I have already related, in the murder of Rasputin. All this has been told, but what has not yet been written is the manner in which the news of the assassination of her favourite was received by the empress.

At first her despair was pitiable to behold, then she quickly rallied, and getting back her energy, proceeded to avenge her murdered friend. The *czar* was at headquarters, and she happened to find herself alone with her children at Tsarskoie Selo. She sent for one of her husband's *aide de camps*, General Maximovitsch, and commanded him to proceed immediately to Petrograd, and to arrest the Grand Duke Dmitry Pavlovitsch, allowing him, however, to remain in his own palace, but with strict orders not to leave it, even for a short walk.

The whole Imperial family protested, but it was of no avail. Mr. Protopopoff was on the side of the *czarina*, and he alone was in command of the police forces of the capital. Any thought of resistance was out of the question. The hated minister would not have hesitated to proceed, even against the relatives of his sovereign, to gratify the revengeful feelings of Alexandra Feodorovna.

How vindictive the latter showed herself to be can be seen out of the severity of the punishments which, at her instigation, were showered upon all those who had taken part in the conspiracy to which Rasputin had fallen a victim. Prince Youssoupoff, with his wife, was exiled in one of his properties in the government of Koursk, and the young Grand Duke Dmitry was ordered to proceed to the front in Persia, which, considering his delicate state of health, was tantamount to a death sentence. When this became known, the whole of the Imperial family wrote to the *czar* in the following terms:—

> May it please Your Majesty, we, whose signatures you will find
> at the bottom of this letter, urgently and strongly beg of you to
> reconsider your decision in regard to the Grand Duke Dmitry
> Pavlovitsch, and show him some leniency. We know for a fact
> that he is physically ill, and morally broken down. You have
> been his guardian in his youth, and you are aware of the deep
> feelings of affection and of respect that he has always enter-
> tained in regard to you, and to our Fatherland. We implore Your
> Majesty in view of his youth, and of the precarious state of his
> health, to allow him to repair either to his own estate of Ous-
> soff, or else to Vilensky.
> Your Majesty is probably aware of the terrible conditions in
> which our army finds itself placed in Persia at the present mo-
> ment, and of the many illnesses and epidemics of all kinds that
> are raging there. To expose the grand duke to those dangers
> is simply compassing his ruin, because he can only come out
> of such a trial a physical and moral wreck, and surely the kind
> heart of Your Majesty will take pity on a youth for whom you
> have had some affection in the past, and in regard to whom you
> have always shown yourself a kind father. We pray to God to
> soften the feelings of Your Majesty, and to induce you to alter
> your decision, and to show some mercy to your own kinsman.

To this letter was received on the next day the following reply:

> No one has the right to commit a murder. I am aware that
> many people are suffering now from qualms of conscience, be-
> cause it is not only Dmitry Pavlovitsch who is mixed up in this
> business. I am surprised at your daring to address me in such
> terms. Nicholas.

The grand duke had to submit. He departed for the Persian front,
accompanied by an officer who had received strict orders to oppose
any attempt that he might feel tempted to make, in order to escape
his doom. A curious incident, very characteristic of the state of mind
prevailing in the capital at that time, then occurred. The comrades of
this officer, upon hearing of his appointment, obliged him to resign
his commission, considering that he had disgraced himself by accepting such a mission.

In the meanwhile, the body of Rasputin was taken at night to

Tsarskoie Selo and buried in a small chapel which had been erected some years before by the empress, quite close to the palace which she inhabited. Troops surrounded it so as to prevent anyone getting near to it, whilst the ceremony lasted, and the funeral was attended by the emperor, the empress, and the intimate friend of the latter, Madame Vyroubieva.

Alexandra Feodorovna used to go every afternoon to pray on the grave of the man whose influence had proved her bane, until at last the Revolution imprisoned her, and threw to the winds the ashes of the greatest enemy that the dynasty of the Romanoffs had ever known. When the body was exhumed by the angry populace, one found on its breast a sacred image, bearing the names of the empress, and of her three daughters, last memento of an affection which had proved so fatal to those who had nursed it.

The murder of Rasputin had one very clear and definite object, that of ridding the *czar* of an individual who had sullied his honour. Those who were courageous enough to send him into eternity had nursed the hope that once this evil influence had disappeared, the counsels of wisdom would prevail, and Nicholas II. might be at last brought to understand that his duty required of him to look bravely into the face of the situation in which he had been thrown together with the Empire over which he ruled. Until that time, no one had been able to talk seriously with him, with hopes of being listened to.

The emperor had acquired the habit of never giving an immediate reply to any proposition that was submitted to him, but deferred his decisions, in order to discuss them first with the empress, who in her turn consulted her favourites Sturmer and Protopopoff, who had taken to a certain extent the place left empty by Rasputin's disappearance. They were all of them working together towards the conclusion of a separate peace with Germany, because they believed that if once this were achieved they would be able to recall the army from the front, and to use it against the *Duma* and the nation, establishing with its help upon a sounder and firmer base their own power and might. None among them gave a thought to the possibility that the troops might practise with the people, and work together with it towards the downfall of the government and of the dynasty.

This desire of the empress to bring about, no matter at what cost, the ending of the war, was suspected by a good many people. A few officers in possession of important commands had an inkling of it, and the leaders of the labour party had also heard about it. The last named, who had worked more than any other class of the nation for the continuation of the struggle in the material sense of the word, and who wanted to avenge their sons fallen before the enemy, became anxious at the possibility of such a peace being concluded; and very distinct threats were uttered not only in Petrograd, but all over Russia, against the ministers, the emperor, and especially the empress. This explains, apart from other reasons, why the murder of Rasputin was hailed with such joy. One hoped that his removal would put an end to a state of things out of which could only result disaster, shame and misfortune.

Unfortunately, things turned out quite differently. Alexandra Feodorovna declared that she considered it her duty to go on doing exactly what her dead and gone friend had advised her to do, and the partisan of a separate peace with Germany found in her more solid protection than the one they had enjoyed before.

She pursued unmercifully all those who had tried to open the eyes of the emperor, and the first thing she did, after having seen the Grand Duke Dmitry sent to Persia and Prince Youssoupoff exiled, was to cause the *czar* to write to the Grand Duke Nicholas Michaylovitsch, who had addressed to him the letter which had incensed her so terribly, and command him to leave Petrograd and repair for two months to an estate which he owned in the South of Russia, in the government of Kherson This order was brought to the grand duke by an Imperial messenger, on the last day of the year 1916 at half past eleven o'clock at night. It was written entirely in the emperor's hand, and was couched in the following terms:

> I command you to start a once for Grouchevka, and to remain there two months Nicholas.

But there was added a postscript that had been probably written without the empress's knowledge, under the vague feeling of remorse for such an unjustifiable action, and which said:

> I beg you to do what I ask you.

Other grand dukes attempted in their turn to shake the influence of Alexandra Feodorovna, and to point out to the *czar* the peril which it represented for the dynasty. Many angry scenes took place at Tsarskoie Selo, between them and the master of this Imperial place, but they all led to nothing, and when the wife of the Grand Duke Cyril, the Grand Duchess Victoria Feodorovna, sought the sovereign on her own initiative, and tried to make him realise the great unpopularity of his consort, Nicholas II. interrupted her with the exclamation:

"What has Alice got to do with politics? She is only a sister of mercy, and nothing else. And in regard to her so-called unpopularity, what you say is not exact."

He then proceeded to show his cousin any amount of letters emanating from wounded soldiers, who thanked the empress for the care which she had taken of them, letters of which not a single one was genuine, and which had been manufactured at the instigation of Sturmer and Protopopoff. The truth of the matter was that the wounded and sick in the different hospitals visited by Alexandra Feodorovna, did not at all harbour kind feelings in regard to her, as they reproached her with giving all her care and attention to the German prisoners, to the detriment of her own soldiers. And among other stories which were related concerning those visits of hers, there was one which had obtained a wide circulation.

It was related that one day the empress, talking to a wounded officer who had been brought to her own hospital at Tsarskoie Selo, had asked him the name of the German regiment against which he had been fighting. The officer had replied that it was a Hessian regiment, upon which Alexandra Feodorovna had turned her back upon him, and had left the room in a violent rage which she had not even tried to control or to dissimulate.

The Grand Duchess Victoria was not discouraged by the manner in which her disclosures had been received by Nicholas II., and she had attempted to discuss the subject with the empress, but the latter, at her first words, had stopped her with the remark:

The people whom you advise us to take into our confidence, are the enemies of the dynasty. I have been for twenty-two years upon the throne, and I know Russia well. We are beloved by the nation, and no one will ever dare raise his hand against us. All this opposition about which you are talking proceeds from a few aristocratic bridge players, and is devoid of any importance.

After this, there was nothing to be done but to allow events to take their course, and to proceed.

They were to develop far quicker than one could have imagined. The army had begun to discuss the position, and to comment upon it. Everyone who had watched the march of affairs during the last months, felt that something was going to happen, but no one knew

MEETING ADDRESSED BY NIKOLAI LENINE IN FRONT OF WINTER PALACE, PETROGRAD

what it would be, or wished even to know it, so general was the discouragement that had taken hold of the public mind. There was, however, one factor left, which towered over the whole of the situation; that was the sincere desire on the part of the different political parties to try and keep back as long as possible a crisis which was recognised to have become inevitable, but which no one wished to see hastened.

This feeling was such a general one that a member of the *Duma*, who for family reasons had come for a few days to Stockholm where I was residing at the time just before the Revolution, told me that no one had been more surprised than he when the news had reached him that it had broken out, because, though he had been convinced it was going to produce itself, yet he had never believed that it could take place so soon.

Whilst this fearful storm was brooding on the horizon and getting nearer and nearer to him with each day that passed, Nicholas II. refused to listen to the thunder which was already resounding close to his ears, and was getting more and more determined to persist in the fatal resolution of holding his own against the tempest, and if necessary of using force in order to conjure and to subdue it. If ever the old Latin proverb, "*Quod Deus vult perdere, prius dementat*," has ever been realised, it was in the case of this unfortunate sovereign, who had fallen into the hands of an ambitious, cold woman, devoid of intelligence and of scruples, and incapable of appreciating the character of the people over whom she had been called upon to reign, and of whom she had been unable to conquer either the esteem, the respect or the affection, during the quarter of a century that she had lived in its midst.

Chapter 4

This discredited monarch, and his hated and despised empress, by whom were they surrounded during those eventful days which preceded their fall? Who were the people whom they trusted, and on whom they relied? Whom do we see advising them? Only a handful of flatterers, of sycophants, always ready to turn against him and to betray them at the first opportunity, together with ministers devoid of any political sense, and without any knowledge or comprehension of the position into which the country had been allowed to drift; without any courage or energy, incapable of imposing themselves or their opinions upon the masses, and of convincing them of the soundness of their views; incapable even of subduing these masses by the use of sheer force.

Apart from these flatterers and these weak advisers, whom could Nicholas II. and his consort trust and believe in? Whom had they got beside them? A discontented army, that was too thoroughly weary of seeing itself neglected and passed over like a negligible quantity, whilst it was fighting for dear life on the frontiers, and who had lost all wish to go on with what appeared to it to have become a hopeless struggle; a few functionaries who cared for nothing but their own advantage or advancement; a handful of adventurers in quest of places, influence and riches, especially of the latter; a police always ready to listen to every kind of low denunciation; that had abused its power, that had destroyed, thanks to its criminal activity, every sense of personal security in the nation, and that prosecuted only those who did not pay it sufficiently to leave them alone.

Blackmailers, spies, and valets; this was all that was left to the *czar* of all the Russias, to watch over him. They were the only people on whom he could rely, and even they would only remain faithful to him as long as the supreme power would remain, at least nominally, in his hands. His family, as we have seen, detested the empress, and was ready and prepared to side against him on the first notice of his downfall, which it effectively did. What was left in Petrograd; of aristocracy had withdrawn itself from him, lamenting over evils which it knew itself powerless to allay, and had come to the sad conclusion that the further it kept from Tsarskoie Selo the better it would be for everybody.

The emperor stood alone, forsaken by jail those who under different circumstances would have considered themselves but too honoured to die for him, let alone defend him against his foes. Alexandra Feodorovna had created a desert around her husband, and, thanks to her, there was hardly a Russian left in the world who did not for some reason or other curse the sovereign whom Providence had destined to become in all human probability the last of the Romanoffs crowned in Moscow. Nicholas II. imagined that he could rely on the devotion and the loyalty of his army. He forgot that this army was no longer the one that had acclaimed him with such enthusiasm at the beginning of the war.

Most of the officers who had been in command of it at the time had fallen on some battlefield or other; the soldiers too had disappeared, and the young recruits who had taken their place had been reared in different ideas, and were ignorant of the old discipline which had inspired the former regiments whose original contingents had been slain. The army had become a national one from the Imperialist it had been before; it was composed of the same elements of discontented minds who before they had been called to the colours had freely discussed the conditions under which the war was being fought, and who had noticed better than it would have been possible for them to do at the front, the mistakes of those in command, the remorseless dilapidation of the Public Exchequer which was going on everywhere, together with all the faults and the carelessness that had brought about all the disasters which had fallen upon the nation.

This army could no longer nurse, in regard to the *czar*, the veneration and almost religious respect which had animated it in earlier days. It had perceived at last that he was not at the height of the duties and responsibilities which had devolved upon him, and as a natural consequence of the fall of the scales from its eyes it had sided against him, together with the *Duma*, from which it was hoping and expecting the salvation which its masters of the present hour were unable to procure for it.

But whilst the whole of Russia was aware of this state of things, Nicholas II. alone refused to see it. He felt afraid of appearing as the weak man that he really was; he refused all the urgent entreaties which were addressed to him, to appeal to his people, and to appoint a popular and responsible ministry, capable once he had called it to power of requiring from him the fulfilment of his former promises, which he had determined beforehand never to keep.

He threw himself from right to left, and from left to right, in quest of councillors after his own heart, or rather after the heart of the empress, because it was she who finally decided everything; and he changed his ministers with a facility which was the more deplorable that those of the morrow did not differ from the ones whom he had dismissed the day before, until at last, thanks to his irresolution and to his obstinacy, he contrived to discredit, not only in Russia, but also abroad and among his Allies, the government of which he was the head, together with his own person and the great Imperial might which he personified. At last even the extreme conservative parties, who until then had been on his side, joined the ranks of his enemies, and this defection of theirs made the disaster an irremediable one, and the fatal catastrophe inevitable.

England at this moment made an effort to save the *czar*, together with his dynasty. Lord Milner, who had repaired to Petrograd to attend the conference of the Allies which was being held there, tried to open the eyes of Nicholas II. as to the dangers which surrounded him, and to persuade him to grant at last a constitutional government to his people, and to entrust the interests of the country to a cabinet in possession of its confidence. His representations proved absolutely useless. The emperor replied to him that if the troubled state of public opinion persisted, he would establish a military dictature.

He forgot in saying so that in order to carry an attempt of the kind it is indispensable to have at one's hand a man strong enough to accept the responsibility of such a post, and an army faithful and loyal enough to back him up. Protopopoff, whom the empress consulted as to the wisdom of the decision which Lord Milner had implored the *czar* to take, declared that he thought it would be an extremely dangerous one to adopt, and that the only thing which could and ought to be done, in the present circumstances, was to resort to rigorous measures; to prorogue the *Duma* and the Council of State; and to repress without the least mercy every demonstration against the government.

He added that he was quite ready to assume the responsibility of the repression which he advised, and if the necessity for doing so presented itself, to give orders to the police to fire on the crowds. At the same time, he inundated the capital, and even the provinces, with a whole army of spies, whose only occupation consisted in denouncing to him all the people who did not pay them sufficiently well to leave them alone. A kind of committee of public safety, such as had existed in France at the time of the Terror, became, thanks to Mr. Protopopoff, the sole master of the Russian Empire, and it disposed, according to its fancy, of the existence as well as of the property and liberty of the most peaceful citizens.

During one night, fifty workmen belonging to the group that was sitting in the industrial war committee, entrusted with the fabrication of ammunitions, as representatives of the labour party, were arrested, without any other apparent reason than the fact that they had allowed themselves to discuss in public the debates which had taken place in the *Duma*, and had been overheard by some spy or other.

This Assembly had met on the 27th of February, 1917, as had already been settled before the resignation of Mr. Sturmer, and the appointment of Prince Galitzyne as prime minister in his place. It became evident from the very first day the session was opened that most violent discussions were about to take place, and that the government would never be able to command a majority, because even the ultra Conservatives who had backed it up before had forsaken it.

170

One more reason for discontent with it had arisen: the almost total lack of food in Petrograd, where, thanks to the mismanagement of the railways and the lack of tracks, no provisions of any kind could arrive. Riots of a more or less serious character took place in different quarters of the town; the population clamoured for bread, and broke the windows in the bakers' and butchers' shops, wherever it could do so. This was one more complication added to all those already existing. The *Duma* thought it indispensable to make an energetic manifestation of its want of confidence in the government's power to grapple with the difficulties of the situation.

The parties composing the moderate left, together with the cadets that had recently united themselves into one group denominated the "*Bloc*," declared by the mouth of their leader, Mr. Chidlovsky, that it was indispensable to call together a cabinet comprising really national elements, in possession of the confidence of the country as well as that of the sovereign, because the one in existence was entirely discredited, even among its former supporters. During the debates which followed upon this motion, the socialist deputies, among others Mr. Tcheidze, expressed themselves in most violent terms, and said, among other things, that the government then in power would never understand the wishes or the needs of the nation, or become reconciled with it, and that between it and the country there existed an abyss which nothing in the world could ever fill.

It had against it the whole of Russia, and it had done nothing and was doing nothing to smooth over the difficulties which it had itself created, and for which it was alone responsible. And Mr. Tcheidze concluded his speech by expressing his conviction that a compromise was no longer possible, and that only a great national movement of revolt could overturn the cabinet and replace it by another one better able to understand the needs of the country and of the army.

One of the leaders of the extreme right who, up to that time, had been famous for his reactionary opinions and sympathies, Mr. Pourichkievitsch, went even further than his socialist colleague, and proceeded to sketch the character of Mr. Protopopoff, accusing him of spending his time in suspecting everybody (the zemstvos, the aristocracy, the *Duma*, and even the Council of State) of conspiracies against his person, and of meditating the suppression of these two institutions within a short time. Mr. Pourichkievitsch added that in what concerned the *Duma* he was personally convinced that it would prefer a dissolution to the alternative of a blind submission to a tyrant like the

Minister of the Interior, and of keeping silent when it knew that the Fatherland was in danger.

Another speaker of great talent, Mr Efremoff, said that he had come with great regret to the conclusion that all means at the disposal of a parliamentary assembly to fight the government had been exhausted, and that the whole country was a prey to deep dissatisfaction with the existing order of things. It was high time, he added, that the system which had ruled Russia for such a long time should give way before a responsible cabinet, the constitution of which was claimed imperatively by public opinion. It was only such a cabinet that would be able to encourage the country to go on with the struggle in which it found itself engaged, against a foe who had obtained so many advantages over it, thanks to the mistakes and to the crimes of the administration represented by Mr. Protopopoff, and by his friends.

But it was the leader of the cadets, Mr. Miliukoff, the greatest statesman that Russia possesses at the present moment, who dealt the last blow to the ministry, thanks to the acerb criticisms which he addressed to the Sovereign and to the latter's advisers, and to his indignant protest against the arbitrary imprisonment of the delegates of the workmen of Petrograd, who had been chosen by them to represent their interests in the industrial war commission. The vice president of this commission, Mr. Konovaloff, joined him in this protest, whilst another deputy belonging to the extreme left, whose name was to become famous very soon, Mr. Kerensky, in language of a violence such as had never been heard before in the *Duma*, prophesied that the time would soon come when this *Duma* would find itself compelled to fight for its rights and for the liberty of the nation, and would adopt decisive measures to put an end to the danger which was threatening the great work of the national defence, if it was allowed to remain in the hands and under the control of people who had so badly understood its claims and its necessities.

After these debates, during which had been voted by an immense majority the immediate release of the arrested workmen, Mr. Protopopoff rushed to Tsarskoie Selo, the metropolitan Pitirim, and Mr. Sturmer (who had remained a *persona grata* at court, notwithstanding the fact that he had been compelled to resign his former functions of prime minister) accompanied him. A conference took place between them and the empress, towards the close of which Nicholas II. was asked to come in and to listen to the decisions that had been arrived at, which he was requested to sanction.

This conference decided that the negotiations already engaged with Germany in view of the conclusion of a separate peace should be hastened; that the *Duma* should be prorogued for an indefinite period of time, and the police armed with machine guns, in order to be able to crush at once, by a display of its forces, every popular manifestation that might be attempted in favour of a change of government, should such manifestation take place in the capital.

Here I am touching in this short sketch of the Russian Revolution upon a point which is still dark, the point concerning this separate peace with Germany, about which there arose at that time so much talk in Petrograd. The idea of a step of that kind, which would have constituted an arrant treason in regard to the Allies of Russia, had been conceived first in the brain of Mr. Sturmer, to whom most probably it had been suggested by his confidential friend and secretary, Mr. Manassevitsch-Maniuloff, about whom I have already spoken in the first part of this book, and who, after the murder of Rasputin, had been finally brought to trial and sentenced to eighteen months' hard labour for blackmail.

He had always been in the employ of Germany, and he had spoken to his patron of the necessity for putting an end to a war which, if it went on much longer, might endanger the very existence of the dynasty. Mr. Sturmer had also sympathies for the "*Vaterland*," and he was but too glad to act according to the hints which were given to him by a man in whom he had every confidence. He found an unexpected ally in Rasputin, who in his turn induced the empress through Madame Vyroubieva to rally herself to his opinion, which was a relatively easy thing to do, considering the fact that she had been already, of her own accord, working towards a reconciliation between the Romanoffs and the Hohenzollerns, the only people whom she thought of any consequence in the whole affair. The difficulty consisted, however, in finding a person willing and disposed to act as intermediary in so grave a matter. Rasputin knew Protopopoff, discussed the subject with him, and found him quite ready to enter into the views which he expounded to him.

At that time Mr. Protopopoff was vice president of the *Duma*. No one knew exactly how he had contrived to secure his election as such, considering his reputation of reactionary and especially of opportunist. He had, however, succeeded in getting himself appointed, and the fact that he held this position gave him a certain weight and prestige abroad. He was given very precise instructions as to what he was to do, and started with several of his colleagues of the *Duma* for England, under the pretext of returning the visit which some members of the English House of Commons had paid to Petrograd a few months earlier.

On his way back, he stopped at Stockholm as I have already related, conferred there with an agent of the German Foreign Office called Mr. Warburg, and settled with him the conditions under which an eventual peace could be concluded. After this Protopopoff returned to Russia, where, however, the story of his Swedish intrigues had already become known so that he was awarded a very poor welcome by his friends. People believed then that his political career had come to an end, when, just at this juncture, the most important post in the Russian Empire, that of Minister of the Interior, became vacant, thanks to the dismissal of Mr. Chvostoff who had tried to get rid of Rasputin with the help of the monk Illiodore, and, to the general stupefaction of the world, the place was offered to Mr. Protopopoff by the empress herself.

By that time one had become used in Russia to every possible surprise in regard to the appointment of ministers, and nothing that could happen in that line astonished those (and they were legion) who knew that it was a gang of adventurers that was ruling the country. The rise of Mr. Protopopoff was not therefore considered by them as something out of the way, but in parliamentary circles it gave rise to deep indignation; an indignation which eventually found its way into the press, where, however, it was very quickly suppressed by the censor, and also in the various speeches uttered in the *Duma*, during which allusions were made for the first time to the unhealthy influence exercised by the empress over her husband. The former was triumphant.

As soon as she became aware of the conditions under which the German Government would consent to conclude peace with Russia, she set herself, in conjunction with her friends, to try to persuade Nicholas II. that his duty in regard to his people required him to put an end to a hopeless conflict during which the best blood in Russia was being spilt for a cause doomed beforehand. She made him observe that if the war went on much longer, the revolutionary elements in the country would wax stronger, in proportion to the sacrifices entailed upon the nation, and that it was quite possible, the latter, exasperated by their magnitude, would attempt to get rid of a government that had not succeeded in restoring to it the tranquillity which it so sorely needed.

It did not take her a long time to convert the *czar* to her point of view, and the negotiations officiously inaugurated by Mr. Protopopoff were officially continued by him together with Mr. Sturmer, whom Alexandra Feodorovna personally entreated to assume their direction in conjunction with her own self.

In spite of the extreme secrecy which had presided at these different conferences between the empress and her favourites, something of their purport had transpired among the general public, and threats had been proffered against those who had accepted to play the sad part of Judas in regard to their country. These threats had been whispered in the corridors of the *Duma*, and Mr. Protopopoff had been informed of their purport by his spies. It became therefore one of his principal aims to get rid of an opposition which, he knew but too well, would only increase in violence as well as in importance as the sorry work he was bent upon performing would come out in the light of day and become known to his numerous adversaries.

Apart from this, he thought it would be better to present himself later on before the *Duma* with an accomplished fact behind him. He therefore persuaded the empress that whilst he would be pressing with the utmost speed the negotiations with the *Kaiser*, begun already, it would be advisable to bring from the front a considerable number of troops to Petrograd, so as to be able with their help to crush any effort at resistance attempted either by the population of the capital or by its garrison, about whose state of mind the minister did not feel quite sure.

The cabinet was so badly informed, in spite of its numerous spies, of what was going on in the army that it imagined the latter would only feel grateful and happy to see the campaign come to an end and be able to go back to its homes, and that in consequence it would lend itself with the greatest pleasure to any attempt made by the monarch and the government to put an end to a struggle for which it did not feel any longer any enthusiasm at heart.

The men who reasoned thus were absolutely mistaken. The army had made up its mind to win the war; the workmen whose importance was increasing with every day that went by, also wished it, because they hoped that out of this victory they were longing for might result a radical change in the form of the administration they had begun to despise more and more as its incapacity became more and more apparent.

The person of the *czar* did not inspire respect or enthusiasm any longer, but on the other hand love for the Fatherland had made considerable progress since the beginning of the war, and the national sentiment which, up to that time, had only existed in the state of an Utopia had become a reality, especially since one had perceived the great strength which it had communicated to Russia's allies, to France among others, where the Republic, which many people were already seeing loom in the distance as a possibility in the land of the *czars*, had inspired so much patriotism to its citizens.

Neither Mr. Sturmer, nor Mr. Protopopoff, nor those who shared their opinions and their views, were able to understand what was going on in the heart and in the soul of the Russian nation. They were far too much absorbed in their own petty, personal interests, to be able to give a thought to such a subject. For them the conclusion of a peace with Germany meant the strengthening of their influence and of their power, together with honours, dignities, and the possibility to enrich themselves, and to have a few more stars attached to the golden embroideries of their uniforms.

It meant also the possibility of getting rid once for all of this spectre of a responsible ministry, of which they stood in such dread. They therefore threw themselves in the struggle against the *Duma* with an ardour that grew as they saw the increasing difficulties with which the accomplishment of their designs was going to encounter in that Assembly, and, as a first step in the course of action they had determined to follow, they submitted to the signature of Nicholas II. the fatal decree which prorogued the *Duma* together with the Council of State, and which was to give the signal for the conflagration of which they were to become themselves the first victims.

Traitors are always to be found in hours of great national peril. Among the people who resided in the palace of Tsarskoie Selo, there was a person who, becoming acquainted by chance of what was going on there, rushed to communicate the news which he had heard to Mr. Kerensky, the leader of the extreme left party in the *Duma*. The latter did not lose one moment in communicating to his colleague the news which had come to his knowledge, and also to the president of the Assembly, Mr. Rodzianko.

Mr. Rodzianko was about the last man whom one would have suspected of being possessed of the necessary determination to resort to a "*coup d'etat.*" He was a chamberlain of the *czar*; he had been brought up in monarchical traditions, and during his whole life he had submit-

ALEXANDER KERENSKY

ted to the one which, in Russia, placed the sovereign in the light of something holy and sacred before his subjects. He was respected but did not enjoy an immense authority in the Chamber that had never taken quite kindly to him, not thinking him possessed of sufficient courage to fight its battles with efficiency.

It is probable that he felt terrified rather than anything else, at the prospect which the communication of Mr. Kerensky opened before him, but things had advanced too far for him to be able to withdraw. There was no alternative left but to perish oneself, or to destroy others. Mr. Rodzianko called together a meeting of several deputies belonging to the moderate parties, with whom he discussed the situation. They very quickly came to the conclusion that if one entered into a struggle with the government in this all important question of war and peace, one would be backed up by the whole country, which did not wish to see the war come to an end until the enemy had been driven out of Russian territory.

There was also another thing which added itself to all the different questions roused by the discovery of the intentions of the court. It was the determination of the radical groups of the *Duma* to proceed to the *"coup d'etat"* on their own accord, and no matter under what conditions, with or without the help of the moderate elements in the Assembly. This might have become extremely dangerous, as they had behind them the whole mass of the working population of the capital.

The question had therefore to be considered as to whether the Revolution was to be made with the concurrence of all the parties represented in the *Duma*, or by the radical socialists alone, who, in the latter case, would have become the absolute masters of the situation, and might have pressed for the immediate proclamation of a Republic which could easily have degenerated into an anarchy, and which in the best of cases would have lacked the necessary dignity, capable of giving it prestige and authority at home and abroad.

Mr. Rodzianko found himself placed in the presence of a dilemma of a most difficult kind and nature. He took the only decision possible under the circumstances, he boldly placed himself at the head of the movement and constituted a provisional government, in place of the one that had foundered under the weight of the contempt of the whole nation.

The first thing that was done by the *Duma* was to refuse to disperse and to resist the *ukaze* of the *czar* that had prorogued its debates for an indefinite time. The socialist deputies went about trying to get the population of Petrograd to join in the vast movement of revolt they meant to bring about. The latter was but too willing to do so, and the want of provisions was the pretext which the people took to organise vast meetings, and a strike in all the factories.

Great masses of men and women paraded the streets, and were dispersed by a formidable police force which had been assembled by Mr. Protopopoff and armed with machine guns that were used against the crowds, whenever these did not obey immediately the injunctions to disperse given to them by special constables and Cossacks gathered together in all the principal streets and squares of the capital. The regular troops had been consigned in their barracks and ordered to keep themselves ready to lend a hand to the police.

But the unexpected happened. The soldiers had been worked upon by delegates from the workmen, and they declared that they would not obey orders, should any be given to them, to fire upon the populace assembled in the streets. The latter seemed quite sure of impunity, because notwithstanding the preparations made by the police to quell the revolutionary movement, the existence of which was already recognised everywhere, it refused to disperse, and on the contrary proceeded to commit the only acts of violence which were performed during the course of the mutiny. It threw itself on the prisons where political offenders were confined, plundered and burned them, and liberated their inmates. A few other excesses were performed, upon which the *Duma* constituted itself an executive committee, which assumed the task of restoring order in Petrograd.

In the meanwhile, the *czar* who had been kept in total ignorance of what was going on in the capital, had left Tsarskoie Selo for headquarters, after having signed the prorogation of the chambers. In his absence, it was the empress who was left sole mistress of the situation, and it is to her and to Protopopoff that were due all the attempts at repression which happily for all parties concerned were not allowed to be executed, at least not in their entirety.

Mr. Rodzianko telegraphed to the *czar*. He informed him that the position was getting extremely serious, that the population of Petrograd was absolutely without any food, that riots were taking place, and that the troops were firing at one another. He implored the sovereign in the interests of the dynasty to send away Protopopoff and his crew, and he drew his notice to the fact that every hour was precious, and that every delay might bring about a catastrophe.

At the same time, he telegraphed to the principal commanders at

REVOLUTIONARY CROWD IN PETROGRAD

the front, asking them to uphold his request for a responsible government capable of putting an end to the complete anarchy that was reigning in the capital, an anarchy which threatened to extend itself all over the country. The commanders replied that they would do what he asked them to perform. Nicholas II. alone made no sign. It was related afterwards that he had telegraphed to the empress, asking her what she advised him to do.

But it is more likely that the telegram of the President of the *Duma* was never handed to him. Mr. Rodzianko, however, sent another despatch to headquarters which contained the following warning:

"The position is getting more and more alarming. It is indispensable to take measures to put an end to it, or tomorrow it may be too late. This is the last moment during which may be decided the fate of the nation and of the dynasty."

To this message also no reply was received. The *czar* seemed unable to understand the gravity of the situation. Others did, however, in his place, and on that same day, the 12th of March, the troops composing the garrison of Petrograd went over to the cause of the Revolution. They marched to the *Duma* in a long procession, beginning with the Volynsky regiment, one of the crack ones in the army, to which joined themselves almost immediately the famous Preobragensky Guards, and they declared themselves ready to stand by the side of the new government.

The President of the *Duma* received them, and declared to them that the executive committee which had been constituted was going to appoint a provisional government; of the *czar*, there was no longer any question. It had become evident that his army would no longer support his authority or fight for him and for his dynasty. Soon the troops composing the garrisons of Tsarskoie Selo, Peterhof, and Gatschina left their quarters and joined the mutineers. The Revolution had become an accomplished fact.

The new executive committee displayed considerable patriotism at this juncture. It might have provoked enormous enthusiasm in its favour had it revealed what it knew concerning the peace negotiations entered into by the empress, but this might have given a pretext for explosions of wrath on the part of the mob, which could easily have ended in excesses, compromising the dignity of the Revolution. It therefore decided to keep back from the public its knowledge on this subject, and contented itself with arresting the ministers, and all the persons whom it suspected of having lent themselves to this intrigue, and it simply empowered two members of the *Duma*, Mr. Goutschkoff and Mr. Schoulguine, to proceed to Pskov, where it was known that the emperor had arrived the day before, to ask the latter to abdicate in favour of his son.

Nicholas II. in the meanwhile, had arrived at headquarters which were then in Mohilev, and where no one seemed to know anything about what was going on in Petrograd. None of the people about him even suspected that a storm was brewing which would overturn in a few hours a power which they considered far too formidable for anything to be able to shake. The only person who was kept informed of the course which events were taking was the head of the staff, General Alexieieff, who had been won over from the very first to the cause of the Revolution, and who, if one is to believe all that one hears, played all the time a double game. It was he who received all the telegrams addressed to the emperor, and who communicated them to him.

The latter at last was shaken out of his equanimity, and gave orders to prepare his train to return to Tsarskoie Selo. He took this decision in consequence of a message from the commander of the palace, addressed to General Voyeikoff the head of the *Okhrana*, where the latter was advised that the presence of the sovereign was necessary, because the troops of the garrison in the Imperial residence had mutinied, and the safety of the empress and of her children was endangered. But in spite of the orders given to press the departure of the Imperial train it somehow could not be got ready as quickly as was generally the case, so that it was only during the night from the 12th to the 13th of March, that it started at last.

It went the usual route as far as the station of Lichoslav, where it was met with the news that a revolutionary government had been formed at Petrograd which had seized the railway lines and appointed a deputy to take them in charge. Another telegram from the military station master of the Nicholas station in Petrograd instructed the officials at Lichoslav to send the Imperial train to Petrograd, and not to Tsarskoie Selo. This was communicated to General Voyeikoff, who, however, gave directions not to heed this warning, but to proceed to Tsarskoie Selo, as had been arranged at first.

At twelve o'clock at night the Imperial train reached Bologoie. There a railway official informed the persons in charge of it that Tosno and Lioubane were in possession of the troops which had mutinied against the government, and that it might be dangerous to proceed any further. General Voyeikoff would not listen to this advice, and the train went on to the station of Vichera, where it had perforce to stop. The general was told that the first train which always preceded the one in which the sovereign was travelling had been seized by the insurgents, and the members of the Imperial suite who were travelling in it had been arrested and conveyed under escort to Petrograd.

The *czar* was awakened. General Voyeikoff informed him that it was impossible to proceed to Tsarskoie Selo, because the railway line was in the hands of the revolutionaries. It was then decided to go to Pskov, where commanded General Roussky, on whose fidelity the sovereign believed that he might rely.

But Roussky had been won over to the cause of the *Duma*, notwithstanding the fact that he had been loaded with favours by Nicholas II. When the latter reached Pskov, where the general met him at the railway station, the troops there had already been sworn over by their commander in favour of the Revolution, and were quite ready to enforce its decisions. The czar knew nothing about this, and after a few moments' conversation with Roussky, who acquainted him superficially with the spirit reigning in the army, he declared to him that he consented to call together a responsible cabinet chosen out of the principal leaders of the different parties in the *Duma*. But the general replied that he feared this concession came too late, and that it would no longer satisfy the country or the army.

On the 15th of March, Roussky succeeded in talking over the telephone with Rodzianko, whom he informed of the details of his conversation with Nicholas II. The president of the *Duma* then told him that the former must decide to abdicate in favour of his son. They spoke for more than two hours, and before their talk had come to an end, Roussky had promised to do all that lay within his power, even to resort to violence if need be, to further the views of the new government that had taken up the supreme authority in Russia. He went then to make his report to the emperor, after which the latter signified his intention to resign his throne to his little boy.

The telegram announcing this resolution, however, was not sent to Petrograd, because in the meanwhile there had reached Pskov the news that the two delegates sent by the Executive Committee, Mr. Goutschkoff, and Mr. Schoulguine, had started on their way thither, in order to confer personally with the *czar*.

At ten o'clock in the evening of that same day, the 15th of March, they reached Pskov. Their intention had been to confer at first with General Roussky, but an Imperial *aide de camp* met them on the platform, and asked them to follow him immediately into the presence of Nicholas II. The latter received them in his railway carriage. With him were old Count Fredericks, the minister of his household, and a favourite *aide de camp*, General Narischkine.

Nothing in the appearance of the emperor could have led any one to suppose that something extraordinary was happening to him. He was as impassable as was his wont in all the important occasions of his life, and he shook hands with the delegates as if nothing whatever was the matter, asking them to sit down. He motioned Goutschkoff to a chair beside him, and Schoulguine opposite. Fredericks and Narischkine stood at some distance from the group, and Roussky, who came in uninvited at that moment, placed himself next to Schoulguine.

Goutschkoff was the first one to speak. He was extremely agitated and could only control his feelings with difficulty, keeping his eyes riveted on the table and not daring to lift them up to the face of the sovereign whose crown he had come to demand. But his speech was perfectly correct, and contained nothing that could have been interpreted in an offensive way. He exposed the whole situation, such as it was, and concluded by saying that the only possible manner to come out of it would be the abdication of the *czar* in favour of his son under the regency of the former's brother, the Grand Duke Michael Alexandrovitsch.

At this juncture Roussky could not restrain his impatience, and, bending down towards Schoulguine, murmured in his ear:

"This is already quite settled."

When Goutschkoff had finished his speech, Nicholas II. replied in a perfectly quiet and composed tone of voice:

"I thought the matter over yesterday, and today, and I have made up my mind to abdicate. Until three o'clock I was ready to do so in favour of my son, but then I came to the conclusion that I could not part from him."

He stopped for a few moments, then went on:

"I hope that you will understand this," and after another pause he continued:

"On that account, I have decided to abdicate in favour of my brother."

The delegates looked at each other, and Schoulguine remarked that they were not prepared for this complication, and that he begged permission to consult with his colleague. But after a short conversation they gave up the point, as Goutschkoff remarked that he did not think they had the right to mix themselves up in a matter where paternal feelings and affection came into question, and that besides a regency had also much to say against it, and was likely to lead to complications.

The emperor seemed satisfied that the delegates had conceded the point, and then he asked them whether they could undertake to guarantee that his abdication would pacify the country and not lead to any disturbances. They declared that they could do so. Upon this he got up and passed into another compartment of his railway carriage. In about half an hour he returned, holding in his hand a folded paper, which he handed over to Goutschkoff, saying as he did so:

"Here is my abdication, will you read it?"

After which he shook hands with the delegates and retired as if nothing unusual had happened, perhaps not realising that with one stroke of his pen he had changed not only his own life, but the course of Russian history, and, in a certain sense, destroyed the work of his glorious ancestor, Peter the Great.

It is difficult here not to make some remark on the part played by General Roussky in this tragedy which without his interference would probably have taken a different course. It is impossible not to come to the conclusion that the unfortunate *czar* whom he induced to abdicate, might have found better and more faithful servants than the people who forsook him in the hour of his peril. Very probably Roussky believed that he was acting in the interests of his country, which in a sense he was also doing, because something had to be attempted in order to stop the nefarious work of Alexandra Feodorovna, and it is certain that her husband would never willingly have consented to be parted from her.

Killing a woman would have been disgracing oneself, together with the Revolution which had been accomplished under such exceptional circumstances; but still one would have preferred that the man who was instrumental in the destruction of the Romanoff dynasty should not have been one who wore on his epaulettes the initials of the sovereign he was helping to dethrone. One would have liked him to feel some pity for the master whose hand he had kissed a few days before he presented to him the pen with which he ordered him to sign his own degradation.

In spite of the impassibility preserved by Nicholas II. during the last hours of his reign, it is likely that the tragedy which took place at

Pskov must have been one of the most poignant that has ever assailed a sovereign, who, after having reigned for twenty-two years, found himself, in the course of a few hours, reduced to utter powerlessness and compelled to give up of his own accord the crown which his father had bequeathed to him, and which he had hoped to leave in his turn to the son, whom fate and perhaps a mistaken feeling of affection had made him despoil.

He was not a bad man after all, although he had done many a bad action; he was a tender father, and the thought of his child must have added to the moral agony of his soul. By what means he was induced to put his name at the bottom of the document which snatched away from him the sceptre which he had dropped on his coronation day in Moscow, remains still a mystery. Whether violence was used, or whether he was persuaded by the eloquence of Roussky alone to give up the inheritance of his race, is a thing which the future alone will reveal to us.

It is probable that he found himself compelled to come to his decision in some way or other, and perhaps the threat to reveal the treason against his allies in which he had participated, and which had been the work of the empress, was the most powerful argument which was used to oblige him to sign his abdication. It was after all better to fall as a weak man than to be covered with shame in the eyes of the world. He was perhaps told to choose between degradation and dishonour, and he cannot be blamed if he refused to resign himself to the latter.

CHAPTER 5

The abdication of Nicholas II. was but one of the acts of a drama the end of which is awaited with anxiety not only in Russia, but in the whole of the world. Like everything else that he had ever done, it was not performed in time, and it was badly executed. His own selfishness, together with that of his wife, had brought about catastrophes which it would have been relatively easy to avoid, by displaying a small amount of political tact, good sense, and knowledge of the real requirements of the Russian people.

If the *czar* had only been able to render to himself an account of all that was going on around him, he would in the interest of his dynasty have given up his son to the care of the nation, and allowed him to take his place under the regency of the Grand Duke Michael. This would have left Russia with a *czar*, and not allowed the people to see that they could very well exist without one, which, as events have proved, has not been a particularly lucky experience for them.

This would also have ensured to Nicholas II. his own liberty, because it is not likely that the Grand Duke Michael would have had his brother and sister-in-law imprisoned. But neither the dispossessed monarch nor Alexandra Feodorovna were characters able to rise to any heights of unselfishness. She had not the faintest knowledge of the duties imposed upon her by her position as empress of Russia, and when she was placed between the alternative of seeing her husband dethroned, or being compelled to give up his crown to their child, she suggested a third one; that of substituting for the latter his uncle, because she thought it would be easier for her later on to overturn him than an emperor who owned her for a mother; and that she already contemplated the eventuality of a protest on the part of Nicholas II. against the abdication to which he had been compelled is a fact that can hardly be denied.

On the other hand, the Grand Duke Michael could not have refused to act as regent for his nephew, though it was, in a certain sense, natural for him to show some hesitation in accepting over the head of his brother, and of his brother's son, the crown of their common ancestors.

Personally, the young grand duke did not care for power or for honours, and the fact that he was married to a lady not belonging to any royal house made it easier for him to resign himself to go on for the rest of his existence living as a very rich private gentleman, which he had done for a number of years. Pressure was also brought to bear upon him, in the sense that he was told by persons interested in his not accepting the throne that if the Constitutive Assembly which it was proposed to call together, would elect him as emperor, it would put him later on in an easier position in regard to his nephew, the little Grand Duke Alexis, and perhaps even allow him to secure the possession of his empire to his own children after him.

All these considerations put together decided him not to avail himself of the immediate opportunity which lay before him, of becoming the *Czar* of All the Russias, and his proclamation on the subject may have been a wise one from a personal point of view; it was, however, disastrous as regarded the future fate of the dynasty, and it is doubtful now whether it will ever be possible for a Romanoff to reign again in Russia.

The men who had made the Revolution were but too well aware of this fact, and they proceeded, immediately after this act of Renun-

BOLSHEVIKI SAILORS BURIED AT MOSCOW

ciation, to organise the government of the country on the new lines which they hoped and wished to follow in the future. Their lead was followed by the nation with an enthusiasm which was so intense that it is no wonder it came to collapse so soon as was the case. Russia seemed to have been seized with a perfect frenzy; she was like a man who after having been unjustly imprisoned for years does not know what to make of his newly acquired freedom.

People were literally mad with joy, and inclined to find that everything their new government wished to do was right. Hardly a voice of discontent arose during these first weeks that followed upon the abdication of Nicholas II., and this absolution, which was granted beforehand to the ministry that had taken into its hands the direction of the affairs of the country, allowed the men at the head of it to decide the fate of the sovereign whom they had helped to overthrow, in a manner perhaps different from what would have been done under other circumstances.

The *czar*, after having parted from Mr. Goutschkoff and Mr. Schoulguine at Pskov, and seen them leave with his abdication for Petrograd, proceeded himself in his own special train to Mohilew, where the headquarters of the army were established. It is not easy to understand the reasons which induced him to do it. Perhaps he thought he would be in greater safety among the troops that had owned him as a chief but the day before than anywhere else. At that time, he had not the slightest inkling of the treason of General Alexieieff, and he might have nursed the vague thought that the latter might lend himself to another effort to subdue the revolutionary movement which had seized hold so rapidly of the whole country.

Others say that he wished to bid goodbye to his army before returning to Tsarskoie Selo to join his wife and family. The real motive of his determination has, however, not been ascertained so far, though the rumours going about at the time would have it that he had been invited to repair to headquarters by Alexieieff, who thought that it would be easier for him to keep his former Sovereign a prisoner there than anywhere else, until the moment when the new government should have decided as to what was to be done with him.

That something of the kind must have been in his mind can be deduced from the fact that from the day of the return of Nicholas II. at Mohilew he was no longer allowed to see any of the officers of the staff, or those attached to headquarters, and that the only person who visited him twice a day, as if to assure himself that he was still there, was General Alexieieff himself, and this only for a few minutes.

It was also the general who insisted on both Count Fredericks, formerly Minister of the Imperial household, and General Voyeikoff, the head of the Okhrana, or personal police guard of the *czar*, being sent away from Mohilew. He explained his request by saying that these two gentlemen were looked upon with such inimical feelings by the garrison and officers stationed at Mohilew, that he could not answer for their safety were they to remain near the emperor. In consequence of this warning both of them left for Petrograd, but on their way thither were arrested, and conveyed under escort to the fortress of St. Peter and St. Paul, from whence Count Fredericks in view of his advanced age (he is over eighty), and of the precarious state of his health, was transferred to the Evangelical hospital.

General Voyeikoff having been invited to tear off the initials of Nicholas II. from his epaulettes, proudly refused to do so, and declared that he had rather take off these epaulettes altogether. He was the only one who did not consent to submit to the orders of the government in that respect, all the other members of Nicholas II.'s military household having shown themselves but too eager to do it, General Roussky divesting himself of his aiguillettes five minutes after the emperor had handed over his abdication to the delegates sent by the *Duma* to require it from him.

The unfortunate monarch returned to Mohilew from Pskov on the 17th of March. On the next day arrived there by special train his mother, the Dowager Empress Marie, who, upon hearing of the misfortunes that had befallen her son, had hastened to his side. Their relations had been more than strained for a long time, thanks to the intrigues of the Empress Alexandra, but in those moments of agony the mother's heart forgot aught else save that her child was in trouble, and she rushed to him to try at least to help him by her presence to bear it.

Nicholas II. felt the nobility of this conduct, and the few days which he spent with Marie Feodorovna did away with much of the bitterness that had presided at their intercourse with each other for some time. But what they must have been for the widowed empress it would be hardly possible to imagine. She understood but too well, if he did not, the perils which awaited her son in the future, and the contrast which his reign had presented with that of his father must have filled her soul with agony and distress. Fate proved itself indeed hard for this noble woman, because it inflicted upon her that last, supreme sorrow, of seeing, before her train carried her back to this town of Kieff which she had made her home for the last two years, Nicholas II. taken away a captive to that palace that was to know him no longer for its master.

If one is to believe all that one hears, it seems that it was General Alexieieff, together with General Roussky and a few socialist leaders, who insisted on the provisional government ordering the arrest of the former *czar* and of his consort. They represented to Mr. Miliukoff and to his colleagues, that it would be the height of imprudence to allow the empress to remain at liberty and able to go on intriguing, as was her wont, against the new administration. On the other hand, sending the Imperial family immediately abroad had also its inconveniences, because their presence in Denmark or in England would only have been a cause of embarrassment to the Allies.

Then again, the hatred of the population of Petrograd for Alexandra Feodorovna had reached such immense proportions that it was feared it would give way to excesses against her, and even attempts to murder her, if some kind of satisfaction were not given to its incensed feelings in respect to a woman who was considered everywhere in the light of the worst of traitors. For this reason or for another, it is not quite clear, but most likely because of the representations made by Roussky and by Alexieieff, the Executive Committee of the *Duma*, which was then the highest authority in Russia, decided to arrest Nicholas II. together with his Consort.

Four members of the *Duma*, Messrs. Boublikoff, Gribounine, Verschinine and Kalinine, were commanded to repair to Mohilew, and to signify to the ex-emperor the decision of the government. It seems that what had hastened it had been the discovery of a correspondence between the empress and Protopopoff, which the latter, in abject fear for his life, had himself given up to the *Duma*, hoping that he would thus be able to drive away from his own person the responsibility for the conspiracy which had been going on at Tsarskoie Selo, under the plea that he had been compelled to obey the orders which had been given to him.

Apart from this correspondence, other things had come to light; amongst others the part that a Thibetan doctor, who had been a friend of Rasputin, and whom Madame Vyroubieva had introduced to the empress, had played in the private life of the Imperial pair. It seems that he had given to Alexandra Feodorovna certain drinks and drugs, which, unknown to him, she had administered to Nicholas II., with the result that the latter had been completely stupefied, and had become a tool in the hands of his enterprising wife.

The fact sounds incredible, and I would not have mentioned it here had it not been that young Prince Youssoupoff, one of those who had executed Rasputin, publicly spoke about it during an interview which after his return to Petrograd from the exile whither he had been sent by the *czar*, he awarded to a correspondent of the *Vovoie Vremia*, where the account of it was published. Both these incidents gave a free hand to those who, from the very first day of the Revolution, had insisted upon the empress being put under restraint, and once this measure was adopted, it was hardly possible not to extend it also to Nicholas II.

The commissioners started on March 20th for Mohilew. General Alexieieff had been privately informed as to the reason of their arriving there, and, unknown to others, gave orders for the emperor's train to be prepared to carry him away at a moment's notice. At four o'clock of the afternoon of March 21st, the commissioners reached their destination, and they sent at once for the general, with whom they held a conference of about twenty minutes. He assured them that he had already made full preparation for the departure of the monarch.

They asked him for a list of the people in attendance on the latter, and noticing thereon the name of Admiral Niloff, who was considered to be one of the staunchest supporters of the empress, they said at once that he could not travel in the Imperial train, and sent for him to acquaint him with the fact. Niloff asked only if he was to consider himself as being under arrest, but the commissioners assured him that they had received no orders to that effect.

Whilst this was going on, Nicholas II. was lunching with his mother in the latter's special train, which all the time of her stay in Mohilew had remained at the station, and which she had not left during these days. General Alexieieff was the one who took it upon himself to tell the *czar* that he had been made a prisoner. He boarded the train of the empress, pushed himself most unceremoniously into the carriage where she was sitting with her son, and acquainted the latter with his fate. Neither the deposed sovereign nor the widowed empress said a word. She simply got up and went to the window. She saw a crowd of people standing around her train, and the one that was about to carry away her son, then she turned back, and folded him in one long embrace. Speech was impossible to either of them and Marie Feodorovna remained tearless all through this tragedy.

On the platform were standing several officers who had formerly been attached to the person of the emperor, whilst he had been in command of the army. They were waiting to say goodbye to their former chief. A guard, no longer of honour alas! was also standing at the door of the railway compartment assigned to him, who a few days before had been the *Czar* of All the Russias, together with the commissioners of the *Duma*, into whose hands Alexieieff delivered his prisoner.

Nicholas II. passed on from his mother's train to his own. Every head was uncovered; he spoke to no one, and no one spoke. A silence akin to that of the grave prevailed. Standing at the window of her carriage could be seen the figure of the Empress Marie watching this sad departure. A few minutes later the train started on its mournful journey. Another act in this drama had come to an end.

Whilst this was going on at Mohilew, the officer in command of the garrison of Petrograd, General Korniloff, had repaired to Tsarskoie Selo. From the station, he telephoned to Count Benckendorff, the head of the Imperial household, asking him when he could see the empress. The count asked him to wait a few minutes at the instrument, and then told him that Alexandra Feodorovna would be ready to receive him in half an hour. At the appointed time the general was introduced into the presence of the sovereign who entered the room dressed in deep black, but as haughty as ever, and asked him in ironical tones to what she was indebted for the honour of his visit.

Korniloff got up, and briefly communicated to her the decision of the government in respect to her person, and warned her that the palace would be strictly watched, and all communications between her and the outside world forbidden. The empress then enquired whether her personal servants and those of her children would be left to her, and after having been reassured as to that point, she withdrew as impassable as ever, though strong hysterics seized her as soon as she was once more alone in her private apartments.

The guard in charge of the palace was changed; the telephone and private post and telegraph office were taken over by a staff which General Korniloff had brought over with him from Petrograd, and the empress was informed that she could not leave her rooms, even for a walk, without the permission of the officer in charge of the troops quartered in the Imperial residence.

Though no orders had been issued in regard to her personal attendants, yet the proud princess was to find that most of them had left her of their own accord. Her children were all ill with a severe attack of measles, but this did not prevent the salaried domestics who up to that moment had been so happy and eager to be allowed the privilege of serving her, deserting her in the hour of her need. The few friends she thought she could rely upon were in prison. She was alone, all alone; and so, she was to remain until the end. The devotion with which Marie Antoinette was surrounded during the tragedy of her existence was not known by Alexandra Feodorovna in the drama of her life. She had made far too many enemies during the time of her splendour and prosperity to find anyone willing to cheer and comfort her in the hour of her misfortune.

And the next day her husband was brought back to that palace of Tsarskoie Selo they had both liked so much, brought back a prisoner to find her captive. What did she think when she saw him again? Did she realise at last all the evil which she had done, all the misery, which, thanks to her influence, had overtaken the emperor whose crown she had shared? How did she feel in presence of this catastrophe, of this wreck of all her ambitions, plans and hopes? Outwardly she made no sign that she understood the full significance of the events that had swallowed her up in their depths, together with her pride and haughtiness.

She only manifested some emotion when told that the body of Rasputin had been exhumed and burned publicly by exasperated crowds. Otherwise she remained silent and if not resigned at least disdainful, even when she was subjected to a close interrogation by General Korniloff, who was deputed to examine her as to certain points in the correspondence which Mr. Protopopoff had surrendered to the Duma. She denied to everyone the right to question her; she proudly refused to reply to the demands addressed to her, and it was only when she was alone in her rooms that she used to give way to terrible fits of despair at the loss of that grandeur by which her head had been turned.

Her children were so ill that they could not even be told of the change that had taken place in their existences and destinies. Her husband was too much crushed by the weight of all the calamities which had fallen upon him to be able to comfort her in any way. Her friends had left her, her attendants had forsaken her, her family had abandoned her. . . . And it was thus, amidst the stillness of sorrow and of anxiety, that the curtain was to fall upon the tragedy of Nicholas II. and of Alexandra Feodorovna, or at least upon one of its principal acts. . . .

Part 3 The Riddle of the Future

CONCLUSION

More than one year has gone by since the events narrated in this book, and it is possible now to throw a retrospective glance on them, as well as on all the tragedies that have followed the fall of the Romanoffs. It has been proved beyond doubt that it is not sufficient to destroy a political system and to overturn a monarchy. These must be replaced by something else, and it is this something else which Russia has been vainly looking for during the last twelve months.

After the abdication of Nicholas II., successors had to be found to take up the power which had been snatched out of his hands owing to the clamours of public indignation at his weakness of character and want of comprehension of the needs of his people. These successors, who were taken here and there in the hazards of an adventure brought about by the intrigues of a few and by the cowardice of many, who were they? What did they represent? And what elements of strength did they possess? They were called upon to take the direction of the destinies of their Fatherland in an hour of national crisis, such as it had never known before in the whole course of its history, and to try to save a situation which had become already so entangled that it had almost reached the limits of desperation.

It is possible today to pass judgment on the first government that assumed authority after the fall of the unfortunate *czar*. And, much as one would like to think well of it, it must be admitted that though it was composed of men of great talent and integrity, it did not possess one single character determined enough and strong enough to deliver it from the demagogues who had secured an entry into it, and from the anarchist elements that had tried from the very outset to impose themselves upon it and their doctrines.

Moreover, these men were devoid of experience, and they believed sincerely (there can be no doubt as to this point) but absolutely erro-neously, that it was sufficient for them and their party to come to the foreground in order to bring about in Russia an era of bliss such as exists only in fairy tales. Among them was found Alexander Kerensky, a Socialist, one of the leaders of the Labour Party, an indifferent lawyer but a most eloquent speaker, who, better than anyone else in Russia, understood the art of stirring the souls and appealing to the passions of the crowds upon which he relied to keep him in power; and who by his wonderful speeches could easily lead these crowds upon any road he wished to have them follow, though it might not land them where they imagined they were going.

Kerensky imposed himself upon the Revolution in the same way he imposed himself upon a jury, and he treated it as he would have treated a jury during a criminal trial. Of politics, he had but a hazy idea; of the art of government he understood nothing. He believed in the value of words, and imagined that he could establish in Russia an ideal State, living upon ideal principles. But at one time he was popu-lar, and people thought him a strong man, whilst he was only an elo-quent demagogue. With this he had an overbearing character, would not admit contradiction, and soon was at variance with his colleagues in the ministry, who, unfortunately for Russia, were as weak as he was himself but with less tyrannical dispositions; they retired when they found that they could not prevent him from carrying out his plans of reforming the army and of abolishing its military discipline, without which no troops in the world could be expected to stand bravely in presence of an attacking foe.

It is a thousand pities that men like Paul Milyukoff, Prince George Lvoff, Rodzianko and others, to whose initiative was due the success of the Revolution, allowed themselves to be overruled by Kerensky, until he was left alone to bear upon his shoulders the whole burden of the government and the whole responsibility of the war, when he collapsed like a weak reed at the first real attack directed against him.

Another misfortune connected with the government that replaced that of Nicholas II. was that it failed to recognise the terrible Ger-man propaganda that was carried on with renewed energy in Russia after the Revolution. It would not believe in its danger, and it could not bring itself to employ violence to put an end to the Socialist or, rather, anarchist agitation fomented by German intrigues and kept up by German money, which alone has rendered possible the triumph of Bolschevikism and the seizure of supreme power by people such as

KERENSKY INSPIRING TROOPS TO SUPPORT REVOLUTIONARY GOVERNMENT

Lenine, Trotzky, Kameneff, and other personalities of the same kind, and the same doubtful or, rather, not doubtful reputation.

And yet it would have been relatively easy to put an end to the career of these men, had one only applied oneself to do so in time and bravely faced the criticisms of the people who were in their pay, or in their employ. The whole story of the Lenine-Trotzky intrigue has not yet been told, at least not here in America; and it may not be without interest to disclose some of its details. When Milyukoff and Prince Lvoff proceeded to form a government after the overthrow of the monarchy, they offered the portfolio of Justice to a Moscow lawyer called Karensky (nothing to do with Alexander Kerensky) who enjoyed the reputation of being one of the most eloquent, and, at the same time, honest members of the Moscow Bar.

They called him to Petrograd, where they held several consultations with him. Karensky declared himself ready to accept the position offered him, but only on one condition: that he would be given an absolutely free hand to proceed with the greatest energy and vigour against all the German spies and agents with which the Capital was infested, and that he would also be allowed the same free hand in his dealings with the anarchists who were beginning to make themselves heard.

Neither Prince Lvoff nor Milyukoff would agree to give him these powers he demanded. They feared that if they did so they would be reproached for doing exactly the same as the government that had crumbled down a few days before; and they also objected to allowing a member of the cabinet to dispose at his will and fancy of such grave questions as those involved in repression exercised against any political party, no matter of what shade or opinion. Karensky thereupon refused the position offered to him, but accepted the post of State Prosecutor under Alexander Kerensky at first, and, afterwards, when the latter had been transferred to the war office, under Mr. Pereviazeff.

This allowed him to watch the growing German agitation, connected with anarchist conspiracies, which was beginning to feel its way previous to its explosion. He had heard about Lenine and Trotzky, and was from the first convinced that they were both in the employ of the *Kaiser* either directly or indirectly, and he set himself to obtain proof that such was the case. He had wondered at the easiness with which Lenine had been able to obtain a passport from the German government authorising him to cross the dominions of William II. on his way from Switzerland to Russia.

He, therefore, had the correspondence of both Lenine and Trotzky watched, and very soon his attention was attracted by the fact that they were both sending and receiving constantly telegrams to and from Sweden and Finland, all of which were deeply concerned with the health of a certain "Kola" who seemed to be always getting ill, and then better, in a sort of regular way which appeared more than strange.

This was the first remark which led to the result that at last, it was established, to the absolute satisfaction of Karensky and of others, that Trotzky, Lenine, Kameneff, a certain Zinovieff, a lawyer called Kozlovsky, a lady going by the name of Madame Soumentay, and the wife of Lenine, had received not less than *nineteen millions of rubles* from the German Government. This money had been sent through so many different channels that it was next to impossible to discover its origin. It had passed through eight banks, and, I do not now remember, through how many private hands. But the people whose names I have just mentioned had received it, partly in Russian banknotes, and partly in banknotes printed in Berlin, which were supposed to be Russian, of a new type with which the German government was beginning to meet its obligations so as not to make them too heavy for its own Exchequer.

Karensky sought Prince Lvoff, who was still prime minister at the time, and asked him to sign an order for the arrest of Trotzky and Lenine. The prince had not the courage to do so, and the State Prosecutor had, perforce, to wait. But in July the first insurrectionary movement, engineered by the Bolscheviki, broke out, and then Karensky thought that his duty obliged him to assume the responsibilities which the ministry did not care to face.

By that time, Prince Lvoff, Milyukoff and others had resigned, and Kerensky was virtually master of the situation. But he was weak, weaker perhaps than any of his colleagues had been, and he openly declared to the State Prosecutor that he felt afraid to arrest the two men who were ultimately to lead Russia to her destruction. Karensky, however, was made of sterner stuff, and he bravely decided to act for himself, and signed alone the order for the incarceration of both Lenine and Trotzky. But the former had been warned, and had fled to Finland.

A thorough search was made of the flat which he occupied, where the sum of one million and a half of *rubles* was found in possession of his wife, who could not explain whence she had this money. Trotzky at the same time was incarcerated and brought before the State Prosecutor. The latter, in order to justify the course of action he had taken, had caused to be published in all the Petrograd and Moscow newspapers an account of the discoveries which he had made, together with the names of the people who had participated in the work of treason he was determined to suppress.

A curious thing in the story is that none of the papers that printed it (and they all did with the exception of the Bolschevik organ *Prawda*), was allowed to get abroad, which accounts for the fact of no publicity having been given to the story. Petrograd then was exasperated against Trotzky to such an extent that Karensky feared he would be lynched, and caused him to be conveyed to the prison called "Kresty" in an automobile driven by his own son, as no chauffeur would undertake to drive him there. What happened later on remains to this day a mystery.

The Minister of Justice, Mr. Pereviazeff, resigned his functions two days after the arrest of Trotzky, and his place was taken by Nekrassoff, who, when asked by the committees of soldiers and peasants who had begun by that time to be all powerful, to give the reasons which had induced the government to resort to this measure, became so embarrassed in his replies that these committees insisted on Trotzky being set at liberty, which was done three days afterwards. Karensky then resigned his functions, and returned to Moscow whence, however, he was obliged to fly and seek a refuge in Kharkov, as soon as the Bolscheviki seized the government.

The latter inaugurated a system of terrorism that claimed more victims than is known abroad, completed the disorganisation of the army, and at last started the negotiations which culminated in the shameful peace signed at Brest Litovsk. After three and a half years' war and a Revolution, Russia as an independent nation ceased to exist, and became virtually, and to all appearance, a German province.

This is the story as it reads, and sad enough it sounds. Germany can look triumphantly on the success of her work and glory in it. Happily, for Russia, for the world and for the cause of civilisation, it is only one chapter of it that has come to an end. Russia, the great Russia of the past, is not dead. She possesses far more vitality than she is given credit for, and she still has sound, true, and honest elements amidst her citizens. When attempting to judge her, one ought to think of the great French Revolution, and to remember that in France, also, it took years before its work was at last consolidated and set upon a sound basis. One must bear in mind that in France, too, a period of terrorism made people despair of the future and fear that the end of

PEACE DOCUMENT OF DELEGATES AT BREST-LITOVSK CONFERENCE

their Fatherland had come.

Our Russian Revolution is hardly one year old, and though perhaps one will be aghast at what I am going to say, I think that she has not yet passed through that phase of real terror which is always a symptom of great upheavals such as Russia has undergone and is undergoing. We may see worse things yet; we may live to look upon the erection of a scaffold on one of the squares of Petrograd or of Moscow. But this will not mean that the end of Russia has come, nor that she has become, or will remain, a German province. The hatred of the Teuton, on the contrary, will grow as events progress and the great disillusion arrives.

A few more months, and the peasants whom Trotzky, Lenine and their crew have lured with false promises will perceive that these demagogues have been unable to fulfil all that they had sworn to them they would do. They will realise that their lot has become under the rule of these new masters ten thousand times harder than was the case before, and they will be the first to rise against these deceivers. If we are to believe all that we hear from people who have arrived here from Russia recently, this movement of reaction has already started, and it is bound to grow stronger with every day and hour which goes by.

The peace signed at Brest Litovsk will remain verily a "scrap of paper" which will end by being thrown into the waste-paper basket. Not one Russian will recognise it, not one Russian will accept it; the Germans feel it themselves, and are preparing for a new struggle which may have a far different conclusion from the one which they are now trying to persuade the world has come to an end.

What has helped them, apart from the treason of Trotzky, Lenine and their followers, who have only had one idea in heart and brain, that of enriching themselves at the expense of the country for which they feel neither affection nor pity, has been the state of confusion into which Russia was thrown by the Revolution that broke up so unexpectedly—a confusion which can only be compared to that which prevails in the house of a man whom sudden ruin has overtaken, when every servant or menial in the place tries to steal and take something in the general disaster or to profit out of it in some way or other.

In Petrograd, in Moscow, as well as all over the country, looting took place, not only of private property, but also of the Public Exchequer, especially of the latter, and the Russian officials, who had always been grasping, became all at once bandits after the style of Rinaldo Rinaldino, or any other brigand illustrated by drama or comedy.

They stole; they took; they carried away; they seized everything they could lay their hands upon. To begin with the silver spoons of the unfortunate *czar* and as many of the crown jewels as they could get hold of, down to the paper money issued by the State Treasury, of which, as the Kerensky government had to own before the so-called National Assembly at Moscow, eight hundred millions were put into circulation every month after the Revolution, in contrast with two hundred millions which were issued formerly.

I do not think that it is a libel on these officials to suppose that part of this fabulous sum found its way into their pockets, instead of being applied to the needs of the nation or of the army. This wholesale plundering, if I may be forgiven for using such a word, was of course not the fault of Kerensky and of his colleagues, under whose ministry it began, but whereas the latter realised immediately that it was taking place and resigned rather than countenance it; the former, though aware of it, found his hands tied in every attempt he made to subdue it, by the fact that those who were principally guilty were either his personal friends or his former partisans, or people with whom he had associated in earlier times, and with whom he had compromised himself to a considerable extent.

With regard to those associates of his former life, Kerensky found himself in the same position as Napoleon III. after his accession, in presence of the Italian *Carbonari*, who claimed from the sovereign the fulfilment of the promises made to them by the exiled Pretender. Kerensky had also given certain pledges at a time when he never expected he might be called upon to redeem them; and when he became a minister he had to give way to the exigencies of all the radicals, anarchists, and extreme socialists among whom he had laboured, and with whom he had worked at the overthrow of the detested and detestable government of the *czar*. He could not cast them overboard or set them aside. He had to listen to them, and in a certain sense to submit to their demands.

For example, in the case of the exile to Siberia of the unfortunate Nicholas II., a measure which in the first days of the Revolution he had declared that he would never resort to, but which he nevertheless executed under conditions of the most intense cruelty, simply because it was demanded from him by persons to whom he could not say no. People who knew him well say that the fact of his powerlessness caused him intense suffering, but he had neither the strength to assert himself in presence of his former comrades, nor, perhaps, the will to do so.

In a certain sense, he was the man of the hour, "*le maitre de l'heure*," as the Franco-Arab proverb says. He was even to some extent the one indispensable element without which it would have been impossible for a Republic ever to become established in Russia. And everybody seemed to agree, one year ago, that a Republic was the only form of government possible after the fall of the Romanoffs. Of this Republic Kerensky rapidly became the symbol and at the same time the emblem of a new Russia; a regenerated and better one, in the opinion of his followers of the moment; a worse one from what it had been formerly, in that of his adversaries, but at all events of a different Russia from the one previously known.

But, unfortunately, Kerensky was neither a statesman like Milyukoff nor an administrator like Prince Lvoff, nor even a business man like Konovaloff. He lacked experience and knowledge of the routine of government. He had but a limited amount of education, no idea of the feelings of people born and reared in a different atmosphere from that in which he had grown up. He was only a leader of men, or rather of the passions of men; and, unfortunately for him, what Russia required was more a ruler than a leader, of whom she had more than she wanted, though perhaps at that particular moment none so powerful as Kerensky.

He had emerged a dictator out of a complete and general chaos; and he was to add to it the whole weight of his unripe genius and of his exuberant personality. After having been the Peter the Hermit of a new Crusade, he was to become the false Prophet of a creed which he had preached with an eloquence such as has been seldom surpassed, but in which it is doubtful whether he himself believed. Had he consented, or had he been able to work in common with more experienced men than himself towards the triumph of the Republican cause, he would have taken in the annals of his country the place of one of its greatest men.

As it has turned out, he will rank among its most interesting and brilliant historical figures, but only as a figure. His disappearance also has had something romantic about it, which will perhaps appeal to certain people in Russia, and which will disgust others. The world is wondering where he has gone and what has become of him; but everything points to the fact that he has either done away with himself, as he often said he would do in case of failure, or else that he has been murdered by the Bolscheviki during those days when the Neva and the different canals of Petrograd were carrying away to the sea hundreds of dead bodies every day. At least this is the opinion of persons who were in Russia at the time Kerensky vanished into space; and very probably this opinion will prove to be a true one.

The moderate liberal parties in Russia, who are the really intelligent, would, of course, wish their country's future government to become a Republic modelled after that of the United States. At the same time, if we are to believe the rare news which reaches us from Petrograd, and especially from Moscow, one hears people say now what they would never have dared to mention a few months ago—*i.e.,* that a constitutional monarchy, if it could be established, would offer certain advantages. I hasten to say that, personally, I do not see where these advantages would come in, unless they were associated with a new dynasty. But at the same time, together with many others, when I look at all that has taken place recently in my poor country, I cannot but feel sad at the great uncertainty as to the morrow which the Revolution of last year has opened, not only before Russia, but before the whole world, and I would like to see this incertitude come to an end in some way or other.

I have but little more to add. It is difficult even to try to guess what the future holds in store for the former realm of the Romanoffs. The only thing which one can say at present with any certainty is that Russia will never honour the signature of Trotzky in regard to the peace treaty concluded with Germany. Any hesitation Russia might have had as to this point in her moments of discouragement, that must have made themselves felt at times, disappeared after the message sent by the President of the United States to the Soviets in Moscow.

This message dispelled any fear the Russians might have had as to whether their allies had abandoned her. At present the country knows that it does not stand alone, and that any resistance it has to offer to its foes will be appreciated and encouraged. This is much; indeed, this is the one thing which was capable of rousing the energies of the whole of that vast land which the Teutons imagine that they have conquered. I can but repeat: Russia is not dead yet. Russia shall show the world that, betrayed as she has been, she can still lift the yoke put upon her, save herself, and help to save the world for the great cause of democracy.

And the conclusion of this book? I do not pretend to offer any. I simply invite my readers to draw the one they like best. I ask them only to do so with kindness and an appreciation of the difficulties of the situation. I have not tried to write a volume of controversy; I have merely attempted to describe, as well as I could, the Revolution and the events which preceded it, among which the extraordinary story of Rasputin figures so curiously.

I have given the narrative as it was related to me by people whose veracity I have no reason to challenge. It is certain, however, that many of its details are still unknown, and it is doubtful whether they will be revealed before the end of the war. At present, there are too many persons interested in dissimulating the part which they have played in the drama, either out of fear, or because they do not think the time opportune. It seems sometimes as if there exists a tacit understanding among the actors of the tragedy to hide the details of the conspiracy which came to an end by the signature of the Manifest of Pskov. This signature was wrenched, no one knows yet by just what means, out of the weakness of Nicholas II!—that unfortunate monarch who has never realised the obligations and duties he owed to the nation that dethroned him.

The last crowned Romanoff had never had, unfortunately for him, and still more unfortunately for his subjects, a sense of appreciation of the real value of facts or of events, which sometimes is even more useful than a great intelligence, to those whom destiny has entrusted with the difficult task of ruling over nations. He believed that his duty consisted in upholding the superannuated traditions of autocracy, and he did not perceive that these traditions had been maintained so long only because there had existed strong men to enforce them. Honest and kind of heart though he was, at least in many respects, he had contrived in spite of these qualities to rouse against him from the very first days of his accession to the throne all the social classes of his country. He had irritated the aristocracy, wounded the feelings of the army and of the people, and excited against himself the passions of the proletariat and of the peasantry, by his weakness of character and his obstinacy in surrounding himself with the most hated and most despised elements in Russia.

A few days before his fall he might still have made a successful effort to save himself and his dynasty, had he only followed the disinterested advice which was forwarded to him by his Allies and consented to the establishment of a responsible ministry. He preferred to listen to his wife and to the people she kept around her. Instead of trying to conciliate his subjects, he threatened them, until the expected occurred, and he lost not only his crown but also his liberty; and has

THE HOUSE AT BREST-LITOVSK WHERE PEACE NEGOTIATIONS BETWEEN THE RUSSIAN BOLSHEVIKI AND THE AUSTRO-GERMANS WERE CONDUCTED.

perhaps forfeited his life and that of his family.

But the future, the future, my readers will ask me, what will be the future, what shall it bring forth for Russia? The only reply possible to this eager question is to quote the words of Victor Hugo in his wonderful *Ode to Napoleon*:

The future belongs to no one, it is controlled by God alone.

Rasputin: His Influence and His Work

By Renee Elton Maud

Five or six years ago some Russian cousins of mine came for a short stay to Paris, and for the first time they pronounced before me the name of "Rasputin," telling me of his disastrous influence at court and particularly over the empress. They told me:

> He has persuaded her that the *tzarevitch* will die if she continues to live with the emperor as his wife, his object being to assure to the enemies of the Romanoffs that their hope will be accomplished and that no other heir will be born to the emperor, which is their great fear.

Besides, at that period the empress was ill and nervous, and at times could not walk, having to be wheeled about in an invalid's chair; to-day, I am told, she has returned to that chair, in Siberia, whither her unqualifiable conduct has led her.

The emperor certainly had an heir, and for once rumour was right as to what had indeed happened to the poor child, and he had been made to forfeit the hope of posterity to the line of which he might well be the last member.

"Therefore, he will not reign," said my cousins.

The emperor had even chosen his successor, a son of one of the grand dukes. (The *tzar's* brother had at this time been excluded from the succession on account of having contracted a morganatic marriage).

Grand Duke Alexis in addition has very feeble health, and the doctors had doubts whether he would live beyond the age of sixteen, which he has not yet reached. They said that also he was attacked by that infirmity which consists in having a skin too few, and consequently a liability to severe haemorrhages.

My cousin told me that one day on getting into his bath, the *tzarevitch* slipped a little and immediately a great "pocket" of blood formed itself; the same thing occurred one day in stepping out of a boat in which he had been for a sail. In fact the poor boy suffered from a strange and disconcerting illness, which is partly explained today, as will be seen later on.

Then I asked who Rasputin was. I was told that he called himself a pope, but in reality he was only a coarse and ignorant adventurer from Siberia; and they spoke with disgust of this intruder and the position he had contrived to acquire.

Rasputin, a name for ever detestable and detested by all who have a grain of feeling of straightforwardness and honesty, is perhaps the most diabolical figure of our century. Some hundreds of years ago he would have been looked upon as a sorcerer.

A native of Pokrovskoe, a little village situated in the province of Tobolsk in Siberia; a mixture of charlatan and satyr; neither monk nor priest, but simply an illiterate peasant; a poor village driver; father of three children left behind in their *izba*, but who later on came to school in Petrograd.

To the most depraved morals he joined a great love of vodka.

After having tried theft several times, and been sentenced to two or three terms of imprisonment, the luminous idea dawned on him one fine day to pose as a saint, thinking the occupation would be more lucrative. He therefore embarked on the life of one of those wandering monks living on alms and of whom I have already spoken.

From the depths of those strange steel-grey eyes came a light endowed with an enormous magnetism, amounting to hypnotism, it seems, and he practised this power on nearly all the women whom he met irrespective of age, surroundings, disposition, bent of mind—whether light or austere.

Naturally he employed this power to surround himself principally with women in the best society, and also with those endowed with large fortunes, this being at the same time more flattering and more practical.

The new religion, if one may so describe the lax and too easy doctrine that he preached, was, I am told, a mixture of those "religions" that flourished in the Middle Ages, and appealed to that *milieu* enormously. He went so far as to preach that a laxity of morals should be regarded as the sin most easily pardoned by the Almighty . . . and women of the best-known families and those placed in the highest position were present *incognita* at these "religious" services.

During each of his so-called "pilgrimages" he continually made new disciples; sister-disciples thronged his progress.

It was at one of these meetings at Petrograd that Madame Vyruboff, of unlucky memory, who is today imprisoned in the fortress of St Peter and St Paul but who was then the favourite lady-in-waiting to the empress—in fact the most intimate confidante of both the *tzar* and the *tzarina*—met him for the first time. This intriguer, like so many others, fell so much under his influence that she became one of his most zealous and devoted followers—later she became his mistress—and formed the project to present him at court.

All the same, this was not brought about without a certain amount of trouble and delay, for the scoundrel, who at the bottom of his heart trembled with joy at the mere notion of this presentation, required pressing, and even gave the impression of rejecting the idea, refusing to accede to it on the pretext that he made no difference between the lowest of the *moujiks* and the great ones of the earth.

He had then arrived at accomplishing "miracles"; his reputation of "miracle worker" had already been established, and was spreading each day, gaining ground like a spot of oil. Thanks to his ingenuity and to that of an accomplice, he had continued to create the appearance of effecting some.

Madame Vyruboff, knowing how vital to the empress was the question of the health of the *tzarevitch*—to whom she wished at all costs to assure the throne of the Romanoffs, in spite of the early death which the doctors had foretold for him—had the "brilliant" idea of first presenting Rasputin, the intriguer, believing that by so doing she would make herself useful and important, conjecturing also that he might perhaps do something to ameliorate the health of that frail being.

The rascal pretended to hesitate, but consented at last, on receiving a message from the empress asking him to come and visit the little patient. He was received with all the eagerness, all the ardour that can be felt by a maternal heart which has borne a long agony of pain and anxiety, and when she saw him stretch his hands over the frail little body of her child in the act of blessing, and thus perhaps produced a healing influence, she, too, while weeping grateful tears felt herself fall under the influence of the strange fascination which he exercised, above all, when turning to her, with that particular manner which made a victim of nearly every woman he met, he promised her a complete cure.

And the *tzarevitch*, as though to lend more weight to his words, seemed to show an improvement after the visits. The empress, full of hope, only saw in this charlatan a saint, a messenger from Heaven sent to cure her child!

From that time, Rasputin took root in the palace and began to "instruct" the ladies of the court; the practical side was not forgotten by him, and if he had made dupes he had also reaped a great harvest of money. He pretended to collect for the monastery built by him in his native village, where the monks lived an austere and most ascetic life of prayer among the most luxurious surroundings, the fruit of the offerings collected by him.

From time to time he would threaten his "sister disciples" to leave the capital and return to the monastery, at hearing which they became desolate, and one and all implored him to remain.

The empress, more than anyone, was petrified at the thought of what might happen, and all the more that, each time that Rasputin went away, a change for the worse was noticed in the health of the precious child.

This may be explained thus: Rasputin was well versed in the composition and effects of certain drugs known in the East, which he obtained from a great friend of his, an Oriental quack doctor, who gave to his patients infusions of herbs brought from Tibet, and he took care to have one of them administered to the Imperial child by Madame Vryuboff when he was absent. This, while making him ill, assured Rasputin's recall, and as may be imagined he was not anxious to cut short his brilliant career. Sometimes it happened that the drug brought the child apparently too near the gates of death. Hence the short despairing and heart-rending notes, of which so much has been said, addressed by a poor distracted mother to the "Saint"!

He made himself even more needed, and did not even reply to the Imperial missives. Then, tiring of the charms of his so-called beautiful and austere monastery, which had never existed, and was in reality but a poor house where his family lived, and, in addition, twelve of his admiring and fanatic "sisters" and where he had, as one may imagine, a lively time, he would reappear, and be greeted as a saviour.

The *tzar* did not like Rasputin, but he tolerated him. His Majesty generally possessed a clear judgment, but never had quite the courage of his opinions; and unluckily his courage stopped short of sending the rascal away.

Among the friends of Rasputin must be mentioned Protopopoff, Minister of the Interior, and Boris Sturmer, who thanks to the former's intrigues had been appointed Prime Minister of Russia. Both were known to be pro-German.

The "monk's" empire at the court became so great that through the intermediary of the empress those who had been remiss to him in any particular lost important posts, and he also caused his unworthy "*protégés*" to be given the highest appointments. This grew to such an extent that he really came to out-emperor the emperor himself, and he knew it—that shameless rascal who endeavoured to make himself look like the picture of Christ.

He had also powerful enemies, among whom was Stolypin, an honest man, and then one of the most powerful men in the Empire. When in 1906 the New Russian Imperial *Duma* assembled for its first session, the question of the redistribution of land became at once the chief topic of the debates. The second *Duma* took it up also, and after the dismissal of the second *Duma* the government considered the same question again.

Monsieur Stolypin, who was prime minister at the time, introduced his very much discussed Land Reform Bill, which provided to a great extent for the distribution of State and Crown land to the peasantry; but this land reserve was big and would not have been exhausted for a long time. The chief object of Monsieur Stolypin's land reform was to break up the communal ownership. There was no appropriation of private owner's land and no private owner was forced to sell his property. As a result, 2,000,000 new farms sprang up in different parts of Russia. Later on, he also paid for his honesty, like so many others, by perishing from a bomb explosion at Kief.

But the enemy Rasputin feared most of all others was Grand Duke Nicholas, who had learnt a great deal about the so-called "Saint" and esteemed him accordingly; Rasputin knew this and was consequently not free from anxiety. I have been assured that at a ball given at the palace since the war, the Grand Duke Nicholas, assisted by young Grand Duke Dmitri Paulovitch, seized the mock monk, who naturally was there, the pupils of his eyes more charged with magnetism than ever, and tearing off the pious emblems with which he was covered—one more fascination—administered the most severe chastisement after having thrown him outside.

Soon after the commencement of hostilities Grand Duke Nicholas was appointed by the *tzar* Commander-in-Chief of the Russian Armies on the German frontier. Later on, he was appointed Viceroy of the Caucasus and the *tzar* took the full command of the Western front upon himself. It was an established fact that the grand duke's transference—which became a burning question—was brought about entirely by the influence of the pro-German group by which the emperor was surrounded, these intriguers finding the presence of the grand duke a great obstacle to the realisation of their dark plans.

A great sportsman, the grand duke had the best pack of hounds in the Empire; his borzois were unrivalled in beauty, strength and speed, and he possessed wonderful shooting preserves in the Caucasus and elsewhere.

Following on the *tzar's* abdication, it was decided by the existing government to reinstate the Grand Duke Nicholas as Commander-in-Chief of the army, in which post he had so greatly distinguished himself at the beginning of the war; and he was actually on the point of leaving for headquarters when the Committee of the Workers' Delegates and the Committee of the Soldiers' Deputies, egged on by the Socialists, protested against the measure. The Labour Party were alarmed that the great popularity of the grand duke with the army might be the cause of their proclaiming him Tzar of Russia; therefore, they insisted on the revocation of his appointment, and Kerensky upheld them, threatening to resign from the cabinet should the grand duke assume the chief command.

From the appearance of Rasputin, Germany was on the watch, realizing what an easy prey Russia might become, and soon the pockets of the "Saint" were bulging over with German gold. Surrounded by pro-German friends, they began to plot for Germany to such an extent, and so successfully, that Rasputin was sent for to Berlin by the *Kaiser*, who it may be imagined did not waste his time. Rasputin, installed in a fine house near the Moika, saw his religion develop every day; then it was that Grand Duchess Olga, the eldest daughter of the emperor, became one of his most fervent "sister disciples," and on his return from his clandestine journey to Germany, in 1916, he began cleverly to insinuate to his admiring female listeners that a separate peace would be very profitable to the great Russian Empire.

It was in vain that Grand Duke Nicholas and others informed the empress what Rasputin really was, and told her of his depraved life and his false miracles, it was in vain that they told her that he and his friends would destroy Russia—all these efforts of persuasion were of no avail.

In vain, also, Grand Duke Nicholas implored the emperor to banish from the court all those Germans by whom he was surrounded, telling him bluntly, "If you do not do so, the House of Romanoff is doomed."

As for Rasputin, feeling himself tracked down like a wild beast, he continued to terrorise the empress on the subject of the *tzarevitch*, saying:

> If any misfortune happens to me, the *tzarevitch* will die too, and that exactly forty days, hour for hour, after me.

Many people disappeared and died in a mysterious manner, many dramas took place even in the "Saint's" house—and some of these, it was said, were by his own hand—but he always succeeded in suppressing the scandal.

A young woman returned from Petrograd, who had the good sense not to become his victim, has told me how she was invited not very long before his tragic end to a tea-party at which the scoundrel was to be present. He entered the room not only with a most self-satisfied air, but one which tried to be also mystical, and began to speak to each of the young women in his hideous jargon, staring with that hypnotic look, which made each one of them his own, at the same time kissing each on the lips, with an incredible and repulsive audacity, as if it were due to him. The witness in question avoided the same fate but with difficulty, upon which the "Saint" took on a puzzled anxious expression, and began to turn round, saying that he felt a current of antipathy in the room and came to a stop in front of her. From the moment she entered the room Rasputin did not appear to be at ease, no doubt because of that contrary current.

He seemed to this young woman to be a coarse creature, not even knowing how to express himself; naturally with no manners, and repulsive in his fatuousness; less than well cared for in his appearance, in fact—abject. Only one thing about him was right—of very fine quality—his linen. The empress, it is said, gave him these very fine shirts; and, when her children were ill, it is said that she insisted that they should wear the "holy tunics" of the "Saint" so that they should not get worse.

It was in 1916 that the power of the mock-monk attained its zenith.

Naturally on the occasion of his visit to England some years ago, the German emperor and his suite—cunningly chosen with a view to such functions—were there as spies, and not, as so many *naïve* people believed, as friends.

Prince Henry of Prussia repeated one of his spying tours and many other Germans avowed their love for England publicly—and that with good reason. Those journeys must have been very profitable for them, and I myself have no confidence in those who are always reiterating the small amount of interest they take in our country, while living in it all the time—what then are they doing in it?

Among the number of those spies one must evidently also count the Queen of Greece, sister of the *Kaiser*, who at Eastbourne on the eve of the declaration of war, pretended to know nothing about it, notwithstanding which she managed to escape just in time. She must therefore have been informed beforehand, or at any rate at the last moment. Since then she has but too much proved herself a fond sister for it to be possible for us to be credulous; it is true that her affection has cost her her throne, much it is said to her fury. In gratitude the *Kaiser*, directly on her arrival in Switzerland, opened an account at a Swiss Bank for her to the amount of £50,000.

Naturally, as the secret agent of the *Kaiser* in Russia, Rasputin was in constant communication with Berlin. They wished to get rid of Brusiloff, then of Korniloff, but failed in the two attempts at assassination, which annoyed Berlin very much. What they desired was the cessation of the great and victorious offensive.

Monsieur Goutchkoff, director of the Committee of War Industries, denounced the "Holy Father" Rasputin to the *Duma*, but again he managed to escape the consequences, and informed the emperor that Heaven would certainly take revenge on him and on his heir for what he himself had to endure.

And the poor deceived emperor did not in the least suspect that Protopopoff was a traitor—that Protopopoff, who had come to England, announcing himself as a friend, and then had gone to France, being received everywhere with a warm welcome—refusing to believe the man to be so double-faced.

Then the "Holy Father," as he was called, told the emperor that he would do well to mistrust Brusiloff, whom he knew to be a traitor to his country, and insisted on this to such an extent that the brave general was on the point of being arrested a few days later.

He also poisoned the emperor's mind against Nebrasoff, the Minister of Communications, who was dismissed, being a powerful obstacle to the pro-German clique, and hindering their projects of internal disorganisation; for they dreamed not only of bringing about famine in different parts of Russia, but also of sowing there, as well as at the front, the most severe epidemics, the dangerous germs of which were sent with great care from Berlin, and distributed in the food in the more populous districts, so that the result should cause greater ravages. No excuses can be found for the empress, for I am assured that Rasputin showed her every line of the correspondence sent and received in exchange between Berlin and her many agents. Not only did she acquiesce in their intrigues, but she incited them to more, encouraging them to make a separate peace, and also to sow epidemics and to create famine; and all the while German gold flowed into the hands of this clique.

Nevertheless, Brusiloff had recommenced his offensive, his successes being followed with anguish at Berlin. Sturmer forced Rumania to enter the war, knowing that she was not ready. It was easy to invade her in spite of the valour of her brave troops, and Russia forgot one by one the promises made to her new Allies, and did not come to her help. Then came the great retreat, fruit of the intrigues of traitors. Certain Russian generals had also joined the side of the traitors. Mackensen won easy laurels, and Sturmer, Protopopoff, Rasputin and Co. hoped that the great retreat and the invasion of Rumania would decide Nicholas II. to make that famous "separate peace." These tools of Germany, these creatures of the *Kaiser's*, hoping for its accomplishment, were delirious with Sturmer deceived his allies, talking loudly of "no separate peace," while, as is known, he was using all his energies in a contrary direction.

But if the court and so many of the great ones of the earth knelt before Rasputin, they did not all do so, and the masses had no belief in him. They laughed at him, and this rascal, who knew more than anyone the blackness of his own soul, went about protected by a coat of mail, for he was not without anxiety as to what Fate had in store for him. If his days sometimes gave the illusion of a veneer of piety, his evenings were those of a libertine; and, if the women had gone mad about him, the fathers, husbands and brothers had a mortal grudge against him.

In Kerensky, a lawyer and a member of the *Duma*, all this vermin scented danger; they wished to be rid of him, aware that he knew rather too much about their secret acts and their profits. An attempt was made to assassinate him in the street, but this fresh scheme of murder failed.

Then followed the accusations, but too well justified, against General Sukhomlinoff. Grand Dukes Nicholas, Dmitri and Serge got to work, and wished to make the allegations public, for matters would have been revealed, strangely deplorable, strangely compromising, for the clique of the "Saint" and his creatures, so much so that it would have meant without doubt the end of their reign, and their anxiety was therefore great. This trial, again by their intrigues, was deferred by the emperor, and was only opened up again since the fall of the latter; the general has been condemned to imprisonment for life, on the grave charges made against him when Minister for War.

The respite of the traitors was, however, not of long duration, for Monsieur Miliukoff, supported by the same grand dukes, conceived the project of unmasking the "Saint" before the whole *Duma*. In vain was it tried to prevent him, to arrest him, to kill him; he was able to escape from the nets spread for him and all attempts failed against this new subject of their apprehension, who, in a packed hall, before most of the ambassadors, and under the presidency of Monsieur Radzianko, made that memorable interpellation unveiling what Rasputin and Co. really were, and gaining the applause of the house—November 14, 1916—and the expression of a unanimous desire, as it seemed, for the continuance of the war.

All Petrograd was stirred. There was a rush for newspapers, but these, being censored, told nothing; private propaganda were organised to make known the truth, and the speech was distributed in a complete form.

★★★★★★

Monsieur Radzianko, as is known, was elected President of the third *Duma*, and again of the fourth, that is to say, he was President at the moment of the Revolution. He married a Princess Galitzine, and was formerly in the *Chevaliers-Gardes*, considered the first Russian regiment. Adored by the peasants on his great estates, he was much in touch with the Zemstvo Party, the friend of the peasants. A great friend of Sir George Buchanan, our late ambassador, his dream for his country was to have a ministry appointed by the *tzar*, though outside the *Duma*, responsible to and dependent upon possessing and retaining its confidence.

The empress, in the palace, breathlessly awaited the result, devoured with anxiety as to the issue which none of them had known how to prevent.

The "Saint," seriously alarmed by the revelations of Miliukoff—the only topic of conversation in the capital—thought it prudent to make himself scarce again, and departed on a so-called "pilgrimage."

The empress was in a terrible state, not only on account of the interpellation, but because since the departure of the scoundrel the condition of her precious child seemed to have become worse every day; hence a desperate summons to return. Madame Vyruboff had evidently received orders to drug the poor boy to such an extent that his condition should be sufficiently serious to madden the poor anxious mother.

The result of the denunciation was the fall of Sturmer; but he received a post at the palace. He was replaced by Trepoff, an honest man, who at once announced his plan of action: "No separate peace, and war on German influence."

Nicholas II. had not the least idea that Rasputin was the creature of the *Kaiser*, and though his instinct did not allow him to regard him with any favour, he bore with him, as I have already said, for the sake of the empress and to avoid family scenes; as he admitted on one occasion: "I would rather put up with this man than have to endure five attacks of hysterics a day."

It is certain that Alexandra Feodorovna was ill, and that her nerves were more than shaken; action should have been taken and on this pretext she should have been sent away. One must admit that there was enough to make her ill. Almost ever since her marriage, in any case since the year before the first Revolution, she lived in constant anguish, asking herself continually what was going to happen to her husband and children; as regards that one cannot blame her—on the contrary. It is said that the empress has sent her magnificent jewels to Darmstadt, her native country, to help the Germans continue the war.

Another dangerous spy of the *Kaiser's* at Petrograd was Grand Duke of Mecklenburg-Strelitz, on the best of terms naturally with Rasputin, and also exercising a great influence at the palace and over the empress. He had naturalied himself Russian in 1914; but who is more to be mistrusted than one who has been "naturalised"?

It was then—at the end of November 1916—that Rasputin was more especially warned that a plot had been made against him. The Grand Duke Nicholas tried again to instil sense into the emperor, but in vain. And the scoundrel paraded the so-called visions which he had never had, alarming the empress more and more on the subject of her son, and continuing his work of threatening his approaching death if the famous separate peace were not signed. The empress had come to believe that if this peace did not immediately become an accomplished fact the Romanoffs were doomed; and this she wished to prevent.

Germany naturally wished much for this peace; but today has to use the greatest circumspection before accepting the proposals of Lenin, whose government is recognized neither by the ambassadors of the Allied powers nor by the Russian Ambassadors in Allied countries.

The dark forces did their best to spread cholera amongst the troops at the front, an epidemic that was luckily stamped out almost at once, to the great disappointment of those who had instigated it. They then tried to poison the Grand Duke Dmitri; but that also failed.

On the 16th of December 1916, Rasputin was invited by Prince Felix Yousoupoff to spend the evening in his father's mansion, under the pretext of meeting a young woman who ardently desired to become a "sister disciple." What I do not understand is, why he should have accepted the invitation, for he had been so often warned against his would-be host. He therefore arrived at the prince's luxurious house, and was received by him, but after a gay supper was left *tête-à-tête* with one of the prince's friends on the pretext of inspecting some *objets d'art* which had attracted his notice previously.

The friend in question did the honours of the princely house with affability, and offered Rasputin wine—into which a strong admixture of poison had been introduced!

The mock-monk sipped a few drops in the manner of a connoisseur, which indeed he had become, having accustomed himself to the taste of the famous vintages of the Winter Palace, and then addressing himself to his interlocutor he appeared to be interested in some special work of art on one of the tables in the room, which the latter felt obliged to show him for closer inspection. On returning to Rasputin's side he noticed the monk had become paler as he passed his hand across his face as if desirous of concealing a strong pang of pain.

The prince's friend positively held his breath, keeping his eyes fixed on his prey as he noticed the glass standing empty beside him; he imagined the inevitable was bound to follow quickly, as the dose was a very strong one.

Upstairs, anxiety grew apace, many hearts were palpitating, every one counting the seconds which seemed eternal. Prince Felix Yousoupoff was there with a few friends who had all sworn to purge Russia, once and for all, of her evil genius.

But, as it happened, at the end of a few minutes the momentary sensation of discomfort seemed to disappear and the rascal became quite himself again to the prince's friend's amazement, who began to wonder whether after all this extraordinary man opposite him was in reality entirely like other men, and not, as some people affirmed, a demon or a sorcerer, gifted with some wonderful and unknown power of resistance. This man who had the power to heal had also the facility to kill, so it was generally believed. And there, in that room, the silent witness of so many festivities of the past, was about to be enacted the last scene of one of the greatest dramas which had ever taken place in the world's history.

Driven at last almost to despair, the hero of the plot, anxious to conclude his task, drew out his revolver and shot the "Saint" as he gloated over the beautiful antiques; but, although wounded, Rasputin still had sufficient strength to stagger into the hall and was on the point of making his way to the street door as, pale with pain and foaming with rage, he yelled out: "For you have tried to kill me, I will revenge myself." Upon which the hearer renewed his attack, emptying the contents of his revolver into the "Saint's" head—and breathed again freely once more, as this time the "monk" was indeed dead. Then was uttered one general shout of joy from the little group of the prince's friends assembled not far off, although in concealment during the tragedy. Rasputin had fired several times, but, as he was very drunk, I was told he only killed a dog.

Prince Felix Yousoupoff, on hearing the first shot, had rushed down the stairs and discharged his revolver; but it is said that owing to nervousness his hand shook and missed proper aim, and it was his friend who gave the *coup de grâce*.

It was afterwards discovered that Rasputin, profiting by his companion's momentary absence, had emptied the contents of his glass into a vase on one of the pieces of furniture which stood close by; this, either from distrust or because he had already indulged in too numerous libations.

It has been said that Rasputin was only killed in order to make clear whether it was really he who was guilty of all that had happened, or whether things would go on the same after his death. But it seems to me that his death came too late, and his evil work had been so well started that with or without him matters could no longer move up against the stream—they could only follow the current on which they had been started.

And there, in the great Neva, all black in the dark night, they threw beneath the ice the body, at last reduced to impotence, of him who had been the bane of the great Empire, cold in death as the deep icy water that engulfed it.

During a whole week everyone wondered what could have become of Rasputin and why he had disappeared so suddenly and mysteriously; the court *camarilla*, his friends and the pro-German *coterie* were at their wits' ends concerning him.

When the body at last was found, the empress came to prostrate herself before the remains, showing the most violent sorrow, going afterwards each day to pray at his tomb and invoking the most terrible vengeance on his murderers.

These had been traced; and Nicholas II. left her free to inflict on them whatever punishment she chose.

The Grand Duke Dmitri was sent to the Persian front, and Prince Yousoupoff and his son were exiled to their estates, for it was not at that time easy to inflict a heavier sentence on such important people as the grand duke and his accomplices.

The empress could not indeed by punishment slake the thirst of her soul for vengeance, and the unhappy mother was maddened by dread, only increased with the passing hours, of the realisation of the sinister words of the dead man:—

If disaster happens to me and I die, the *tzarevitch* will die forty days, hour for hour, after me!

The hour of the Revolution of March 10, 1917, struck; the emperor being at the time at the Front, the moment had been well chosen, or rather arranged. The red rag of revolt was carried in triumph above the heads of a delirious crowd; ensigns on monuments and everything that could recall an Empire were burned in the great fires lighted in the streets. The emperor started to return precipitately to the empress and his children at the palace of Tsarkoe-Celo, where all the Imperial children were suffering from measles. His first thought was of resistance, and to send his troops against the rebels of Petrograd.

The Grand Duke Nicholas, then Commander-in-Chief in the Caucasus, and General Alexieff, Chief of the General Staff, siding with the *Duma*, insisted on the abdication of Nicholas II., seeing in that act the only chance of salvation for Russia, and accordingly telegraphed their decision to Miliukoff who had just been appointed to the Ministry of Foreign Affairs.

The nation knew little or nothing of the course that events had taken, and the abdication was only the desire of a few scores of men; now, many deem it a great mistake.

Generals Russky and Brusiloff also telegraphed to Miliukoff, stating the adhesion of the armies to the new regime, and declaring that all was well.

Grand Duke Michael-Alexandrovitch, brother of Nicholas II., was nominated Regent, but without delay made it known that he would only accept the Regency with the approval of the people. This never came; of course the people did not have a chance of expressing an opinion; Kerensky seized the reins of government and what followed is only too well known.

At first everyone was contented with the Revolution; it was hailed as a saviour by those who thought themselves free from the pro-German clique. Matters went well, everything seemed new-born, but when once anarchy broke through its bounds faces began to lengthen, —and a feeling of despair arose—which feeling has gone on increasing ever since.

Today in the depths of her exile, and in her invalid's chair, Alexandra Feodorovna wears mourning for happier days, in the depths of that Siberia to which she never dreamt she herself would be deported one day, that Siberia that she at least has so well deserved by her ignoble treachery, and where she has been sent as a precautionary measure in case of a reactionary movement. And there near the birthplace of her hero now dead, she still mourns more than all else the disappearance of the "Saint."

"All this was bound to happen," she says. "It is the just vengeance for the 'Holy Father,' the Romanoffs must end and perish."

The Russian people accused the empress of bringing bad luck to everyone; but even at Darmstadt she was considered a bird of ill-omen.

As for Nicholas II. he has become completely imbecile, if rumour is correct, and will never recover his reason; the best thing that could have happened, perhaps, as far as he is concerned.

During his imprisonment at Tsarkoe-Celo, the revolutionary party was obliged often to change the soldiers who guarded him in order to be sure of their fidelity to the new regime, so great was known to be the ascendancy of the "Little Father" over his soldiers.

When he left the palace for exile, many people knelt and piously

IMPERIAL PALACE AT TSARKOE-CELO

crossed themselves as he passed, just as they would had they been shown a holy picture with miraculous powers. That which had been the religion of these humble people, they retained still for their emperor who was losing his throne through his family affections, obstinacy and weakness.

The outcome of the first Revolution had for result the creation of the *Duma*, which was intended to be the Saviour and Regenerator of the Empire—it has witnessed its end. Gapon, the idol of the masses, the precursor of Rasputin, appears no more but as a shadow pale, and fugitive.

The outcome of the second Revolution has been the fall of the Romanoffs and the institution of a self-styled Republic, which it was said would bring glory in the field of battle and happy liberty to a great people. I never believed it.

May the damaged walls of the *Kremlin* express to this great people—whose passions were being let loose at the same time that they were being deceived—the shame felt by them at the sight of the blood spilt around them, blood shed among brothers by a Revolution which has brought them only a civil war and mortal struggles, and will soon have produced more victims than all the Romanoffs together have done with their sentences of exile to Siberia— many but too well deserved, though accounted to them as a crime.

May a Romanoff worthy of the name that he bears rally the real Russia—she who endures and is silent, not being able to do more for the moment—and so make of her again a great power worthy of respect and gaining it, the terror of her ignoble neighbour, Germany— and not her vassal.

That is my most heart-felt wish, and also my most sincere prayer for that great country which is a little mine, and which from the bottom of my heart I love as my second country.

Inquire of an anti-Semite the meaning of the Russian Revolution, and he will expose to you the whole of the Jewish drama which unfolds itself in all its force before you. It is a fact that ever since the Revolution of March all the various governments which have succeeded each other so rapidly have in every instance been profitable to the Jews only and have done their utmost to upset all the opposing barriers which the *ancien régime* had deemed good for Russia—by setting these up as a rampart against their invading greed. Now that General Allenby has accomplished what Richard Coeur de Lion and the whole of Christendom failed to do—namely, the conquest of Jerusalem from the Turk it makes one hope that the time has come about for them all to *s'en aller caravaner* back whence they came so many centuries ago.

Lorsque la grande guerre ou le grand soir révolutionnaire auront passé sur le monde, il ne restera plus dominant toutes ces ruines que la Banque juive.

The above is a quotation from the great Russian author Dostoievsky, which my father, Monsieur Gaudin de Villaine, Sénateur de la Manche, and one of the most valiant leaders of the Right in the French Senate, has made use of on more than one occasion in his interpellations when addressing that body and in an article which was of course boycotted by the Press. It seems to justify itself more forcibly every day.

With the exception of Lenin, who is not a Jew and whose real name is Ullianoff—others say Lehrann and that he is a German—all the members of the Direction of the Soviets are Jews sailing under assumed Russian names. Thus, Trotsky's real name is Braunstein and that of the miserable wretch Zenovieff, who is one of the most active German agents, is really Apfelbaum—and so on!

Lenin comes from a revolutionary stock, his brother having been hung in 1887 for conspiring against the Tzar Alexander III.

I have some Russian cousins living in Italy, where they have been for a great many years, and I hear that according to Lenin's laws they are considered as emigrants, consequently their property in Russia has been confiscated, and should they return they would be imprisoned.

Krylenko, appointed by Lenin as *generalissimo* of the Russian Army, is a man of very mediocre intelligence; he was up to a few months ago residing near Montreux in Switzerland and was merely a lieutenant of the reserve of the Russian Army. He is not a Jew, but he is known by his friends as Father Abraham, a sobriquet of which he is very proud.

The great Russian people appear to me like a huge ball sent helter-skelter, rolling down a slide from an eminence—the slide is the Revolution.

One government will continue to replace another until the abyss of anarchy is reached. Germany's plan and interest are therefore to help all the smaller separatist non-Russian people, Finland, etc., to stand on their own feet as free political entities and autonomies.

May this revolutionary night not delay much longer to envelop the country of the German *Kaiser*, whose greatest pleasure seems to be in shaking and overturning the various thrones of the earth in order to consolidate on their ruins his own—a dangerous game to play, for the revolutionary mirage develops into a very virulent germ once spread amongst a discontented populace.

This emperor of whom a German diplomat before the war once said jokingly:

> If he goes to a christening he wants to be the child; if to a marriage, he wants to be the bridegroom; and if to a funeral, he wants to be the corpse!

Today this emperor has been nicknamed the "Red *Kaiser*," the War *Kaiser*, the *Kaiser* of the Ruins, the *Kaiser* of the Massacres, and of all the horrors which have been committed.

But, vengeance will come, and justice will make itself felt. Sooner or later, vengeance must come.

That which is not generally known, but what I know authoritatively, is that France might have obtained for herself and her Allies a separate peace with Austria. The brothers of the Empress of Austria were educated in France and are very French at heart, they had gone so far as to open peace negotiations through the intermediary of the Vatican, and all would have gone well had it not been for the regrettable pride of the Italians and the Masonic Lodges!

And today, December 1917, before closing these pages, I look back once more in the direction of the dear great Russia and I salute her; there, towards the great *Steppe* beneath its almost perpetual whiteness, where the silence makes itself felt; towards the luminous and pure atmosphere of the beautiful country of the Don Cossacks, where there seems still to be a ray of hope, perhaps, if only it could assert itself and render back to the *moujik* his religion venerated in his *izba* during centuries past, not only his sacred pictures, but afar, in a dream of purple and gold his God, his All—a *tzar*!

LEONAUR

ALSO FROM LEONAUR
AVAILABLE IN SOFTCOVER OR HARDCOVER WITH DUST JACKET

A DIARY FROM DIXIE by *Mary Boykin Chesnut*—A Lady's Account of the Confederacy During the American Civil War

FOLLOWING THE DRUM by *Teresa Griffin Vielé*—A U. S. Infantry Officer's Wife on the Texas frontier in the Early 1850's

FOLLOWING THE GUIDON by *Elizabeth B. Custer*—The Experiences of General Custer's Wife with the U. S. 7th Cavalry.

LADIES OF LUCKNOW by *G. Harris & Adelaide Case*—The Experiences of Two British Women During the Indian Mutiny 1857. A Lady's Diary of the Siege of Lucknow by G. Harris, Day by Day at Lucknow by Adelaide Case

MARIE-LOUISE AND THE INVASION OF 1814 by *Imbert de Saint-Amand*—The Empress and the Fall of the First Empire

SAPPER DOROTHY by *Dorothy Lawrence*—The only English Woman Soldier in the Royal Engineers 51st Division, 79th Tunnelling Co. during the First World War

ARMY LETTERS FROM AN OFFICER'S WIFE 1871-1888 by *Frances M. A. Roe*—Experiences On the Western Frontier With the United States Army

NAPOLEON'S LETTERS TO JOSEPHINE by *Henry Foljambe Hall*—Correspondence of War, Politics, Family and Love 1796-1814

MEMOIRS OF SARAH DUCHESS OF MARLBOROUGH, AND OF THE COURT OF QUEEN ANNE VOLUME 1 by A. T. Thomson

MEMOIRS OF SARAH DUCHESS OF MARLBOROUGH, AND OF THE COURT OF QUEEN ANNE VOLUME 2 by A. T. Thomson

MARY PORTER GAMEWELL AND THE SIEGE OF PEKING by *A. H. Tuttle*—An American Lady's Experiences of the Boxer Uprising, China 1900

VANISHING ARIZONA by *Martha Summerhayes*—A young wife of an officer of the U.S. 8th Infantry in Apacheria during the 1870's

THE RIFLEMAN'S WIFE by *Mrs. Fitz Maurice*—*The Experiences of an Officer's Wife and Chronicles of the Old 95th During the Napoleonic Wars*

THE OATMAN GIRLS by *Royal B. Stratton*—The Capture & Captivity of Two Young American Women in the 1850's by the Apache Indians

LEONAUR

ALSO FROM LEONAUR
AVAILABLE IN SOFTCOVER OR HARDCOVER WITH DUST JACKET

THE WOMAN IN BATTLE *by Loreta Janeta Velazquez*—Soldier, Spy and Secret Service Agent for the Confederacy During the American Civil War.

BOOTS AND SADDLES *by Elizabeth B. Custer*—The experiences of General Custer's Wife on the Western Plains.

FANNIE BEERS' CIVIL WAR *by Fannie A. Beers*—A Confederate Lady's Experiences of Nursing During the Campaigns & Battles of the American Civil War.

LADY SALE'S AFGHANISTAN *by Florentia Sale*—An Indomitable Victorian Lady's Account of the Retreat from Kabul During the First Afghan War.

THE TWO WARS OF MRS DUBERLY *by Frances Isabella Duberly*—An Intrepid Victorian Lady's Experience of the Crimea and Indian Mutiny.

THE REBELLIOUS DUCHESS *by Paul F. S. Dermoncourt*—The Adventures of the Duchess of Berri and Her Attempt to Overthrow French Monarchy.

LADIES OF WATERLOO *by Charlotte A. Eaton, Magdalene de Lancey & Juana Smith*—The Experiences of Three Women During the Campaign of 1815: Waterloo Days by Charlotte A. Eaton, A Week at Waterloo by Magdalene de Lancey & Juana's Story by Juana Smith.

NURSE AND SPY IN THE UNION ARMY *by Sarah Emma Evelyn Edmonds*—During the American Civil War

WIFE NO. 19 *by Ann Eliza Young*—The Life & Ordeals of a Mormon Woman During the 19th Century

DIARY OF A NURSE IN SOUTH AFRICA *by Alice Bron*—With the Dutch-Belgian Red Cross During the Boer War

MARIE ANTOINETTE AND THE DOWNFALL OF ROYALTY *by Imbert de Saint-Amand*—The Queen of France and the French Revolution

THE MEMSAHIB & THE MUTINY *by R. M. Coopland*—An English lady's ordeals in Gwalior and Agra duringthe Indian Mutiny 1857

MY CAPTIVITY AMONG THE SIOUX INDIANS *by Fanny Kelly*—The ordeal of a pioneer woman crossing the Western Plains in 1864

WITH MAXIMILIAN IN MEXICO *by Sara Yorke Stevenson*—A Lady's experience of the French Adventure

AVAILABLE ONLINE AT www.leonaur.com
AND FROM ALL GOOD BOOK STORES
07/09

LEONAUR

ALSO FROM LEONAUR

AVAILABLE IN SOFTCOVER OR HARDCOVER WITH DUST JACKET

THE 9TH—THE KING'S (LIVERPOOL REGIMENT) IN THE GREAT WAR 1914 - 1918 *by Enos H. G. Roberts*—Mersey to mud—war and Liverpool men.

THE GAMBARDIER *by Mark Severn*—The experiences of a battery of Heavy artillery on the Western Front during the First World War.

FROM MESSINES TO THIRD YPRES *by Thomas Floyd*—A personal account of the First World War on the Western front by a 2/5th Lancashire Fusilier.

THE IRISH GUARDS IN THE GREAT WAR - VOLUME 1 *by Rudyard Kipling*—Edited and Compiled from Their Diaries and Papers—The First Battalion.

THE IRISH GUARDS IN THE GREAT WAR - VOLUME 1 *by Rudyard Kipling*—Edited and Compiled from Their Diaries and Papers—The Second Battalion.

ARMOURED CARS IN EDEN *by K. Roosevelt*—An American President's son serving in Rolls Royce armoured cars with the British in Mesopatamia & with the American Artillery in France during the First World War.

CHASSEUR OF 1914 *by Marcel Dupont*—Experiences of the twilight of the French Light Cavalry by a young officer during the early battles of the great war in Europe.

TROOP HORSE & TRENCH *by R.A. Lloyd*—The experiences of a British Lifeguardsman of the household cavalry fighting on the western front during the First World War 1914-18.

THE EAST AFRICAN MOUNTED RIFLES *by C.J. Wilson*—Experiences of the campaign in the East African bush during the First World War.

THE LONG PATROL *by George Berrie*—A Novel of Light Horsemen from Gallipoli to the Palestine campaign of the First World War.

THE FIGHTING CAMELIERS *by Frank Reid*—The exploits of the Imperial Camel Corps in the desert and Palestine campaigns of the First World War.

STEEL CHARIOTS IN THE DESERT *by S. C. Rolls*—The first world war experiences of a Rolls Royce armoured car driver with the Duke of Westminster in Libya and in Arabia with T.E. Lawrence.

WITH THE IMPERIAL CAMEL CORPS IN THE GREAT WAR *by Geoffrey Inchbald*—The story of a serving officer with the British 2nd battalion against the Senussi and during the Palestine campaign.

Ingram Content Group UK Ltd.
Milton Keynes UK
UKHW041336270723
425894UK00001B/18